# UNDERSTANDING THE ALEF-BEIS

# UNDERSTANDING THE ALEF-BEIS

## Insights into the Hebrew Letters and the Methods for Interpreting Them

**Dovid Leitner**

FELDHEIM PUBLISHERS
JERUSALEM NEW YORK

Paperback edition

ISBN: 978-1-59826-010-6



10 New Hall Road
Manchester, England M7 4EL
email: teleshop@talk21.com
tel: (0044) 161 792 7321



Design and layout by E. Chachamtzedek

Distributed by:
FELDHEIM PUBLISHERS

208 Airport Executive Park
Nanuet, NY 10954

www.feldheim.com

# Contents

*RABBI* O.Y. *WESTHEIM.*
Dayan, Manchester
Rav of Beis Hamedrash Zeirei Agudas Yisroel

**אשר יעקב ועסטהיים**
דומו"צ בק"ק מאנשעסטער
רב דביהמ"ד צא"י בק"ק הנ"ל

15, Broom Lane,
Salford M7 4EQ
Tel: 0161 792 4939
Fax: 0161 792 5124

בס"ד

ג' חשון ה'תשס"ז לבה"ע

In this outstanding publication, Reb Dovid Leitner נ"י reveals some of the magnificent and breathtaking endless breadth and depth of the *Kedusho* [sanctity] and wisdom that lie beneath the surface of the letters of the *Alef – Beis* and words of the *Torah* and *Tefilloh.* This knowledge greatly enhances not only our appreciation and understanding of what we say and learn, but also our *Kavono* in our *Tefilos,* because it makes us realise how much more complexion and meaning there is to the words we utter.

This publication is therefore recommended to all those who are searching to elevate their *Torah* and *Tefillos* to higher levels, and to bring them closer to *Hashem Yisborach* with vibrant feelings and emotions.

אשר יעקב ועסטהיים
15 BROOM LANE
SALFORD M74EQ
ENGLAND
דומ"צ מאנשעסטער

Y. Ch. Horowitz
Rabbi of Stamar Community
Salford M7, Manchester

ישראל חיים הורוויץ
הרב דקה"ק ויואל משה סאטמאר
מאנשעסטער יצ"ו

בס"ד

הנה גברא יקירא מקמי עירנו מוה"ר הרבני התורני ירא וחרד לדברי ה'
כמוה"ר דוד לעווענטאל נ"י הנני מכירו רבות בשנים כולם שוין לטובה
אשר לבד ישרותו בוער בקרבו אהבת התורה, ושוקד על דלתותי'
לאחרונה רחב לבו ורשם על גליון רעיונות לה' בדבר הא"ב
אשר אף אמנם שלא מובן לי היטב שפת המדינה, מ"מ באשר
את הר' המחבר הנ"ל שליט"א הנני מכיר היטב, וחזקה שאינו
מוציא מתחת ידו דבר שאינו מתוקן, וכל שאופן עובדה ועוסק
בתורה, אין צורך החשבונות, ושכר הטוב הצפון למוחזק במזכה גם
את הרבים ויקבעו בדפוס להועיל גם לאחרים
אשר על כן ברכתי אליו שיהיה ה' עמו ויצליחהו בכל אשר יפנה
ונזכה בקרוב לראות בשורקיים מאהבה ומלאה הארץ דעה גו' בגאולה

כ"ה י"ב סיון תשס"ו לפ"ק
מאנשעסטער יע"א

ישראל חיים הורוויץ

# Acknowledgments

FROM THE DAY I undertook to begin writing this book, I have witnessed open *hashgachah pratis* (Divine Providence) at every stage. It began some five years ago in shul, on a Sunday morning after *Shacharis*. An extremely heavy rainstorm was raging outside, and so I decided to spend a few minutes learning while waiting for the weather to improve. I randomly selected a *sefer* from the shelf, and in it I found the unique explanation of Rabbi Saadiah Gaon on the alphabetic structure of the *alef-beis*—which was to become the backbone to this entire book.

A few weeks later, I went to *daven Minchah* in a newly opened *beis ha-midrash* near to my home. The *gabbai* was unpacking some *sefarim* that had been donated, and placed a copy of *Osios d'Rabbi Yitzchak* on the table where I was sitting. I obtained permission to borrow this out-of-print *sefer*, which proved extremely valuable and provided much of the material for the chapters dealing with the letters. I began writing down some of interesting points that I saw in that *sefer*, and from other *sefarim* that he quotes. These notes resulted in a series of twelve articles that appeared in the Jewish Press which were subsequently translated and used in a similar series in a Swiss weekly.

As a direct result of these articles, I was invited to lecture on the subject of the *alef-beis* at a S.E.E.D. Encounter Conference in Manchester. I accepted the invitation, although it meant that I had less than two weeks to prepare. The lecture was well attended and the enthusiastic audience asked some thirty relevant questions. What struck me as an open act of *hashgachah pratis* was that the answers to all of the questions posed, I myself had only seen during the ten days that I had to prepare for the talk. Moreover, the answers were found in a variety of *sefarim*, which were not even directly related to the subject of the *alef-beis*.

In researching this vast and fascinating subject, I collected insights and explanations from many *Rishonim* and *Acharonim*. The thoughts contained in this book are not my own; my job has been simply that of a compiler. Full credit for all the information contained in this book is due entirely to the originators. I am extremely thankful to Hashem, for granting me the opportunity to dissipate these Torah gems to the English reading public.

I am very grateful to my *mechutan*, Rabbi Abittan who introduced me to the *sefer Ginas Egos*, which has proved a valuable source of basic information for this publication. Many thanks are due to my friend Rabbi H. Shalom of Gateshead who kindly lent me his copy of the *sefer Magen David*, a book that focuses on various aspects of the Hebrew alphabet and its letters.

My deepest appreciation is due to my dear parents, who invested all their energies to ensure that all their children received the best possible education. They were unique in our community in that they succeeded in providing us all with the best possible Torah *chinuch*, together with a broad secular education. Our exemplary Torah education included the family's close personal connections with all our *Rabbeim* at the Manchester Yeshiva, including the *Rosh haYeshiva*, Rabbi Yehudah Zev Segal *zt"l*, and his son-in-law Rabbi Meir Zvi Ehrentreu *zt"l*. I also merited to learn in Ponevezh Yeshiva in Eretz Yisrael, where the Torah giants of our generation imbued me with an extra appreciation for Torah learning.

I am grateful to R' Yaakov Feldheim of Feldheim Publishers, for accepting this publication into his outstanding library of Torah literature and handling all aspects of production and distribution.

I wish to thank Mrs. Esther Chachamtzedek, who has displayed much patience and wisdom in her editing of the original manuscripts by adding structure and constructive suggestions that produced this book. I am grateful, as well, to Mrs. Zippy Thumim, who has surpassed my expectations in her beautiful cover design. A special thanks to my son, Yaacov Yisroel for his artistic input and drawings.

My heartfelt thanks to my brothers, who have provided constant encouragement, office facilities, and help during the entire project.

Last but not least, to my wife Mirjam, who allowed me to disappear for hours on end in order to research, compile and edit the original manuscript — her continuous support has enabled me to bring this book to fruition.

Dovid Leitner
Manchester, England
Chanukah 5767

# Introduction

SHORTLY BEFORE GIVING THE Torah on Mount Sinai, Hashem introduced the forthcoming event in the *pasuk*: אנכי בא אליך בעב הענן—"I will come to you in the thickness of the cloud" (*Shemos* 19:9). The Me'or V'Shemesh discusses the significance of giving the Torah through the medium of "the thickness of the cloud." This phrase implies something hidden, just as a thick cloud blocks the view of objects that are behind it. In order to see these obscure objects specialized equipment is required.

Similarly, the Torah can only be fully understood by using various specialized methods of interpreting it. The numerical value of the words בעב הענן is equal to that of the word ברמז, "by a process of hints," alluding to the fact that these methods of interpreting the Torah, passed down at Mount Sinai, contain many concealed facets that provide extra hidden meanings to the Torah's teachings. When Hashem created the letters of the *alef-beis,* He implanted within them Divine wisdom and knowledge.

In no way does this book purport to be a comprehensive understanding of the wisdom concealed within the Torah; however, it is possible to gains insights and/or a deeper understanding by implementing different tools for interpreting the letters of the *alef-beis*. For example, letters or words can be equated through their numerical values and used to draw comparisons and connections between concepts, providing additional insights into their meanings.

The Rokeach, in his *Sefer HaChochmah*, explains seventy-three methods of interpreting each letter, word or phrase in the Torah. Some of the more common concepts are:

***Alef-Beis*** — the letters of the *alef-beis* in alphabetic order

***Roshei Teivos/Sofei Teivos*** — the first/last letters of each word in a phrase or a *pasuk*

***Gematria*** — the numerical value assigned to each letter of the *alef-beis*

**Large/Small Letters** — letters that are written larger or smaller than the rest of the text

**Ascending/Descending Order** — the order that the letters appear in a word, phrase or *pasuk*, vis-à-vis an ascending or descending alphabetic order

**Triangular Values** — a letter value which is the sum of all the integers up to and including the numerical value of that letter

The first *pasuk* of the Torah contains indications as to the existence of the concepts listed above. The *pasuk* states: בראשית ברא א-להים את השמים ואת הארץ — "In the beginning of Hashem's creating the heavens and the earth" (*Bereishis* 1:1).

***Alef-Beis***: The first concept listed above is indicated by the word **את**, which is formed by using the first and last letters of the *alef-beis*. They therefore represent and symbolize the entire *alef-beis* from beginning to end. Actually, the word **את** appears twice in the phrase **את** השמים ו**את** הארץ. Rabbi Nasan Neta Shapiro, author of *Megalleh Amukos*, interprets this duplication as representing both the twenty-two-letter and twenty-seven-letter alphabetic structures (see pp. 3 and 14).

***Roshei Teivos***: The existence of this concept is indicated by the total numerical values (thus also incorporating the concept of ***Gematria***) of the first letters of the seven words contained in the first *pasuk* of the Torah: **ב**ראשית **ב**רא **א**-להים **א**ת **ה**שמים **ו**את **ה**ארץ.

They total twenty-two, corresponding to the twenty-two letters of the basic *alef-beis*.

**Large/Small Letters:** Although there are no capital letters in Hebrew, there are occasions when a letter will appear in the Torah double the size — or half the size — of the remaining letters in that word, which has significance vis-à-vis the text. The existence of this concept is indicated by the first letter of the Torah, the ב in בראשית, as it is twice as large as the rest of the letters.

**Ascending/Descending Order:** The existence of this concept is found in the first word of the Torah itself. The six letters that make up the first word בראשית incorporate the first two letters and the final three letters of the *alef-beis* (**ב**ר**א**שית and בראשית). In Hebrew, every letter has a corresponding numerical value and the alphabetic sequence of the letters follows an ascending or descending order. An ascending order signifies a natural progression and represents the attribute of mercy. When the letters follows a descending order, they represent an enforced attribute of justice. The first word of the Torah combines both of these aspects together. The highlighted letters in the word בראשית follow a normal ascending alphabetic order, while those of בראשית follow a descending order. Thus, the letters in first word בראשית combine both of these attributes together, as Creation itself took place through the combined attributes of justice and mercy.

**Triangular Values:** Studying the sum of the numerical values of the letters reveals the full potential that is incorporated within them. The fact that the first *pasuk* in *Bereishis* has seven words, comprising a total of twenty-eight letters, alludes to this concept in that the triangular value of the number seven is twenty-eight (1 + 2 + 3 + 4 + 5 + 6 + 7 = 28).

All of these concepts, as well as many others will be explained in greater detail throughout this book. Since many of them are interrelated and utilize other methods, it was necessary in the earlier chapters to mention concepts that will only be explained in a later chapter. However, effort has been made to provide abbreviated explanations or cross-references to the appropriate topic.

◆ ◆ ◆

I have divided this book into seven chapters, incorporating some of the insights and wisdom contained in the *alef-beis*:

Chapter 1 deals with the alphabetic order, the regular and final letters, and simple and composite letters.

Chapter 2 enumerates alphabetic transformation methods and the phonetic groupings of the letters.

Chapter 3 discusses the letters as they appear in Tanach, including deviations in size or positioning — such as large, small or suspended letters — as well as the crowns that appear on the top of many of the letters.

Chapter 4 introduces the concept of numerical values, commonly known as *gematria*. Several other numerical values — such as *mispar katan* and triangular values — will also be explained.

Chapter 5 discusses some interesting properties of the letters, such as letter fulfillments (*millui* and *nistar*), *notrikon*, *roshei teivos/sofei teivos*, and letter permutations.

Chapter 6 contains some insights into the individual letters.

Lastly, Chapter 7 contains some explanation as to the meaning of the vowels used in combination with the Hebrew *alef-beis.*

◆ ◆ ◆

The *alef-beis* is the first thing a young Jewish child is taught when he begins his schooling, and thus it forms the foundation of Torah learning. Yet, it is probable that since those early formative years, many have never spent much time expanding their knowledge of the letters and the wisdom embedded within them.

It is the aim of this book to provide the tools to enhance our understanding of the *alef-beis.*

# UNDERSTANDING THE ALEF-BEIS

CHAPTER 1

# An Overview of the Alef-Beis and Its Structure

OUR SAGES TELL US that the Torah existed two thousand years before the creation of the world and that Hashem used it as a blueprint for Creation, as the Gemara states: "Hashem looked into the Torah and created the world" (*Pesachim* 68b).

Furthermore, in Tractate *Berachos* (55a), *Chazal* inform us that the letters of the *alef-beis* themselves were used in Creation. The spiritual, creative force and wisdom that Hashem imbued within them were harnassed to create the world. The Torah was transmitted using the *alef-beis*.

In addition to the letters, vowels were necessary to enable us to vocalize and pronounce the written word, which would allow the transmission of the oral teachings of the Torah to future generations. The letters of the *alef-beis* can be compared to a human body, which only comes to life with the addition of the soul. Similarly, the letters themselves would remain utterly silent without the inclusion of the vowels.

Rabbi Moshe Cordovero, in the introduction to his work *Pardes Rimonim*, explains the unique status of the Hebrew alphabet. He states there that one should not think that the letters of the *alef-beis* are a symbolic convention — that the Sages determined that certain signs would represent specific sounds. If this were the case, there would be no difference between the Hebrew letters and those of other alphabets, where the written word is nothing more than a vehicle to publicize the intent of the writer.

For example, a doctor who writes a book about medicine does not intend that the contents be used as a cure. His goal is for the reader to become familiar with the information that he is writing about. The book itself contains no intrinsic therapeutic importance. And if, after reading the book many times, the reader fails to comprehend its contents, he has failed to obtain any benefit from it. He has wasted much time and effort, without gaining further understanding.

The letters of the Torah, however, are all of Divine origin. Each letter, when written in its proper shape on parchment and with the correct ink, contains spiritual concepts and is imbued with spiritual forces. Therefore, when a person reads the Torah, even if he does not understand its meaning, he nevertheless is affected by the letters and reaps a spiritual benefit.

Nevertheless, the letters of the *alef-beis* can be better understood — both in their written and articulated forms — by studying the various their properties and the methods used to interpret them. By way of analogy, a serious chemistry student will obtain much basic information and insight from studying the Periodic Table of Elements in great detail. This will provide him with a further understanding of the molecular composition, structure and properties of each of the elements. In a similar way, a better understanding of the letters of the *alef-beis*, the order in which they appear, their groupings, and their respective numerical properties and attributes, will enhance our comprehension of the Torah.

## THE LETTERS OF THE ALEF-BEIS

The standard Hebrew alphabetic structure is made up of twenty-two letters — beginning with the letter א (*alef*) and ending with the letter ת (*tav*) — each one possessing a numerical value. The following are the standard letters, with their corresponding numerical values:

| ת | ש | ר | ק | צ | פ | ע | ס | נ | מ | ל | כ | י | ט | ח | ז | ו | ה | ד | ג | ב | א |
|---|---|---|---|---|---|---|---|---|---|---|---|---|---|---|---|---|---|---|---|---|---|
| 400 | 300 | 200 | 100 | 90 | 80 | 70 | 60 | 50 | 40 | 30 | 20 | 10 | 9 | 8 | 7 | 6 | 5 | 4 | 3 | 2 | 1 |

This alphabetic structure, with all the secrets contained therein, was taught by Hashem to Adam haRishon. Rabbeinu Bechaye writes (see *Bereishis* 37:3) that this knowledge was then transmitted via Adam haRishon's grandson, who in turn taught it further, until it reached Yaakov Avinu at the yeshiva of *Shem v'Ever*.

Yaakov Avinu subsequently taught this knowledge to his son Yosef. When the letters of the names Yaakov and Yosef are written out fully (יוד עין קף בית / יוד ואו סמך פה — this is referred to as the letters' fulfillments; see p. 157 for an explanation of this concept), there are a total of twenty-two letters, corresponding to the number of letters in the *alef-beis*.

## THE ALPHABETIC ORDER

As stated above, every letter of the *alef-beis* has a corresponding numerical value and that value begins at one for the א and continues in a natural progression based on the decimal system. The natural structure follows an ascending order, which represents the attribute of mercy. Conversely, letters appearing in a descending order represent an enforced attribute of justice. This order is referred to by the acronym of the last four letters of the *alef-beis* in reverse order (ת'ש'ר'ק'), *tashrak*. Thus, when letters within words, phrases or passages appear in reverse alphabetic order, they have a power of justice or judgment. For example: the letters of the word מלך, "king," appear in reverse alphabetic order. Appropriately, a king is responsible for maintaining law and order in his kingdom.

### ◈ The Alef-Beis: A Proclamation of the Aim of Creation

Rabbi Saadiah Gaon explains that the order of the letters of the twenty-two-letter *alef-beis* represents a proclamation of the aim of Creation — that all mankind will acknowledge Hashem as the eternal ruler (ה' ימלך לעולם ועד). He points out that the middle four letters of this alphabetic sequence are the letters *yud*, *chaf*, *lamed* and *mem*, which form the word ימלך, "[He] will rule."

אבגדהוזחט<u>יכלמ</u>נסעפצקרשת

As these are surrounded by nine letters on either side, this alphabetic sequence represents a royal procession, with the King in the center, flanked on either side by his guards.

Rabbi Saadiah Gaon points out a numerical connection to this idea in the order of the *alef-beis*: The first nine letters — from א to ט — have a total numerical value of forty-five (1 + 2 + 3 + 4 + 5 + 6 + 7 + 8 + 9 = 45), the same as that of the word אדם, the human being, whose purpose in creation is to proclaim Hashem's sovereignty. The final nine letters — from *nun* (נ) to *tav* (ת) — have a total numerical value of 1,350 (50 + 60 + 70 + 80 + 90 + 100 + 200 + 300 + 400 = 1,350), which is forty-five (אדם) multiplied by thirty, representing the thirty ways that kingship is attainable (See *Pirkei Avos* 6:6).

With this explanation, we can understand why many of the additional *selichos* and *piyutim* that are said during the month of Elul — as well as those additions which are incorporated into the Rosh Hashanah and Yom Kippur prayers — follow an ascending order of the *alef-beis*. During a period when our primary objective is to acknowledge Hashem as the King of the universe, it is appropriate to include prayers that follow this ascending alphabetic order, as this sentiment is implied by this structure.

### ◈ Pesukim That Contain All the Letters of the Alef-Beis

Rabbi Saadiah Gaon's explanation is reinforced by the fact that throughout Scripture there are exactly twenty-six *pesukim* that contain the entire *alef-beis*. Twenty-six is the numerical value of Hashem's Name of י-ה-ו-ה. This again stresses the fact that the *alef-beis* structure is an automatic proclamation of ה' ימלך, for which purpose the world was created. The twenty-six *pesukim* are listed by the Mesorah on *Yechezkel* 38:12. They are:

*Shemos* 16:16
*Devarim* 4:34
*Yehoshua* 24:13
*Melachim* II 4:39
*Melachim* II 6:32
*Melachim* II 7:8
*Yeshayahu* 5:25
*Yeshayahu* 66:17
*Yirmeyahu* 22:3
*Yirmeyahu* 32:29
*Yechezkel* 17:10
*Yechezkel* 38:12
*Hoshea* 10:8
*Hoshea* 13:2
*Amos* 9:13
*Tzefaniah* 3:8
*Zechariah* 6:11
*Koheles* 4:8
*Esther* 3:13
*Daniel* 2:15
*Daniel* 2:43
*Daniel* 4:20
*Daniel* 7:19
*Ezra* 7:28
*Nechemiah* 3:7
*Divrei HaYamim* II 26:11

*Tzefaniah* 3:8 is unique in that it is the only *pasuk* in all of Scripture that contains the twenty-two letters of the *alef-beis* as well as the five final letters (these will be explained further on). Similarly, the Ten Commandments also includes the entire *alef-beis*.

The Baruch She'Amar writes that in all of Scripture there are twenty-six occurrences of the word עליון, the Highest Power, with reference to Hashem. These correspond to the twenty-six *pesukim* that incorporate all the letters of the *alef-beis*, both of which symbolize His eternal power.

*Shemos* 16:16 is the first *pasuk* that contains all twenty-two letters. That chapter describes how the Jewish nation received their daily portion of Manna, the heavenly bread. Rabbeinu Bechaye writes:

> This *pasuk* incorporates two important concepts: the twenty-two letters of the *alef-beis* and the provision of sustenance. Nothing exists in the universe that is not incorporated and represented by the twenty-two letters of the *alef-beis*. Similarly, there is no living creature that does not require sustenance. For this very reason, Chapter 145 of *Tehillim*, commonly known as *Ashrei*, is incorporated into our daily prayers and is of such importance. The first letters of these *pesukim* follow the order of the *alef-beis*, and also incorporate that vital *pasuk* that encapsulates our requirement for sustenance: פותח את ידך ומשביע לכל חי רצון — "You open Your hand and satisfy the desire of every living thing" (v. 16).

Of all the *pesukim* that contain the entire *alef-beis*, only two are found in the Chumash: *Shemos* 16:16, which speaks of the sustenance that Hashem provided for the Jewish People in the wilderness; and *Devarim* 4:34, which mentions how Hashem redeemed us from Egypt with great signs and wonders. The Ba'al HaTurim connects these two *pesukim* with the following comment: "This comes to teach that every person who keeps the Torah's commandments will be provided sustenance with ease, just as He did to those who were fed with Manna."

Rabbi Chaim Erlanger *zt"l* of Lugano points out that *Shemos* 16:16 is composed from eighteen words, which correspond to the eighteen *berachos* of the *Shemoneh Esrei*, a prayer that is recited twenty-two times each week.

The ninth *berachah* in the *Shemoneh Esrei*, in which we pray for sustenance, begins with the word ברך and ends with השנים. The Written Torah begins with the letter ב and the Oral Torah ends with a ם. We can extrapolate from here that in the merit of keeping the entire Torah, Hashem provides us with ample sustenance.

## ◈ The First Written Reference to the Alphabetic Order

It is interesting to note that we do not find any written reference to the alphabetic order of the *alef-beis* until some three thousand years after Creation, during the reign of David haMelech.

In his explanation of this concept, the Ben Ish Chai cites *Shmuel* I, Chapter 8, where we learn that at the latter part of Shmuel haNavi's life, he was approached by the elders of the Jewish nation requesting that he appoint a king. The passage reads (ibid. 8:5–7):

> They said to him, "…so now appoint a king to judge us, like all the nations." And the matter was displeasing in the eyes of Shmuel when they said, "Give us a king to judge us," and Shmuel prayed to Hashem. And Hashem said to Shmuel, "Listen to the voice of the people, according to all that they will say to you, for they have not rejected you, but they have rejected Me from reigning over them."

The Jewish People's request for the appointment of a Jewish monarch was interpreted by Hashem and the prophet Shmuel as a rejection of the sovereignty of Hashem. This, in itself, is difficult to comprehend, because the Torah commands us to appoint a monarch, as the passage stipulates: "When you come to the land that Hashem, your God, gives you, and possess it, and settle in it, and you will say, 'I will set a king over myself, like all the nations that are around me.' You shall surely set over yourself a king whom Hashem, your God, shall choose..." (*Devarim* 17:14–15). Were the Jewish People not fulfilling the Torah commandment by seeking to appoint a monarch? If so, why was Hashem displeased with their request?

The Ben Ish Chai reconciles this difficulty with the following explanation: From the time of Creation until the reign of David ha-Melech, any mention of the alphabetic order of the *alef-beis* would automatically convey the message that Hashem will reign for all eternity. Hashem planned that the Jewish People should firstly settle down in their newly acquired land. They should then build the *Beis haMikdash* as the earthly abode for His *Shechinah*. This building of Hashem's palace on earth was to be given first priority.

Once this was established, a Jewish monarch was to be appointed who would act to reaffirm Hashem as the King of the universe. The monarchy would act as a miniature replica of the Kingdom of Hashem. By leading his people in the ways that are dictated by Hashem in His Torah, the Jewish king would reinforce the Kingdom of Hashem. The populace would obey the king, who, in turn, would ensure that they abide by His commandments.

Therefore, when the Jewish People asked for the appointment of a Jewish monarch prior to the building of the *Beis haMikdash*, Hashem saw this as a rejection of His Kingship. They were giving priority to the authority of a monarch who would be appointed by a mere mortal. In order to correct this mistake, David haMelech and his son Shlomo wrote down the *alef-beis* in its ascending alphabetic order. By so doing, they remind all future generations of the correct priority—that Divine Monarchy takes preference over that of a human one.

The entire *alef-beis* in its correct order is found only in three books in Scripture: *Tehillim* (composed by David haMelech), *Mishlei* (composed by Shlomo haMelech), and *Megillas Eichah* (written by Yirmeyahu haNavi). The fact that the acronym of these three books (תהלים משלי איכה) spells out the word אמת, "truth," hints at the *true* priority of acknowledging Hashem's Kingship before that of a human monarch.

In order to demonstrate this, David haMelech vowed not to personally enjoy the comforts of his palace until he had prepared a home for Hashem and His *Shechinah*. He states this clearly in

*Tehillim* 132, which is one of the fifteen *Shir haMa'alos* (*Tehillim* 120–134), which David haMelech composed while the foundations for the *Beis haMikdash* were being laid. Interestingly, *Tehillim* 132 is the only one of these fifteen that contains all of the twenty-two letters of the *alef-beis*.

The same message is reiterated again in *Shmuel* II 7:2, when he writes: "Behold, how can I dwell in a cedar palace, when the Ark of Hashem rests within a mere curtain?"

This lesson, which David haMelech wished to impart, can be demonstrated in a pictorial manner: Hashem's Kingdom on earth — which, as we have explained, should have been established first — can be represented by writing His holy Name of י-ה-ו-ה. The kingdom of David haMelech was to be established later, thus his name should have been written behind Hashem's Name. By superimposing the Name of Hashem over that of David haMelech's — the way that it should have been —

י ה ו ה

we are left with three *yud*s (since the letter ה is composed by combining the letters ד and י together [see p. 213]), which have a combined numerical value of thirty (each י equals ten; see Chapter 4, for more on numerical values), an allusion to the thirty ways in which kingship is attainable (see *Pirkei Avos* 6:6). In this way, the human monarchy of David haMelech remained in the shadows of the Kingdom of Hashem.

Yehudah received the blessing from his father Yaakov that לא יסור שבט מיהודה — "Royalty should never depart from him." The Midrash points out that the spelling of the name Yehudah (יהודה) incorporates the four letters that comprise Hashem's Name, with the addition of the letter ד. This extra letter represents David haMelech (דוד המלך) who only used his royal powers to enhance and promote the Kingdom of Hashem, and not for his own personal glorification. The numerical value of the name יהודה is also thirty.

As a direct reward for David haMelech's self-sacrifice of his own personal comfort for Hashem's honor, he merited that he and his descendants would be the only ones allowed to sit in the *Azarah* section of the *Beis haMikdash*. This is clearly stated in the Gemara: אין ישיבה בעזרה אלא למלכי בית דוד בלבד — "Only descendants of David haMelech are allowed to sit in the *Azarah*" (*Yoma* 25a).

Rav Saadiah Gaon has explained how the *alef-beis* sequence proclaims ה' ימלך — the eternal Kingdom of Hashem by the natural alphabetic order in which the letters appear. David haMelech and his son Shlomo haMelech represent the pinnacle of Jewish monarchy throughout our history. They were both eager to confirm the priority that must be given to the Kingdom of Hashem, reinforcing this priority by committing the *alef-beis* order to writing.

The book of *Eichah* laments the destruction of the *Beis haMikdash* and the royal power of the Jewish monarchy. It uses the same *alef-beis* sequence to offer comfort to the Jewish People, and to provide them with hope and encouragement that the redemption will eventually come. This alphabetic order serves to remind us that the aim of Creation remains unchanged, even though the House of Hashem has been destroyed. The universal acknowledgment of ה' ימלך will be accomplished, despite the temporary destruction of the *Beis haMikdash*.

### ◈ ה' ימלך לעולם ועד — "Hashem Will Rule Forever and Ever"

Since the order of the *alef-beis* portrays the aim of Creation, with the ultimate declaration of ה' ימלך לעולם ועד — "Hashem will rule forever and ever" (*Shemos* 15:18), this *pasuk* warrants further analysis. This proclamation appears in the Song by the Sea, the praises that the Jewish nation sang to Hashem after miraculously crossing the *Yam Suf*. In the relatively short period of time that it took them to cross the dry passage of land that was created by the parting of the sea, they all personally witnessed numerous miracles, through which Hashem revealed to them His Divine powers. This revelation reciprocated a song of praise to Hashem, as explained by Rashi in *Shir HaShirim Rabbah* (3:9). Rashi states there: "He revealed Himself to them in His Glory, and they could point to Him with a finger. Even a maidservant saw that which the prophet Yechezkel did not see."

In Ramban's commentary on the above *pasuk*, he explains that the inclusion of the words of ה' ימלך לעולם ועד was meant to be a prayer to Hashem — i.e. that in the future the Jewish nation should merit many more such open revelations of His Glory, similar to those that they had just witnessed at the miraculous splitting of the *Yam Suf*.

Radak poses the question: Why is it necessary to use both the words לעולם and ועד when declaring Hashem's eternal Kingship? Would it not have sufficed to write simply the word לעולם, "for eternity"? He explains that by using the word לעולם alone, one might mistakenly understand this to refer to only a limited time-period, as we find when the term לעולם is used regarding the limited period of fifty years of *Yovel* (see *Devarim* 15:17). In order to express the eternal Kingship of Hashem, it is necessary to use a double expression of לעולם ועד.

This explanation is reinforced by the Gemara (*Eiruvin* 54a), which states that when the words נצח, סלה or ועד are mentioned in Scripture, they convey a meaning of eternity. The terminology used in the Gemara is: אין לו הפסק לעולם ולעולמי עולמים — "without interruption and for all eternity." When referring to the eternal nature of Hashem, we therefore need to use this double expression of לעולם ועד, "forever and ever."

Hashem was the first King, and will remain King until the end of time, when all other powers have long been destroyed and vanished from existence. This is confirmed by the *pasuk*: אני ראשון ואני אחרון ומבלעדי אין א-להים — "I am the First and I am the Final One, and beside Me there is no other God" (*Yeshayahu* 44:6). His eternal

Kingship of Hashem is expressed in the declaration that Hashem shall reign for all eternity.

Both *Pirkei d'Rabbi Eliezer* (ch. 11) and the *Targum Sheni* on *Megillas Esther* (1:1) explain that there are a total of ten periods in history where there was or will be a single king who ruled or will rule over the entire universe.

The kings are:

1) Hashem, Who ruled alone at the time of Creation
2) Nimrod
3) Pharaoh during the lifetime of Yosef
4) Shlomo haMelech
5) Achav
6) Nevuchadnetzar
7) Koresh, the King of Persia
8) Alexander
9) Mashiach
10) Hashem, Who will be recognized by all at the End of Days

The Mesorah comments that the expression לעולם ועד appears a total of nine times in all of Scripture, an allusion to the nine kings who have had or will have sole rulership. Hashem alone remains as the first and final King — which, as we have said, is appropriately expressed by the phrase לעולם ועד, since Hashem's Kingdom is eternal. The nine places that the phrase of לעולם ועד is found in Scripture are:

| | | |
|---|---|---|
| *Shemos* 45:15 | *Tehillim* 45:15 | *Tehillim* 145:2 |
| *Michah* 4:5 | *Tehillim* 119:44 | *Tehillim* 145:21 |
| *Tehillim* 9:6 | *Tehillim* 145:1 | *Daniel* 12:3 |

Significantly, six of these nine places are to be found in *Tehillim*, which was composed by David haMelech. Of these six times, three are in Chapter 145, which, as we mentioned before, follows the *alef-beis* order.

## Simple and Composite Letters

With regard to their composition, the twenty-two letters of the *alef-beis* are divided into two groups: simple letters and compound letters. The simple letters are the seven letters whose shape is unique; they are: ז'כ'ר'נ'י'ו'ד'. (The letters are written in this order as a mneumonic, known as *zikaron yud.*) The remaining fifteen letters are composed from a combination of simple letters, and belong to the group of compound letters. For example, letter *alef* is formed by combining the letter *vav* with two *yuds*.

The following is a listing of the usual compositions for the letters of the *alef-beis*:

| Letter | Composition | Letter | Composition |
|---|---|---|---|
| א | י + ו + י | ל | כ + ו |
| ב | ו + ו + ו | מ | כ + ו |
| ג | י + ז | נ | נ |
| ד | ד | ס | כ + ו |
| ה | ד + י | ע | ז + ו + נ |
| ו | ו | פ | כ + י |
| ז | ז | צ | נ + י |
| ח | ד + ו | ק | ר + ן |
| ט | נ + ו or כ + ו | ר | ר |
| י | י | ש | ו + ו + ו |
| כ | כ | ת | ר + ו |

It is interesting to note that he natural ratio of a circle (π [pi], obtained by dividing the circle's circumference by its radius) is 22:7, which corresponds to the ratio between the total number of letters in the *alef-beis* and the number of simple letters. The spherical shape of the circle alludes to the complete cycle of creation — the fulfillment of the aim of Creation with the coming of Mashiach, which, as we have said, is displayed in the letters of the *alef-beis* itself.

◈ ◈ ◈

The composite letters of a compound letter can be used to provide further meaning to a word or phrase. For example:

The Jewish People have a custom to sing extra *zemiros* on Shabbos, both as part of the extra *Pesukei d'Zimrah* (verses of praise said during prayer) and the songs that one sings during the Shabbos meals. We are commanded: זכור את יום השבת לקדשו — "Remember the Shabbos day to sanctify it" (*Shemos* 20:8). The two middle letters of the word **זכור** are the composite letters which form the letter **מ**. By combining them into that letter, **זכור** becomes **זמר** — the Hebrew word for "song." By singing these extra *zemiros* on Shabbos, we are thereby fulfilling the positive commandment of "remembering the Shabbos day."

It is also possible to use the numerical values of the composite letters of a compound letter or word in interpreting the Torah and uncovering deeper understandings (see pp. 140–141 for examples and further explanation).

## The Five Final Letters

There are five letters of the *alef-beis* which, when they appear at the end of a word, have a different format — although they are pronounced the same as their corresponding normal letters. These five final letters combine with the twenty-two-letter *alef-beis* to produce the complete twenty-seven-letter *alef-beis*. They are known as the letters of *mantzpach*, an acronym of the letters מ'נ'צ'פ'כ' (*mem*, *nun*, *tzaddi*, *pei* and *chaf*), which become ם'ן'ץ'ף'ך', respectively.

Since both formats articulate in a similar fashion, the final letters should be viewed as part of their corresponding normal letters. If the final letters were to be additional ones to the twenty-two letters of the *alef-beis*, then it would be expected that they would also have different pronunciations. The fact that they do not differ in their pronunciation means that they are only extensions of the regular corresponding letters. However, when added to the twenty-two-letter *alef-beis*, the combination creates a new alphabetic structure — the twenty-seven-letter *alef-beis*.

The Megalleh Amukos explains that there are actually two separate alphabets, one with twenty-two and the other with twenty-seven letters. In other words, when a word incorporates a final letter at the end of it, the other letters in this word also originate from the twenty-seven-letter *alef-beis*.

The obligation for a father to teach his son Torah is derived from the passage: והיו הדברים האלה אשר אנכי מצוך היום על לבבך ושננתם לבניך ודברת בם וכו' — "And these words which I command you today shall be upon your heart. You shall teach them to your sons and you shall speak mainly about them..." (*Devarim* 6:6–7). The Chidah points out that the obligation to teach Torah to one's son is introduced with the word והיו. This word has a numerical value of twenty-seven, which corresponds to the total number of letters in the complete twenty-seven-letter *alef-beis*.

## ◈ Numerical Values of the Final Letters

We have already mentioned that each letter of the twenty-two-letter alphabet has a numerical value, ranging from one to four hundred. These final five letters continue this progression:

| ך | ם | ן | ף | ץ |
|---|---|---|---|---|
| 500 | 600 | 700 | 800 | 900 |

Thus, the number cycle begins with one for the numerical value of א and continues until nine hundred for the final letter ץ, which brings us back to the א in that the word אלף can be read either as *alef* (אָלֶף), with a numerical value of one, or as *elef* (אֶלֶף), meaning one thousand — thereby completing the number cycle.

Each of these five final letters can also be interpreted as having the same numerical value as its respective normal counterpart as well. In other words, the letter ך has the dual value of twenty or five hundred, the letter ם of forty or six hundred, the letter ן of fifty or seven hundred, the ף can have a value of either eighty or eight hundred, and the letter ץ as ninety or nine hundred. The total of the lower numeric values of these five letters (20 + 40 + 50 + 80 + 90 = 280) is equal to the total numerical value of the three highlighted words in the proclamation: **ה' מלך ה' מלך ה' ימלך**—"Hashem is King, Hashem was King, and Hashem will be King," which is Hashem's revelation with respect to time (present, past and future).

The Gemara (*Chagigah* 12a) explains that there are a total of seven ascending levels of spiritual firmaments, and each one is spaced at a distance of five hundred years apart. These years are measured by the amount of time it would take a person to walk this distance. Their total distance is therefore thirty-five hundred walking years.

The higher numeric values produce a total of thirty-five hundred hundred (500 + 600 + 700 + 800 + 900 = 3,500). Rabbi Yitzchak ben R' Yehudah haLevi, author of *Pane'ach Raza*, explains that this figure represents the full splendor of Hashem's Glory throughout the entire universe, which is His revelation with respect to space.

This duality of values represented by the *mantzpach* alphabet displays His full Glory throughout the entire universe, spanning its complete history in both dimensions of space and time.

In this vein, Ibn Ezra, in his commentary to *Shemos* 3:15, provides an explanation as to why the final letters have the same pronunciation as their corresponding normal letters. He points out that the final letters simply represent a different dimension of the normal letters, and this is indicated by their shape. The normal letters represent the dimension of breadth and therefore have a base running from right to left, as we see in the letters נ'צ'פ'כ'. Their corresponding final letters represent the dimension of depth and are appropriately bent vertically as in ן'ץ'ף'ך'. Mathematically, these two formats represent the x and y axis.

## ◈ The Origin of the Five Final Letters

The Megalleh Amukos gives a profound and lengthy explanation as to the origin of these five final letters. He explains that initially, at the time of Creation, only the twenty-two letters of the *alef-beis* existed. It was only after Adam haRishon sinned, by eating from the forbidden fruit, that the five final letters were introduced. When partaking of this food, Adam made use of his five senses — touch, smell, speech, sight and hearing. This transgression was the prime cause that allowed death, exile and destruction to become part of our daily lives.

Each of these five final letters was introduced in order to repair the damage caused by this transgression. Each symbolizes a period of redemption, and our ultimate return to the spiritual level that man possessed before the sin was committed.

The following passage appears in *Zechariah* (13:2) in reference to the arrival of Mashiach: והיה ביום ההוא וכו' יזכרו עוד וגם את הנביאים ואת רוח הטומאה אעביר מן הארץ — "It will happen on that day…I will also remove the [false] prophets and the unclean spirit from the world." The Final Redemption will ultimately lead to the removal of the unclean spirit from the world. The numerical value of the words רוח הטומאה, "unclean spirit," is 280, the same as the lower numerical value of these five final letters.

With the exception of the final ם, the final letters are formed by elongating and straightening the base of the equivalent normal letter. This symbolizes the drawing of a sword in readiness for battle. They are positioned at the rear flank for extra protection, representing an extra vigilance and strength of character that is required at the end of our exiles, in order to merit the salvation that is represented by the final letters.

The Megalleh Amukos further points out that the composition of these five letters are actually built up from a total of eight letters, in the following manner:

| LETTER | COMPOSITION | NUMERICAL VALUE |
|---|---|---|
| ם | כ + ו | 26 |
| ן | ו | 50 |
| ץ | י + ן | 60 |
| ף | ך + י | 30 |
| ך | ך | 20 |
| | TOTAL: | 186 |

The total numerical value of these composite letters (using the lower values) is 186, the same as that of the word מקום, which means "place" or "space." This word is used to represent Hashem (as will be discussed more fully on p. 153). After the transgression of Adam haRishon, it became necessary for Hashem's Name to be "filtered down" into a more attenuated form, to enable a person to connect to Him. This is represented by the tangible parameters of מקום, space. A direct result of this transgression was that these five final letters were added to the *alef-beis.*

Furthermore, the fact that the five letters are composed from eight individual letters points to a connection between the letters ה and ח, whose numerical values are five and eight, respectively. Moreover, they are also very similar in shape. Elsewhere we explain that the shape of the letter ה represents repentance, and these five final letters serve as a rectification for Adam haRishon's sin, as each letter represents one of the five redemptions.

### ◈ Mantzpach: The Alphabet of Redemption

*Pirkei d'Rabbi Eliezer* (Chapter 48) refers to the *mantzpach* alphabet as the "Alphabet of Redemption," since these letters appear at the end of a word, similar to a redemption — which is the final stage at the end of an exile.

*Pirkei d'Rabbi Eliezer* explains:

> Rabbi Eliezer explained that each of the five final letters represent the kernel of "salvation." Avraham Avinu was redeemed from Ohr Kasdim by the use of the final letter ך when he was commanded to leave his homeland, with the words: לך לך מארצך — "Go for your sake from your land..." (*Bereishis* 12:1).
>
> Using the final letter ם, Yitzchak Avinu was saved from the hands of the Philistines, as expressed in the phrase: לך מעמנו כי עצמת ממנו מאד — "Go away from us for you are too wealthy" (ibid. 26:16).

It would appear from this quotation, that the use of two regular *mems* has the same effect as using the equivalent final letter. It is for this reason that the phrase לך מעמנו כי עצמת ממנו מאד is used to display this salvation that took place through the power of the final letter ם.

*Pirkei d'Rabbi Eliezer* continues:

> The final letter ן was used to save Yaakov Avinu from his troubles, when he cried out: הצילני נא — "Please save me" (*Bereishis* 32:12). The final letter ף was used in the redemption from our Egyptian exile as we are told: פקוד פקדתי אתכם — "I shall surely remember you" (*Shemos* 3:16). It is through the letter צ that the Final Redemption will be effected at the time of Mashiach, as expressed in the prophecy: הנה איש צמח שמו ומתחתיו יצמח ובנה את היכל ה' — "Behold, a man whose name is Tzemach, who will spring up out of this place and build the Temple of Hashem" (*Zechariah* 6:12).

Here again the double use of the regular letter *nun* in the phrase הצילני נא is equivalent to the final ן; the double use of the letter פ appears to have the equivalent power as the final ף; and the Final Redemption will be brought about through the use of the double letter צ.

Rabbi David Luria in his commentary to *Pirkei d'Rabbi Eliezer* appends an explanation from Rabbi Shimon Ostropolia, quoting the *pasuk* that states: מכנף הארץ זמרת שמענו צבי לצדיק ואמר רזי לי רזי לי — "From the end of the earth we heard songs, 'The righteous shall be elevated,' and I said, "I have my secret; I have my secret" (*Yeshayahu* 24:16). He points out that the first word, מכנף, is composed from four letters that also have a counterpart in the final letters.

The four redemptions represented in these letters have already taken place. Their songs have already been heard. What is still awaited, however, is the future redemption, which is represented by the double letters of צ in the words **צבי לצדיק**.

The Ben Ish Chai mentions another insight on *Yeshayahu* 24:16. He expounds on the phrase מכנף הארץ, "from the ends of the earth" by looking at the fulfillment of the word ארץ, which is **אלף ריש צדי**. (The concept of "fulfillments" is explained in great detail on p. 157ff.) These letters' hidden fulfillments have a total numerical value of 434. This is equal to the sum of the numerical value of the repeated words רזי...רזי, "my secret…my secret." And who is destined to reveal these secrets to us? Mashiach. The Hebrew words משיח בן דויד also have a numerical value of 434. Thus, the secrets will be revealed from the ends of the earth with the arrival of Mashiach.

Alternatively, the Ben Ish Chai says that the Final Redemption will come about through the final letter ץ, as is explained in *Pirkei d'Rabbi Eliezer*. Therefore, he interprets the phrase מכנף הארץ to mean "from the end of the *word* ארץ." In other words, the final letter of the word ארץ — which is the final ץ — alludes to this Final Redemption, when a new "song of salvation will be heard."

◈ ◈ ◈

The Gemara (*Shabbos* 104) states that the positioning of the final letters of *mantzpach* was forgotten until it was reinstituted by the prophets. There, Rabbi Yirmeyahu is cited as saying (although some people are of the opinion that it was Rabbi Chiya bar Abba): "The letters of *mantzpach* were instituted by the early prophets." The Gemara questions this, since — based on the *pasuk* in *Vayikra* (27:34) — even the prophets are not permitted to add new concepts to the existing Torah.

The Gemara reconciles this by suggesting that the concept of the letters of *mantzpach* already existed, but that their correct position in the word sequence was not yet known, and that the prophets established that these letters of *mantzpach* should appear only at the end of a word. To this suggestion the Gemara again poses the same objection, because if it were so, it would still come under the category of adding a new concept to the Torah. The Gemara concludes that even their position was known to previous generations, as it was a Torah-ordained concept; however, through the passage of time, their position in a word was forgotten, and it was the prophets who re-established their correct position at the end of a word.

These prophets are referred to by the title of צופים — those who are capable of looking into the future. This again indicates that they prophesied regarding future redemptions, which are represented in these final letters.

At the end of Yaakov Avinu's life, as he was lying on his death bed, he summoned his twelve sons in order to bless them. The *pasuk* states: ויקרא יעקב אל בניו ויאמר האספו ואגידה לכם את אשר יקרא אתכם באחרית הימים — "And Yaakov called for his sons and said, 'Assemble yourselves and I will tell you what will happen to you in the End of Days'" (*Bereishis* 49:1), to which Rashi comments: "Yaakov wished to reveal the date of Final Redemption to them, but the *Shechinah* departed from him and he was unable to do so." Here, too, we clearly have the concept of "forgetfulness" when discussing the topic of redemption.

◈ ◈ ◈

There are five occasions in the Torah when Moshe was asked a question to which he openly admitted that he did not know the correct answer. He had to go and ask Hashem for the correct ruling. All of these five subjects incorporate an element of forgetfulness.

These five topics also form the acronym of מנצפ"ך, the five final letters, as highlighted below:

- **מ** *Bemidbar* 15:32 speaks of one who gathered (**מ**קשש) wood on Shabbos: ויהיו בני ישראל במדבר וימצאו איש מקשש עצים ביום השבת — "The Children of Israel were in the wilderness and they found a man gathering wood on Shabbos." We are then told: "They placed him in custody, for what should be done to him had not been clarified" (ibid. 15:32).
- **נ** *Vayikra* 24:11 speaks of a blasphemer (**נ**וקב שם ה'): ויקב בן האשה הישראלית את השם — "The son of the Israelite woman pronounced the Name and blasphemed..." regarding whom the next *pasuk* tells us: "They placed him under guard until the penalty could be specified by Hashem" (ibid. 24:12).
- **צ** In *Bemidbar* (Chapter 27), the daughters of Tzelofchad (**צ**לפחד) had a grievance regarding their father's portion, since he died leaving no male heirs. We are then told: "Moshe brought their case before Hashem" (ibid. 27:5).
- **פ** In the second year after the Exodus, when the *Bnei Yisrael* were in the wilderness and it was time for them to bring the *korban Pesach*, there were those who were ritually unclean. They came to Moshe Rabbeinu upset that they would not be able to bring the sacrifice. "'Wait here,' replied Moshe. 'I will hear what orders Hashem gives regarding your case'" (*Bemidbar* 9:8). Hashem then told Moshe that all those who could not bring the sacrifice in Nisan could bring it on the same day in the following month. This day is thus called *Pesach Sheni* (**פ**סח שני).
- **כ** In *Bemidbar* (Chapter 25) we are told of Pinchas's zealotry in slaying Zimri and Kozbi (**כ**זבי) for their immorality. However, initially the people thought that Pinchas had committed a wanton act of murder, until Hashem told Moshe Rabbeinu

that Pinchas had in fact acted correctly. Rashi explains that the law which applied to this situation was concealed from Moshe.

### ◈ The Order of Mantzpach

The Bnei Yisaschar explains why the final letter ך appears at the end of the *mantzpach* order, while in the numerical values it appears first, with a value of five hundred. He points out that these five final letters can be grouped into three sets: the מ with נ, and the פ with the צ — as both of these pairs follow each other in the alphabetic order — and the כ on its own, since it has no neighboring letter in the *mantzpach* sequence. This is analogous to the structure of a hand, the four fingers are close together and the thumb is singly more distant from the rest. The final letter ך is represented by the thumb. Just as the thumb will be on one side of the hand when the palm is face up and on the other side when the palm is face down, the final letter ך is the first letter in the *mantzpach* when it represents the numerical value and is the last when it represents ימלך, Hashem's kingship.

However, according to the previously mentioned explanation given by *Pirkei d'Rabbi Eliezer*, the letters should be listed in alphabetic order — ך'ם'ן'ף'ץ' — since they correspond to the respective salvations that took place in our history. Chronologically, Avraham (ך) precedes Yitzchak (ם), who precedes Yaakov (ן) and the Egyptian Exodus (ף). This is followed by the Final Redemption with the arrival of Mashiach (ץ). This follows the logical ascending alphabetic sequence.

However, the order that these five letters appear in their acronym of *mantzpach* (מנצפ"ך) is not alphabetic. If *mantzpach* were to follow an ascending alphabetic order, the final two letters (פ and כ) should appear earlier. However, these two letters appear at the end because these five final letters represent the various periods of redemption of the Jewish People throughout history, as will be explained below. A period of salvation portrays and displays the open hand of Hashem as He maneuvers the events of world history. It would be appropriate, therefore, to connect these five final letters with a proclamation of Hashem's Kingship and rulership.

### ◈ The Underlying Message of Mantzpach

Of all the passages of the set prayers, there is only one that does not actually appear in Scripture at all, but is compiled from three different sources. It is composed from phrases in *Tehillim* (10:16, 93:1) and in *Shemos* (15:18). This unique phrase proclaims Hashem's Kingship: ה' מלך ה' מלך ה' ימלך לעולם ועד — "Hashem is King, Hashem was King, and Hashem will be King forever."

The numerical value of each of the words מֶלֶךְ and מָלָךְ is ninety, whereas the word ימלך has a numerical value of one hundred. This corresponds exactly to the order of the letters of *mantzpach*. The sum of the lower numerical values of the first two letters, ם and ן, is ninety, corresponding to ה' מֶלֶךְ; the middle letter, the letter ץ, also has a lower numerical value of ninety and corresponds to ה' מָלָךְ; and the final two letters, the ף and ך, have a combined lower numerical value of one hundred, corresponding to the proclamation of ה' ימלך. The final letters of *mantzpach* proclaim the complete history of the world — its present, past and future epochs. It also proclaims the complete aim of Creation, the acknowledgment by the entire human race of Hashem's Kingship over the entire universe. The order of the letters of *mantzpach* correspond to this grouping:

| ימלך | מלך | מלך |
|---|---|---|
| ף ך | ץ | ם ן |
| [Hashem] will be King | [Hashem] was King | [Hashem] is King |

The teachings of *Pirkei Avos* (6:6) that kingship is attainable through thirty ways is hinted at in this proclamation as it is comprised of thirty letters. Moreover, in the Torah itself we find several allusions to the fact kingship is attainable through thirty ways. Previously, we cited *Devarim* 17:20 as the *pasuk* that instructs us to appoint a Jewish monarch. The Ba'al HaTurim comments that this *pasuk* begins and ends with the letter ל, whose numerical value is thirty. In the fifteenth *pasuk* of the same chapter, the Torah commands us: שום תשים עליך מלך — "You shall surely appoint for yourself a king...." The Ba'al HaTurim states that the numerical value of the words שום תשים עליך equals 1,226, the same as that of the words שלשים מעלות, the "thirty ways" through which kingship is attainable. The Rokeach points out that the letters of the words שלשים מעלות all appear in the phrase שום תשים עליך מלך.

Furthermore, the *Shemoneh Esrei* prayer of Rosh Hashanah and Yom Kippur have three extra paragraphs inserted in the third *berachah* of אתה קדוש. These paragraphs begin with the phrases ובכן תן כבוד, ובכן תן פחדך, and ובכן יתקדש שמך, respectively. The Avudraham explains that these passages all begin with the word ובכן, which corresponds to the phrase in *Megillas Esther* (4:16) which states: לך כנוס את כל היהודים הנמצאים בשושן וצומו עלי ואל תאכלו ואל תשתו שלשת ימים לילה ויום גם אני ונערתי אצום כן **ובכן** אבוא אל המלך אשר לא כדת — "Go, assemble all the Jews who are present in Shushan and fast on my behalf, and neither eat nor drink for three days, day and night; also I and my maidens will fast in a similar manner; *then* I will go to the king contrary to the law...."

These three passages are introduced by the word ובכן to signify that despite all the preparations and the repentance we have performed during the month of Elul in anticipation of the forthcoming Day of Judgment on Rosh Hashanah, we approach Hashem with the conviction that we have made insufficient preparations. This is an exact analogy to Queen Esther's approach to King Achashverosh. Therefore, we begin our prayers with a similar word. We are approaching the King in an unsuitable state, which is contrary to the law.

ובכן is also chosen to introduce our prayers because it has a numerical value of seventy-eight, which corresponds to three times the numerical value of Hashem's Name (twenty-six). In the declaration of ה' מלך ה' מלך ה' ימלך — "Hashem is King, Hashem was King, and Hashem will be King," Hashem's Name is proclaimed three times. On Rosh Hashanah, we proclaim Hashem as the universal ruler. Thus, it is appropriate to introduce these extra prayers with the word ובכן, thereby reinforcing our proclamation of His rulership and, at the same time, admitting to our human failings on the Day of Judgment.

The Rokeach points out that seventy-eight is also the total numerical value of the phrase אנא י-ה-ו-ה, "Please, Hashem," which we use when we implore Hashem to save us and grant us success: אנא ה' הושיעה נא אנא ה' הצליחה נא — "Please, Hashem, save now! Please, Hashem, grant success now!" (*Tehillim* 118:25). The Unity of Hashem is represented in various ways by the number seventy-eight. First of all, the three letters of the word אחד, whose numerical value is thirteen, has six permutations. The total numerical value of these six permutations equals seventy-eight (6 x 13 = 78). Secondly, seventy-eight is also the triangular value (see pp. 149–151 for an explanation of this concept) of twelve, as the Unity of Hashem was brought about through the combination of the twelve tribes of Israel in their service of Hashem.

### ◈ פ'ך — Salvation Through the Ages

It is interesting to point out that the two final letters of *mantzpach* (פ'ך) — the ones that represent the message of ה' ימלך — appear to be instrumental in our salvation at every crucial period in our history.

Shortly before he passed away, Yaakov called his children and wanted to reveal to them the date of the Final Redemption. The *pasuk* states: ויקרא יעקב אל בניו ויאמר האספו ואגידה לכם את אשר יקרא אתכם באחרית הימים — "Then Yaakov called his sons and said, 'Gather yourselves and I will tell you what will befall you in the End of Days'" (*Bereishis* 49:1). Using the Av–Gad transformation method (see p. 68 for an explanation of this method), the letters of the word הימים, in the phrase באחרית הימים, become וכנכן.

These letters introduce the response that Hashem gave to Pharaoh in order to annul his evil decree. During the exile in Egypt, Pharaoh wanted to annihilate the Jewish male children under the pretext that they may be a risk to the internal security of the country during a time of war. Pharaoh decreed that all male children should be drowned, as stated in *Shemos* 1:10, with the pretext פן ירבה, "lest [they] become too numerous." Hashem responds by ensuring that they multiply and become more fruitful than ever before, as the *pasuk* confirms: וכאשר יענו אתו כן ירבה וכן יפרץ — "But as much as they would afflict them, so they would increase and multiply" (ibid. 1:12). Hashem responded by using the expression of **כן** ירבה **וכן** יפרץ. The highlighted letters (כ'ן'ו'כ'ן) are the same as those produced by the expression באחרית הימים, as explained above.

With his evil decree, Pharaoh wanted to annihilate the Jewish nation. This would interfere with Hashem's plan of creating a chosen people who would proclaim Him as supreme ruler of the world. Thus, Pharaoh was attacking His plan to create a nation that would proclaim ה' ימלך to mankind. When this principle is placed in jeopardy, the appropriate use of the פ'ך' is employed to counteract it. Pharaoh said **פן** ירבה, "lest [they] become too numerous," and Hashem responded with the words **כן** ירבה, so that [they] will become too numerous." These two letters represent the eternity of Hashem's plan of ה' ימלך לעולם ועד, that Hashem will rule forever and ever.

◈ ◈ ◈

Similarly, Haman plotted to exterminate all the Jews in a single day. In the *Al haNisim* prayer we say: כשעמד עליהם המן הרשע

בקש להשמיד להרג ולאבד את כל היהודים מנער ועד זקן טף ונשים ביום אחד — "When Haman the wicked rose up against them and sought to destroy, slay and exterminate all the Jews, young and old, infants and women, on the same day...." The entire Jewish nation was threatened with extermination, which would result in the destruction of the people chosen to proclaim ה' ימלך לעולם ועד to the world. Hashem could not allow this to happen; so Haman's evil decree was overturned, as the *Megillah* states: והחדש אשר נהפך להם מיגון לשמחה — "...a month that was overturned from mourning to rejoicing" (*Esther* 9:22).

Once again, the salvation that ensures the continuity of the Jewish nation is accomplished through the use of the letters of פ'ך, as incorporated in the word **נהפך**.

◆ ◆ ◆

In the narrative of the story of the miracle of Chanukah, we are told how the Greeks attempted to impose their culture upon the Jewish People and forbade them from learning Torah and performing many important mitzvos. The Greeks eventually entered the *Beis haMikdash* and defiled its contents. After a courageous fight by the *Kohen Gadol* Mattisyahu and his sons, they overcame the superior Greek military power and rededicated the *Beis haMikdash*. The Gemara (*Shabbos* 21b) relates:

> שכשנכנסו יונים להיכל טמאו כל השמנים שבהיכל וכשגברה מלכות בית חשמונאי ונצחום בדקו ולא מצאו אלא פך אחד של שמן שהיה מונח בחותמו של כהן גדול — When the Greeks entered the *heichal*, they defiled all the oils. When the Hashmonites overcame them, they searched and found only one bottle of oil that was sealed with the seal of the *Kohen Gadol* [and thus had remained pure].

The Greeks tried to disconnect the Jewish People from Torah learning and the observance of its mitzvos, and there was a real danger that they would lose their Jewish identity. Their salvation again came though the use of these very same letters, used in the phrase פך אחד של שמן, the one jug of undefiled oil. This was the source of the miracle of the Chanukah lights, through which we celebrate our spiritual salvation, that enables us to continue in our mission of proclaiming ה' ימלך to the world.

The Ten Commandments contain a total of 620 letters. This corresponds to the 613 Torah commandments, adding to it the seven positive Rabbinically-ordained mitzvos. Historically, of these seven Rabbinically-ordained ones, the lighting of the Chanukah lights was the last one to be instituted. The final word of the Ten Commandments is לרעך, and the final letter ך corresponds to that of the Chanukah lights. The letter ך is spelled out as כף, whose letters can also spell out פך, the jug of oil that was instrumental in the miracle of Chanukah.

It is customary during the Chanukah festival to "play *dreidel*." After lighting the Chanukah *menorah*, the family sits around the table and plays together. In essence, the *dreidel* is a four-sided die with a pointed bottom. The letters ש'נ'ה'ג' appear one on each side. Each family member spins it in turn, and waits in anticipation to see which letter will come up that time, when the *dreidel* stops spinning and falls on one side.

The Bnei Yisaschar points out that these four letters spell out the word גשנה, "in Goshen." When Yaakov, together with his twelve sons and their immediate families, descended to Egypt, they settled together in the district of Goshen. Remaining together as a community was important to them, in that it ensured their ability to survive the hardships of the Egyptian exile.

Such community spirit provides help and encouragement to every individual in times of personal trouble. Similarly, this same lesson is taught annually, when family members sit together near the festive spiritual light of the *menorah* and are reminded of how important the community concept of "Goshen" is to our Jewish survival.

Furthermore, the sum total of numerical values of the four letters ג'ש'נ'ה' equals that of Mashiach. By spinning the *dreidel* and waiting eagerly for the resulting outcome, we are in fact displaying our eagerness for the anticipated arrival of Mashiach.

### ◈ Mantzpach and the Dagesh

The acronym of מנצפ"ך, *mantzpach*, can be divided into two groups: the first three letters follow an ascending alphabetic order and the final two letters a descending one. This represents the combined attributes of mercy and judgment that were incorporated into Creation itself (see Introduction). They are also required to bring about its aim, by being the catalyst for the redemptions from all our exiles.

In the Ben Ish Chai's analysis of the *mantzpach* alphabetic structure, he points out that the first three (ם'ן'ץ') have the same pronunciation in both their regular and final forms; they differ only in their written formats. Conversely, the final two (ף'ך') differ both in their written shape and in the way they are pronounced depending upon whether or not they take a *dagesh*, as they can be written either with or without the *dagesh*.

The letter ף can be read as *pei* or *fei*; the letter ך, as *kaf* or *chaf*. The word *pei* means "mouth" and represents the Oral Torah, since it is articulated with the mouth. The word *chaf* means "palm of the hand," which is instrumental in performing the Torah's commandments. The combination of these two final letters represent both Torah learning and the performance of the mitzvos. Only through this will we merit to proclaim that ultimate ה' ימלך with the arrival of Mashiach.

In the complete *alef-beis*, there are another three letters which have alternative pronunciations depending upon whether they are spelled with or without the *dagesh*, or, in the case of ש, depending upon where the dot is placed. They are: ב, which is pronounced either as *beis* or *veis*; ש, which is articulated either as *shin* or *sin*; and

ת, which is pronounced either as *tav* or *sav*. These three letters spell out the word שבת, Shabbos.

Thus, the message of these five letters that have alternative pronunciations is that the universal proclamation of ה׳ ימלך, as represented by the ף׳ and the ך׳, will only be accomplished when the Jewish People observe the Shabbos.

These five letters provide another special message as well. In order to pronounce them correctly, a person uses the faculty of sight to read them. To differentiate between their pronunciations, he uses his faculty of hearing. On Shabbos we appear differently from the rest of the week, dressed in our Shabbos clothes; our homes are also different, ready to greet the Shabbos Queen. The Shabbos meals and the *zemiros* that are sung, the Shabbos prayers, and even the things we talk about during the Shabbos, are all different from those of a weekday. A Shabbos atmosphere is both audibly and visibly different from the remainder of the week.

### ◈ The Significance of the Number Thirteen vis-à-vis the Twenty-Seven-Letter Alef-Beis

As mentioned earlier, the twenty-two-letter *alef-beis* can be expanded into a twenty-seven-letter one by incorporating the five final letters of *mantzpach* into its alphabetic structure. This can be done in one of two different ways. They can be added at the end of the twenty-two-letter alphabet, thereby producing their own individual numerical values, or each of the final letters can be inserted after their respective regular letter, as follows:

א ב ג ד ה ו ז ח ט י כ ך ל מ ם נ ן ס ע פ ף צ ץ ק ר ש ת

Using this format, the middle letter is the fourteenth letter, the regular letter מ. It is flanked on either side by thirteen letters. Using a similar interpretation as that given previously in the name of Rabbi Saadiah Gaon for the twenty-two-letter *alef-beis*, we arrive at an interesting conclusion. The middle letter, מ, representing *malchus*, is a reference to the King (**מלך**). The thirteen letters on either side correspond to the numerical value of the word **אחד**, "one," which represents the Unity of Hashem. The entire twenty-seven-letter alphabetic order, therefore, represents the proclamation of: **ה' אחד ושמו אחד** — Hashem is *One* and His Name is *One*.

The lessons alluded to in both alphabetic structures appear in the passage with which we end each of our daily prayers: כי המלכות שלך היא ולעולמי עד תמלוך בכבוד ככתוב בתורתך **ה' ימלך לעלם ועד** — ונאמר והיה ה' למלך על כל הארץ ביום ההוא יהיה **ה' אחד ושמו אחד** "For the kingdom is Yours and You will reign for all eternity in glory, as it is written in the Torah: *Hashem shall reign forever and ever*; and it is said: Hashem will be King over all the world — on that day *Hashem will be One and His Name will be One*."

Moreover, doubling the number thirteen gives us the number twenty-six, which is the numerical value of Hashem's Name of י-ה-ו-ה. The Patriarchs and Matriarchs made it their task in life to publicize His existence to mankind. The names of the three Patriarchs — אברהם, יצחק, יעקב — contain a total of thirteen letters. Similarly the names of the four Matriarchs — שרה, רבקה, רחל, לאה — also contain thirteen letters. From these ancestors came the Jewish People, who continue to disseminate this same teaching of Hashem's Oneness to the world.

### ◈ The Exceptional Final Letter

In all of Tanach there is only one instance where a final letter is used in the middle of a word. It is the final ם that appears in the *pasuk*: **ל**ם**רבה המשרה ולשלום אין קץ על כסא דוד** — "To him who increases the authority and peace without end on David's throne" (*Yeshayahu* 9:6), referring to the kingdom of Mashiach. Furthermore, there is one instance where the regular מ comes at the end of a word: בחומות ירושלים אשר **המ** פרוצים ושעריה אכלו באש — "...the walls of

Jerusalem which had been breached, and its gates consumed by fire" (*Nechemiah* 2:13).

This anomaly can be explained as follows. The *pasuk* in *Yeshayahu* refers to the present, hidden nature of David haMelech's monarchy, which will manifest itself only with the arrival of Mashiach. With his arrival, the gaps in the walls of Jerusalem will again be closed, as Hashem will protect us entirely. The Bnei Yisaschar explains these changes as being analogous to those that occur at childbirth. During pregnancy the child receives his nourishment through the umbilical cord, while his mouth remains closed. After birth, this is reversed — the cord is closed and nourishment enters through the mouth. The arrival of Mashiach will herald the birth of a completely new era; at that time, the spelling of these two words will be reversed and will follow the standard rules of the normal and final letters.

### ◈ The Twenty-Seven-Letter Alef-Beis in Scripture

In all of the twenty-four books of Scripture, there is only one *pasuk* that contains the twenty-seven letters of the complete *alef-beis*; it states:

> לכן חכו לי נאם ה׳ ליום קומי לעד כי משפטי לאסף גוים לקבצי ממלכות לשפך עליהם זעמי כל חרון אפי כי באש קנאתי תאכל כל הארץ — "Therefore, wait for Me, says Hashem, for the day that I will rise to meet with you. For it is My judgment to assemble nations, to gather kingdoms, to pour out My fury on them, by all the kindling of My wrath, for with the fire of My jealousy all the earth shall be consumed." (*Tzefaniah* 3:8)

Being that the twenty-seven-letter *alef-beis* displays the ultimate proclamation of Hashem's Oneness, it is therefore appropriate that the above *pasuk* should be followed by: כי אז אהפך אל עמים שפה ברורה לקרא כלם בשם ה׳ לעבדו שכם אחד — "For them I will convert the peoples to a pure language that all of them call in the Name of Hashem, to worship Him of one accord" (ibid. 3:9).

Ibn Ezra explains that this pure language — which was the original language universally used from the time of Creation until the Dispersion, almost two thousand years later — is לשון הקודש, the "holy language." The introductory *pasuk* to the story of the Dispersion alludes to this: ויהי כל הארץ שפה אחת ודברים אחדים — "And the whole earth was of one language and unified words" (*Bereishis* 11:1). The words שפה אחת, "one language," have the same numerical value as the words לשון הקדש, the language of Creation, which is articulated through the letters of the *alef-beis*.

## Applications of the Alphabetic Order

As stated earlier, when the letters of the *alef-beis* appear in an ascending order, they represent a natural progression and the attribute of mercy; when they appear in the reverse descending order, they represent the attribute of strict justice.

Rosh Hashanah is the appropriate time of the year when we affirm Hashem as מלך — the universal King. The Torah provides guidelines regarding the appointment of a Jewish monarch. A Jewish king should be chosen מקרב אחיך — "from amidst your brethren" (*Devarim* 17:15).

Moreover, he is advised neither to have too many horses (לא ירבה לו סוסים [ibid. v. 16]), nor too many wives (ולא ירבה לו נשים [ibid. v. 17]), nor to amass too much money (כסף וזהב לא ירבה לו מאד [ibid.]). These limitations are to ensure that he will not become haughty, and that ולא יסור לבבו — "he will not be led astray" (ibid.).

Rashi states that if a Jewish monarch follows this advice, he will merit to have his kingdom endure and he will remain on his throne (כסא). The Ben Ish Chai points out that the word כסא is an acronym for כסף (money), סוס (horse) אשה (wife) — the three areas of restriction.

The actual spelling of the word מלך portrays this advice: These three letters are all middle letters — מ is the middle letter of the complete twenty-seven-letter *alef-beis,* and כ and ל are the middle two letters of the twenty-two-letter *alef-beis* — alluding to the fact that the king has to be chosen "from *amidst* his brethren."

The Jewish monarch is the most influential and important person in the nation — this is indicated by the ל, the tallest and most regal of all the letters. Yet the word מלך ends with the final letter ך, whose foot descends lower than that of all the letters. The usage of both of these letters teaches that although the king is the most powerful person, he must remember to remain humble.

These important lessons are all incorporated in the actual shape of the letters, and their relative positions in the *alef-beis.* Moreover, as we said before, the fact that they are juxtaposed in a reverse alphabetic order indicates the attribute of justice — as the Jewish king is responsible for judging his people and maintaining law and order.

◆ ◆ ◆

Another example that illustrates how the alphabetic order provides added meaning to words is found in the names of the months of the year. The destruction of both Holy Temples took place during the months of **ת**מוז (Tamuz) and **א**ב (Av). The first letters of these two words follow a reverse alphabetic order (first ת and then א), representing the attribute of justice. The actual destruction took place on the ninth day of **אב**. Yet the spelling of the name of this month follows an ascending order. Tradition tells us that the forthcoming Mashiach will be born on this day, and the ninth of Av will become the most joyous festival of the year. This potential is displayed by the ascending order of its spelling.

The next two calendar months are reserved for repentance and return to Hashem, and are commonly referred to as the Days of Mercy. The acronym of these two months, **א**לול (Elul) and **ת**שרי (Tishrei), follow an ascending alphabetic order from *alef* to *tav,* and therefore symbolize the attribute of mercy. Yet, it is during Tishrei that Hashem judges the universe. Appropriately, the spelling of the word תשרי follows a descending alphabetic order.

◈ ◈ ◈

As mentioned earlier, Hashem imbued the letters of the *alef-beis* with latent divine powers, and with these letters He created the world. Being that the letters of the *alef-beis* are the building blocks of Creation, they must also incorporate the basic laws of nature. Amazingly, some five hundred years ago, the Yalkut Reuveini wrote that this same alphabetic order also reveals the hidden powers of nature.

All naturally occurring materials are made up from ninety basic substances called elements. The smallest part of an element is an atom, which has at its center a nucleus made up of protons and neutrons. This nucleus has a positive electrical charge caused by the charge of the protons, and contains almost the whole mass of the atom. Its size, however, is tiny, when compared to the rest of the atom. If the atom was the size of a large wedding hall, the nucleus would be no larger than a pea, situated at its center.

Negatively charged electrons move around the nucleus, similar to way that the planets move in their orbits in space. Although electrons are very small, they cover a lot of space, and their orbit size determines the size of an atom. They traverse relatively large distances, traveling through empty space — since the vast majority of an atom consists of empty space. Electrons always occupy shells — or energy levels — around the nucleus, with those nearest to the nucleus being filled first. The first and smallest shell will only hold two electrons, the second one eight and the third one eighteen, following a prescribed formula. Atoms will always try to have full electron shells, and if they are not full, will react with another atom, in a chemical reaction, to complete their outer shells. Electrons and protons always carry equal but opposite electrical charges and provide a neutrality to the entire atom.

Atoms of different elements have different numbers of protons in their nuclei, and therefore a different number of electrons in orbit. The lightest element — that of hydrogen — has one proton and one electron, while the heaviest naturally occurring one, uranium, has ninety-two. In order to obtain a vast amount of energy quickly, we can split the atomic nucleus. By splitting uranium, the nucleus becomes unstable and splits into two lighter nuclei of roughly equal mass, shooting out two or three neutrons in the process. This splitting process is called nuclear fission, or atomic fission, and with these fragments a substantial amount of energy is released in a very short space of time.

Empty space in Hebrew is known as הבל (*hevel*). Every element consists primarily of *hevel* — shells of empty space through which electrons spin around the central nucleus. Uranium, being the heaviest natural element, has the largest number of shells, with a total of seven such energy levels, through which its electrons travel.

The book of *Koheles* begins by referring to *hevel* a total of seven times, which can be taken as an allusion to the composition of all the elements, since they possess up to a maximum of seven hevel shells of empty space. Thus, in the first *pasuk* of *Koheles* the phrase הכל הבל can be interpreted to mean "all [matter consists of a maximum of seven shells of] *hevel*."

A large massive amount of energy can be obtained by arranging for two light elements to fuse together and form a single nucleus. This process is called nuclear fusion and, like fission, it results in the release of a large amount of energy. Fusion, however, produces far more energy for a given mass of material than any fission reaction. This is the principle behind the production of the hydrogen bomb.

This vast amount of energy that can be released by either atomic fission or fusion was mathematically predicted by Albert Einstein. What is, however, truly remarkable is that more than four hundred years before Einstein, the Yalkut Reuveini quotes a Midrash which makes the following observation:

*Chazal* explain that the creation of the universe took place through the use of four basic ingredients: fire (אש), water (מים), air (רוח) and dust (עפר); and of these four, fire is the source of energy. In the progression of the *alef-beis*, the first letter *alef*, represents **אש**, as it begins with that letter. Since there are four basic ingredients, every subsequent fourth letter in the alphabetic order represents the latent power **אש**. This produces the following pattern:

**א**בגד**ה**וזח**ט**יכל**מ**נסע**פ**צקר**ש**תךם**ן**ףץ

When grouped together, these letters spell out אהטמ פשן, "atom fission/fusion." At the end of the passage the Yalkut Reuveini admits that he was not aware of the meaning of this revelation.

Thus, atomic fission/fusion is incorporated into the alphabetic sequence of the *alef-beis*.

Rabbeinu Bechaye explains that *Chazal* derived that from the word ארץ, "earth," everything can be broken down into one or a combination of these four basic ingredients, through which the entire universe was created.

Commenting on Rabbeinu Bechaye, *Tosefos YomTov* explains that the word ארץ corresponds to the ingredient of עפר (dust), since they have similar meanings, and that the letters of the word ארץ correspond to the remaining ingredients: א represents **אש**; ר represents **רוח**; and the letter צ has a numerical value of ninety, representing **מים**, which also has a numerical value of ninety.

The Ohr HaChayim points out that of these ingredients only fire is not specifically mentioned in the narrative of Creation, as Hashem wanted to obscure the destructive and potentially deadly power of fire. However, the first word of the Torah, **בראשית**, spells out the words **ברית אש**, "covenant of fire."

If we take these words literally, we could say that Hashem made a covenant with fire. What might this mean? That it was a precondition at Creation that nuclear power be harnessed for peaceful purposes, and not be used to cause the total destruction of the world.

## The Gemara's Grouping and Explanation of the Alphabetic Order

The Gemara in *Shabbos* (104) explains the alphabetic order of the *alef-beis,* while at the same time interpreting the meaning of each individual letter. (Since this passage is fairly long, I have divided it into sections, in order to make it more readable and easier to understand. I have used a different bolded typeface in order to highlight the actual words of the Gemara and its translation. Ordinary typeface is used for the various explanations that are given to interpret them.) The relevant passage begins:

### ◈ Alef–Beis: Study Torah

**אל"ף בי"ת אלף בינה — *Alef, beis:* Study [the Torah] and gain insights...**

The word אלף means to teach or to study (see *Iyov* 32:32). בינה is the understanding that one gains by the process of deduction from previously acquired knowledge. The Maharsha explains that the lesson of these two opening letters of the *alef-beis* is that when employing this self-taught understanding to propose new Torah insights, one must use only those guidelines and rules that have been previously taught by one's Torah teacher (the אלף), and not rely on one's own intellect. This lesson forms the basis of the opening part of *Pirkei Avos,* which teaches us the method that the Torah was transmitted from one generation to the next. Genuine Torah needs to be transmitted from teacher to disciple. There first has to be an אלף, the mentor to teach the בינה, the understanding, to the next generation.

The numerical value of the fulfillments of אלף and בית totals 523, the same as the number of chapters in the Six Orders of the Mishnah. Thus the first two letters of the *alef-beis* represent the entire Oral Torah.

### ◈ Gimmel–Dalet: Give to the Poor

**גימ"ל דל"ת גמול דלים מ"ט פשוטה כרעיה דגימל לגבי דל"ת שכן דרכו של גומל חסדים לרוץ אחר דלים ומ"ט פשוטה כרעיה דדל"ת לגבי גימ"ל דלימציה ליה נפשיה ומ"ט מהדר אפיה דדל"ת מגימ"ל דליתן ליה בצינעה כי היכי דלא ליכסיף מיניה — *Gimmel, dalet*: Aid the needy. Why is the [left] leg of the letter *gimmel* extended towards the letter *dalet*? Because it is indeed the manner of the one who bestows kindness to run after the needy** [to help them]. **And why is the leg of the letter *dalet* extended towards the letter *gimmel*?** In other words, why is the stem of the *dalet* slanted backwards towards the *gimmel* and not forwards towards the letter *hei*? This is to indicate that the poor man **should make himself available to his benefactor.** The poor man also has an obligation to perform kind deeds, and by making himself easily available to his benefactor, he is able to reciprocate the kindness. **And why is the face of the letter *dalet* turned away from the letter *gimmel*?** To indicate that the **benefactor should give charity discreetly, in order not to embarrass the recipient.**

The Maharsha clarifies this explanation by quoting the Gemara in *Sukkah* (49b), which states:

> We are taught: In three ways is performing acts of kindness greater than charity. Firstly, charity can only be performed by giving money, while kindness can be performed through good actions or with money. Secondly, charity can only be performed by giving to poor people, whereas kind deeds can be performed to both the rich and the poor. Thirdly, charity can only be given to the living, whereas kind deeds can be performed to both the living and the dead.

In order to stress this distinction between charity and kind deeds, the Maharsha explains that the grouping and juxtaposition of these two letters teaches us that one should pursue the enhanced option of performing kind deeds with the poor.

Giving charity is viewed by the Torah as a privilege that the rich man has. It emulates the way that Hashem Himself created and established the world, as it fulfills His infinite desire to perform kindness with His creation. The actual letters of the word חסד, kindness, can be read as חס + ד, meaning that one should have pity (חס) on a poor person (represented by the ד) and never send him away empty handed.

The alphabetic sequence of א'ב'ג'ד' represents the rich man who leaves his home to provide for the poor. The ב fulfills as בית, meaning a house, and is followed in the alphabetic order by the letter ג, which pictorially is the profile of a person walking away from his home (ב ג). These are followed by the letter ד, which fulfills as דלת, the doorway where the poor man (the דל) normally stands in order to collect alms. The home owner is represented as the lord of the house, the א, whose profile (the ג) is seen leaving his house towards the poor man to perform acts of kindness.

True kindness is when the rich man takes the trouble to deliver the charity discreetly to the poor man, rather than waiting for him to come collecting.

◈ ◈ ◈

The Toras Chayim, in the introduction to his commentary to the Gemara in *Sanhedrin*, offers a unique explanation for the Gemara's interpretation of the *alef-beis* sequence. The first two sets of letters, the Gemara explains, represent learning Torah and the performance of kind deeds, respectively.

Thus the explanation for אל"ף בי"ת אלף בינה and גימ"ל דל"ת גמול דלים, incorporate the pillars of Torah and kindness, upon which the entire universe exists. They form the title and main theme, so to speak, that the remainder of the *alef-beis* comes to explain. Thus, the Toras Chayim explains the meaning of the remainder of this passage in the Gemara vis-à-vis how each pair of letters fit into these two categories.

### ◈ Hei–Vav: Hashem's Name

**ה"ו זה שמו של הקב"ה** — *Hei, Vav:* These [two letters] represent **the Name of Hashem.**

Rashi explains that these two letters, ה and ו, compose the Name of Hashem that we say in *davening* on Hoshana Rabbah: אני והו הושיע נא — "Hashem, bring salvation now." The Name of Hashem of והו is both the first and the forty-ninth set of the seventy-two-letter Name of Hashem, known as the *Shem haMeforash.*

The Maharsha explains that these two letters, ה and ו, form the second half of the four-letter Name of Hashem (י-ה-ו-ה). The numerical value of ה is five and that of ו is six, representing the five books of the Written Torah and the six orders of the Oral Torah, respectively.

In *Tehillim* 19 there are six phrases that describe the beauty of the Torah. They are:

1) תורת ה' תמימה משיבת נפש — "The Torah of Hashem is perfect, restoring the soul."
2) עדות ה' נאמנה מחכימת פתי — "The testimony of Hashem is trustworthy, making the simple one wise."
3) פקודי ה' ישרים משמחי לב — "The orders of Hashem are upright, gladdening the heart."
4) מצות ה' ברה מאירת עינים — "The command of Hashem is clear, enlightening the eyes."
5) יראת ה' טהורה עומדת לעד — "The fear of Hashem is pure, enduring for ever."
6) משפטי ה' אמת צדקו יחדו — "The judgments of Hashem are true, altogether righteous."

Each of these six *pesukim* contains five words, correlating to the six orders of the Oral Torah and the five books of the Written Torah, respectively. Moreover, the second book of the Written Torah is known as שמות—a word that translates as "names." Appropriately, the second word of each of these phrases is the Name of Hashem.

The ה and ו also represent the reward that Hashem bestows on those who perform kind deeds and acts of charity, as alluded to in the following Gemara (*Bava Basra* 9b):

> Rabbi Yitzchak taught that one who gives a coin to a poor man will be blessed with six blessings, whereas one who comforts him with kind words will be blessed with eleven blessings.

The six blessings that are given as a reward for giving charity are symbolized by the letter ו, while the eleven blessings are symbolized by the combination of the letters ה and ו, which have a combined numerical value of eleven. These eleven blessings are bestowed on all who offer kind words of encouragement to the needy.

The Ben Ish Chai adds that these eleven blessings are also alluded to in the language used by the Gemara (כל הנותן פרוטה לעני), as the letters that make up this charitable contribution—the פרוטה—rearrange to spell out פרט + וה, which translates as "specifically, eleven." These eleven blessings are bestowed as a result of performing specific charitable acts.

The lesson taught by the alphabetic order of the first six letters is exhibited in the Gemara in *Sanhedrin* 98b: מה יעשה אדם וינצל מחבלו של משיח? יעסוק בתורה ובגמילות חסדים—"What should a person do in order to be saved from the birth pangs of Mashiach? He should toil in Torah and perform kind deeds."

As we said, the first two letters represent learning Torah, the second set represents the performance of kind deeds, while the third set represents the latter half of Hashem's Name—that will reattach itself to spell out His full Name, when the evil forces have been eradicated at the time of Mashiach (as explained in the Av–Gad transformation method, on p. 68).

### ◈ Zayin–Ches, Tes–Yud, Chaf–Lamed: The Reward for Giving to the Poor

**ז"ח ט"י כ"ל ואם אתה עושה כן הקב"ה זן אותך וחן אותך ומטיב לך ונותן לך ירושה וקשר לך כתר לעוה"ב** — *Zayin–Ches, Tes–Yud, Chaf–Lamed*: **If you do this** (i.e. study the Torah and help the needy), **then Hashem will sustain you and favor you, bestow you with goodness, provide you with an inheritance, and bind for you a crown for the World to Come.**

The Toras Chayim explains that this grouping is representative of the reward for performing charitable acts for the poor, and divides the six letters into two sets.

The first three letters, ז'ח'ט', form the first set, and correspond to the phrase: **זן** אותך **וחן** אותך **ומטיב** לך — "[Hashem] will sustain you and favor you, [and] bestow you with goodness"; this is the reward given for performing acts of charity to the needy. We acknowledge this in the first blessing of the Grace aAfter Meals: הזן את העולם כלו **בטובו בחן** בחסד וברחמים — "Who nourishes the entire world, in His goodness with grace, kindness and with mercy," which correspond to the three basic provisions that are required — food, clothing and housing. Hashem will reward charitable acts with all three types of sustenance.

The second set of three letters, י'כ'ל', represent the reward that corresponds to the learning of Torah, which is represented by these letters in the above Gemara ונותן לך **ירושה** וקשר לך **כתר לעוה"ב** — "He will provide you with an inheritance, and bind for you a crown for the World to Come."

### ◈ Mem and Final Mem: Revealed and Hidden Teachings of the Torah

**מ"ם פתוחה מ"ם סתומה מאמר פתוח מאמר סתום** — The **open** *mem* and **closed** *mem* refer to an **open statement** and a **closed**

**statement**, respectively. Some Torah studies should be taught openly and revealed to other people, whereas secrets of Kabbalah should remain concealed from the general public.

The Torah itself was given after Moshe was in Heaven for forty days, a number that equates to the numerical value of the letter מ. The open and closed letters מ allude to both the revealed and hidden teachings of Torah knowledge. The letter מ fulfills as מם, which incorporates both the open and closed letters *mem*.

If we continue the expansions of the open letter מ and present them in a pictorial form, we obtain:

מ

מ ם

מ ם ם

מ ם ם ם

As the open letter מ represents the revealed Torah, and the final ם represents the hidden secrets contained therein, the above illustration demonstrates, how continued learning reveals further insights of hidden knowledge.

◈ ◈ ◈

The Maharsha explains that Creation took place through a total of Ten Divine Utterances, as enumerated in the fifth chapter of *Pirkei Avos*. These utterances are בראשית ברא א-להים, and the nine times that the phrase ויאמר א-להים appears in the narrative of Creation. The nine utterances of ויאמר א-להים correspond to the open speech commands of the מאמר פתוח. The first utterance is portrayed in a more obscure form: בראשית ברא א-להים—corresponding to the closed statement of the מאמר סתום, the hidden utterance.

One of the reasons given for this disparity between the first and the other nine utterances of Creation is that Hashem's initial Creation was יש מאין, a concept of creating something from nothing, *ex nihilo*, through the utterance of בראשית.

The Chasam Sofer points out that this *ex nihilo* creation is alluded to in the word בראשית itself. The letters ש and ת have a total numerical value of seven hundred, which corresponds to the higher numerical value of the final letter ן. If we replace these two letters, with the final letter ן in the spelling of the word בראשית, we obtain the letters ב'ר'א'י'ן', which can also spell out the words ברא אין — the *ex nihilo* creation. (Note: When expounding upon an interpretation, a letter that appears in the middle of a word can be duplicated when that word is broken apart, being attached to each of the two new words. This is especially so when the letter is an א or a ה, as they are not pronounced.)

## ◈ Nun and Final Nun: Be Humble

> **נו"ן כפופה נו"ן פשוטה נאמן כפוף נאמן פשוט — Bent *nun* and simple *nun*:** This refers to a **faithful person in a bent position** and to an **erect one.**

Rashi explains that this represents a righteous person who always remains humble in this world but will stand tall and erect in the World to Come.

The Maharsha explains that the bent letter *nun* represents the humble person who keeps his eyes downcast, whereas the final letter *nun* symbolizes the heart of this righteous, humble person, as he always looks upwards in his aspirations of gaining new spiritual heights.

The Toras Chayim explains the juxtaposition of the letters מ and נ in the alphabetic order, and the way they have been expounded by the Gemara. If one wants to learn Torah and its hidden secrets, which are represented by מ"ם פתוחה מ"ם סתומה מאמר פתוח מאמר סתום, then it is essential that one possess humility, which is represented by the teachings of נון כפופה נו"ן פשוטה **נאמן** כפוף **נאמן** פשוט. Moshe Rabbeinu, as the humblest of all men, had all the secrets of the Torah revealed to him. He is appropriately referred to as

נאמן in the *pasuk*: לא כן עבדי משה בכל ביתי נאמן הוא — "Not so is My servant Moshe, in My entire house he is trusted" (*Bemidbar* 12:7).

### ◈ Samech–Ayin: Help the Poor

**ס"ע סמוך עניים ל"א סימנין עשה בתורה וקנה אותה** — *Samech, ayin*: **Support the poor** with encouraging words. **Alternatively, it can be explained as: Make mnemonics for the Torah in order to acquire it.**

The Toras Chayim continues to explain this statement in a similar fashion. The first part of the interpretation refers to supporting the poor with the acts of charity (see the explanation for *Gimmel-Dalet*, p. 40). The second part, of making mnemonics (a method or system for improving one's memory) in order to acquire Torah knowledge, refers to the אלף בינה.

Referring to concepts by the number of categories from which they are composed is an example of a mnemonic found in the Gemara, such as: ארבה אבות נזיקים — The *Four* Principle Causes of Damage (*Bava Kama*); חמש עשרה נשים פוטרות צרותיהן — The *Fifteen* Categories of Women (*Yevamos*); ל"ט מלכות — The *Thirty-Nine* Categories of Forbidden Work (*Shabbos*).

### ◈ Pei and Final Pei: Know When to Speak

**פ' כפופה פ' פשוטה פה פתוח פה סתום** — **Bent** *pei* and **simple** *pei*: alludes to an **open mouth** and a **closed mouth.**

Rashi explains that this teaches a person to take a leadership role when no one else is available, but to refrain when there is a more senior person present.

Similarly, a basic respect for one's teacher is taught by these two letters. Students need to close their mouths and pay attention when their teacher opens his mouth to teach.

## ◈ Tzaddi and Final Tzaddi: Be Very Humble

**צד"י כפופה וצד"י פשוט היינו נאמן כפוף נאמן פשוט הוסיף לך הכתוב כפיפה על כפיפתו מכאן שנתנה התורה במנוד ראש** — This represents a **bent *tzaddik*** (righteous person) **and an erect *tzaddik*. Although this is the same as the interpretation for the straight and final letter *nun,* the Torah added an extra degree of bending to the righteous person's bent state. From here we can derive that the Torah was given with a trembling of the head** (i.e. a person merits acquiring Torah knowledge through possessing extraordinary humility).

This double dose of humility required to learn Torah correctly is referred to in the Mishnah: מאד מאד הוי שפל רוח — "Be very, very humble" (*Avos* 4:4). The numerical value of the words מאד מאד is ninety, the same as the numerical value of the letter צ, alluding to this very same lesson. Both the interpretations of the normal and final letters נ and צ teach the importance of humility. Moshe Rabbeinu is referred to as "trusted" (נאמן) as well as being the humblest of all men, in the two *pesukim*: והאיש משה ענו מאד **מכל האדם** אשר אל פני האדמה — "And the man Moshe was very humble, more than any person on the face of the earth" (*Bemidbar* 12:3); and: לא כן עבדי משה בכל ביתי **נאמן** הוא — "Not so is My servant Moshe, in My entire house he is trusted" (ibid. 12:7).

The Toras Chayim points out that the numerical value of the word מכל is ninety, corresponding to the humility represented by the letter צ of the same numerical value. The numerical value of the next word, האדם, is fifty, corresponding to the humility represented by the letter נ, of the same numerical value. Moshe possessed this extreme humility that is displayed by both the letters of נ and צ together. The numerical value of the words of צדיק נאמן totals 345, the same as the numerical value of משה, the humblest of all men.

According to the Gemara, the letter נ represents a humble person, and the letter צ an extremely humble one. Bending the vertical arm of the letter נ towards the left denotes an extra degree of humbleness. On achieving this extreme humbleness, the *Shechinah* rest on this person. This is displayed by adding the letter י to the right hand side of the bent letter נ, thereby forming the shape of the letter צ.

The Toras Chayim poses an interesting question as to the order of the *alef-beis* and the five final letters in the way the Gemara interprets them. There is a striking similarity between the explanations given for the letters מ'ם'נ'ן and those of the letters פ'ף'צ'ץ. This similarity is more apparent when they are grouped together as:

מ  מ"ם פתוחה מ"ם **סתומה** מאמר פתוח מאמר סתום
נ  נון כפופה נו"ן **פשוטה** נאמן כפוף נאמן פשוט

פ  פ' כפופה פ' **פשוטה** פה פתוח פה סתום
צ  צד"י כפופה וצד"י **פשוט** נאמן כפוף נאמן פשוט

Being that these sets are so similar in the message that they convey, the Toras Chayim asks why the alphabetic sequence is interrupted by the insertion of the letters ס and ע. He answers that the insertion indicates that there are other ways to interpret the alphabetic order — apart from the one which the Gemara explains here. He quotes two examples, one where the alphabetic order provides medical information, and another one that provides halachic rulings. Both of these require the letters ס and ע to be placed in their present position, in order to portray these new teachings.

A reference to the medical information that is contained in the alphabetic order of the *alef-beis* is found in the Gemara quoting Shemuel, who himself was a medical doctor: נו"ן סמ"ך עי"ן נונא סמא לעינים — "*Nun, samech, ayin*: fish is medication for the eyes" (*Nedarim* 54b). The juxtaposition of the three letters נ'ס'ע' in the *alef-beis* teaches us that fish have therapeutic properties which are beneficial to a person's eyesight. Fish have an abundant supply of Vitamin A, which is vital in order to maintain good vision.

The Rokeach explains that all twenty-seven letters of the *alef-beis* have therapeutic properties — alluded to in the request for health that we make in the *Amidah* prayer of רפאנו, which, in *nusach Ashkenaz*, contains exactly twenty-seven words. Each has its own special healing properties, and together they provide the complete prescription required to heal all ailments.

The halachic teachings that can be derived from the alphabetic order of the letters is hinted at in the laws relating to finding lost property, as taught in *Bava Metzia*. Normally a lost article is returned to its rightful owner if the owner is able to provide a *siman*, a sign of identification to indicate that the article belongs to him. However, the Gemara stipulates that if the person who loses the object is a Talmudic student, then he can be believed even without providing any characteristic markings on the object. He is believed by simply viewing the article and verifying that the object is his.

This halachic ruling is indicated by the juxtaposition of the letters ס'ע'פ'צ' in the alphabetic order. This represents the rule that we can rely on the verbal confirmation of the Talmudic student, to verify the ownership of an article. We rely (**סמך**) on the sighting (**עין**) and the verbal confirmation (**פה**) of the righteous student (**צדיק**).

These extra teachings can only be taught by inserting these two letters of ס and ע in their present positions.

## ◈ Kuf Kadosh: A Reference to Hashem

**קוף קדוש** — The letter ***kuf*** represents **the Holy One**, referring to Hashem. In Chapter 4 we explain that the letters of Hashem's Name have a multiplication value (see "Squared Numbers," p. 152) of 186, which is the numerical value of letters which spell out the articulated form of the letter ק (קוף). The letter ק, therefore, represents the Holy One.

## ◈ Kuf and Reish: The Kadosh and the Rasha

**רי"ש רשע מאי טעמא מהדר אפיה דקו"ף מרי"ש אמר הקב"ה אין אני יכול להסתכל ברשע ומאי טעמא מהדרה תגיה דקו"ף לגבי רי"ש אמר הקב"ה**

**אם חזר בו אני קושר לו כתר כמוני ומ"ט כרעיה דקו"ף תלויה דאי הדר ביה ליעייל. וליעול בהך מסייע ליה לריש לקיש דאמר ר"ל מ"ד (משלי ג) אם ללצים הוא יליץ ולענוים יתן חן. בא ליטמא פותחין לו בא ליטהר מסייעים אותו** — [The letter] *reish* represents a *rasha* (an evil person). **Why is the face of the *kuf* turned away from the *reish*? For as Hashem says, "I am unable to look at the face of the evil person." And why is the crown of the *kuf* turned towards the *reish*? Hashem says, "If he repents, then I will bind him with a crown like My own. And why is the leg of the *kuf* suspended?** (The left leg is not connected to the main body of the letter.) **So that if the evil person repents, he can enter and join** [the domain of Hashem, as represented by the letter ק]. **But** [why is it necessary to have two holes? Let him enter through the bottom opening!] **This supports Reish Lakish who asked: What is the meaning of the *pasuk* (*Mishlei* 3:34): "With the cynics he will act cynically, but to the humble He will grant favor"? It means that if one comes to defile himself, they provide an opening for him, but if one wants to purify himself, they will actually help** him to achieve this.

The letters ק and ה are unique in that they are the only ones in the entire *alef-beis* that are composed from two noncontiguous parts. The Gemara gives almost identical explanations of both of their shapes. Whatever is explained with regards the letter ק applies equally to the letter ה.

## ◈ Shin and Tav: Falsehood and Truth

**שי"ן שקר תי"ו אמת מאי טעמא שקר מקרבן מיליה אמת מרחקא מיליה שיקרא שכיח קושטא לא שכיח ומ"ט שיקרא אחדא כרעיה קאי ואמת מלבן לבוניה קושטא קאי שיקרא לא קאי — The letter *shin* represents falsehood, the letter *tav* represents the truth. Why are the letters that make up the word שקר juxtaposed** in the alphabetic order **whereas the letters of the word אמת are spread**

**out? And why do the letters that spell out שקר each stand on one leg, while the letters spelling out the word אמת all have a sturdy base? Because the truth stands and remains, whereas falsehood [has no legs and thus] cannot stand.**

The Gemara states that the letter ש represents שקר, falsehood, while the letter ת represents אמת, truth. The question is: Why is the first letter of the word שקר used to represent that word while the last letter of the word אמת is used to represent it? The answer lies within the Gemara's discussion of the alphabetic order. Of the three letters that spell out the word שקר, the letter ש appears last in the alphabetic order of ק-ר-ש. Until we reach the letter ש, we are unable to fully spell out the word שקר. The letter ש, therefore, represents שקר, as it is only with this letter that we can correctly spell out the complete word. Similarly, in order to spell out the word אמת, we need to fully complete the alphabetic order. It is only when reaching the last letter ת that we can complete its spelling. It is therefore, the letter ת that represents the word אמת, despite the fact that it appears at the end of the word.

◈ ◈ ◈

Next, the Gemara gives an explanation of how various alphabetic tranformation methods are implemented. These methods are dealt with in the next chapter. The continuation of the Gemara will be cited there.

# CHAPTER 2
# Alphabetic Transformation Methods

## Alphabetic Structures

Although the normal alphabetic sequence of the letters begins with the א and ends with the ת, the Ohr Zaruah lists another seven different methods of grouping the letters together. In each method, the letters are grouped together in different sets, and individual letters within the same set can be substituted one for another, thereby uncovering different meanings to the words. Each method of transformation is used to provide a different type of revelation to the Torah.

These seven different methods are identified by the acronym of their initial sets:

| | |
|---|---|
| At–Bash | א"ת ב"ש |
| Al–Bam | א"ל ב"מ |
| At–Bach | א"ט ב"ח |
| Av–Gad | א"ב ג"ד |
| Achas–Beta | אח"ס בט"ע |
| Ayik–Bekar | אי"ק בכ"ר |
| Avag–Beged | אב"ג בג"ד |

There are an additional two alphabetic methods that are not mentioned by the Ohr Zaruah, namely Aiy–Bak and Ach–Bi.

### ◈ The At–Bash (א"ת ב"ש) Method

Earlier we mentioned the significance of the alphabetic order. When letters appear in an ascending alphabetic order, they represent a natural progression that displays the attribute of mercy. When they appear in a descending alphabetic order, they symbolize the attribute of strict justice. The At–Bash (א"ת ב"ש) method combines both the ascending and descending orders. The first letter א is exchanged for the final letter ת, the second letter ב for the penultimate letter ש, and so on. These combine to produce the acronym of א"ת ב"ש.

In mathematical terms, this method would be classified as a transformation of the letters. Within this structure, the first half of the alphabet follows an ascending order, while the second half a descending one, as illustrated below:

א ב ג ד ה ו ז ח ט י כ transforms into
ת ש ר ק צ פ ע ס נ מ ל

The source of the At–Bash structure is to be found at the end of the Chumash in the passage that describes the events leading up to the giving of the Torah. The *pasuk* states: מימינו אשדת למו — "From His right hand He presented a Law of Fire to them" (*Devarim* 33:2). Rashi explains that this Law of Fire was a law of contrasts, of black fire written upon white fire. This corresponds to the black lettering on white parchment in every Torah scroll. Similarly, each "black" letter must be entirely surrounded by "white" parchment, such that it does not touch any other letter.

The Rokeach points out that the numerical value of the word אשדת — which is a reference to the Torah — is equal to that of באת בש, which can be translated as "through [the use of] At–Bash [alphabetic transformations]. Thus, the Torah itself indicates that it can be interpreted using the At–Bash method. Furthermore, the letters ד'ת'ל'מ'ו', which appear in that *pasuk* (מימינו אש **דת למו**) spell out the word תלמוד, the Talmud, which incorporates the entire Oral Torah — the Mishnah, as well as the Gemara.

Moreover, a hint to the usage of the At–Bash method is found in the first word of the Torah. The Rokeach explains that letters of the word בראשית can be combined to form the following pairs of letters: א"ת ב"ש ר"י, which he reads as: "[Use] At–Bash [to transform] ר"י." In At–Bash, the ר becomes a ג and the י is exchanged for a מ, which spells out גם, "also." Therefore, the first word of the Torah (בראשית) tells us that the Torah can *also* be explained using the At–Bash alphabetic transformation.

◈ ◈ ◈

On the third day of Creation, Hashem commanded the earth to sprout forth vegetation of plants that produce seed: תדשא הארץ דשא עשב מזריע זרע — "Let the earth sprout vegetation of plants bringing forth seeds..." (*Bereishis* 1:11). *Sefer HaRemazim* writes that this large variety of vegetation is an analogy to the Torah, whose explanations and interpretations grow continuously.

Symbolically, this sprouting forth of new vegetation, the תדשא, has the same numerical value as the phrase באת בש, which, as we have said, means: "through [the use of the] At–Bash [alphabetic transformations]. These different alphabetic transformations sprout forth new interpretations to the words of the Torah.

Not only can the Torah be explained by using the words the way that they are actually written, they can also be transformed using the At–Bash method to produce a new array of meaning to these very same words, producing a "new species" of meaning to the original words.

◈ ◈ ◈

In *Hilchos De'os*, the Rambam gives advice on how to work towards eliminating bad character traits. For example, if a person wants to control his bad temper, he should go to the other extreme, and never become angry even if circumstances arise that would justify a degree of anger. Once the person achieves this self-control, explains the Rambam, he can move towards the "golden middle way," using his temper only when justified. This advice will help a person improve his character traits.

The At–Bash alphabetic structure, which transforms the letters from the outer extremities towards the center, symbolizes this advice. This is illustrated by the highlighted letters in the following grid:

**א** ב ג ד ה ו ז ח ט י כ ל מ נ ס ע פ צ ק ר ש **ת**
א **ב** ג ד ה ו ז ח ט י כ ל מ נ ס ע פ צ ק ר **ש** ת
א ב **ג** ד ה ו ז ח ט י כ ל מ נ ס ע פ צ ק **ר** ש ת
א ב ג **ד** ה ו ז ח ט י כ ל מ נ ס ע פ צ **ק** ר ש ת
א ב ג ד **ה** ו ז ח ט י כ ל מ נ ס ע פ **צ** ק ר ש ת
א ב ג ד ה **ו** ז ח ט י כ ל מ נ ס ע **פ** צ ק ר ש ת
א ב ג ד ה ו **ז** ח ט י כ ל מ נ ס **ע** פ צ ק ר ש ת
א ב ג ד ה ו ז **ח** ט י כ ל מ נ **ס** ע פ צ ק ר ש ת
א ב ג ד ה ו ז ח **ט** י כ ל מ **נ** ס ע פ צ ק ר ש ת
א ב ג ד ה ו ז ח ט **י** כ ל **מ** נ ס ע פ צ ק ר ש ת
א ב ג ד ה ו ז ח ט י **כ** **ל** מ נ ס ע פ צ ק ר ש ת

The highlighted At–Bash transformation letters form a funnel shape. At the narrow neck of the funnel are the letters י'מ'ל'כ'. These four letters correspond to ה' ימלך, the universal acknowledgment of Hashem as the King of the universe — which, as we have said, is the ultimate aim of Creation. The wider opening of the funnel is formed at the top by the letters א'ת'ב'ש'. These letters spell out the word שבתא — the single Shabbos that must be observed by the entire Jewish nation in order to precipitate the coming of Mashiach, and thus the proclamation of ה' ימלך. Shabbos observance is the litmus test as to whether or not a Jew is observant.

In the first major *piyut* of the morning prayers of Rosh Hashanah and Yom Kippur, we proclaim aloud the *pesukim*: ימלך ה' לעולם א-להיך ציון לדור ודר הללוי-ה ואתה קדוש יושב תהלות ישראל — "Hashem shall reign forever, your Lord, O Zion, for all generations. You, Holy One, are enthroned by the praises of Israel." The last letter in each of the words **קדוש יושב תהלות** spells out the word **שבת**, Shabbos. Only through the correct observance of Shabbos, will we merit to proclaim Hashem King, together with Mashiach.

The Gemara in Shabbos (104a) explains that At–Bash alphabetic structure is referred to as the "Alphabet of Repentance." Ultimate repentance can be brought about either by blowing the *shofar* on Rosh Hashanah, as a universal call for repentance, or alternatively, by the observance of Shabbos. This idea is supported by the *halachah* that the *shofar* is never blown on Shabbos, as both the *shofar* and Shabbos produce the same final results.

The At–Bash structure represents a unification of the Jewish People in their correct observance of the Shabbos. The Ben Ish Chai stresses the importance of learning the laws of Shabbos to enable one to observe it correctly. These laws can be correctly understood only by learning *Maseches Shabbos*, which begins with the word **תנן** and ends with the word **אנא**. The first and final letters of this tractate correspond to the first set of the א"ת ב"ש alphabetic formula, as this tractate forms the mouth of the Shabbos funnel.

In this alphabetic order, the four middle letters, which spell out the word ימלך, appear in the order of י'כ'ל'מ'. To coronate Hashem as the universally-known King of the world, we have to create His crown. This is produced by the Jewish People observing Shabbos correctly. When the four letters י'כ'ל'מ' are joined together to form a circular crown shape, they produce a continuous ימלך proclamation. His crown, known as the כתר, will become fully visible with the forthcoming redemption. In the At–Bash alphabetic structure the word גאל, "redeemer," transforms into the word כתר, "crown."

Alternatively, in reverse order the letters י'כ'ל'מ' spell out the word מלכי, "my King." An individual acceptance of Hashem as "my King" will procure the universal pronouncement of ה' ימלך.

The Rokeach points out that when Moshe approached the burning bush, Hashem called out to him: אל תקרב הלם של נעליך מעל רגליך כי המקום אשר אתה עומד עליו אדמת קדש הוא — "Do not come closer, take off your shoes from your feet, for the place upon which you are standing is holy ground" (*Shemos* 3:5). Moshe was told not to approach this holy place, as the time was not yet right to observe the full revelation of Hashem. It would have to wait until the arrival of Mashiach, which, as we have said is represented in the proclamation of: ה' מלך ה' מלך ה' ימלך. These letters are found in the above *pasuk*; **הלם של נעליך** spell out the word מלך, and **מעל רגליך כי המקום** spell out the word ימלך. Here, too, the letters that spell out ימלך are in a different order from the way the word is articulated. However, when these are formed into a circular crown shape, they read continuously as ימלך, similar to that formed by the At–Bash method.

We can also look at the At–Bash alphabetic structure from a different perspective. Imagine that all the letters of the *alef-beis* are placed around the circumference of a circle. Connecting each letter with the one on the opposite segment forms the At–Bash alphabetic structure:

One of the properties of a circle is that any given circle can be surrounded by another six circles of equal size. The outer six circles represent the six weekdays which surround the central circle of Shabbos. Without the central circle, each outer circle has contact at only one point with its adjacent circle. For example, Monday connects to Sunday and Tuesday at one point only, which is nightfall. However, Monday has no connection to any of the other days of the week. Each day is just another day in our lives, devoid of any substance. Yet when we insert the "central circle," the Shabbos, then immediately all the days of the week become interconnected. Every day is fulfilled by the central theme of Shabbos.

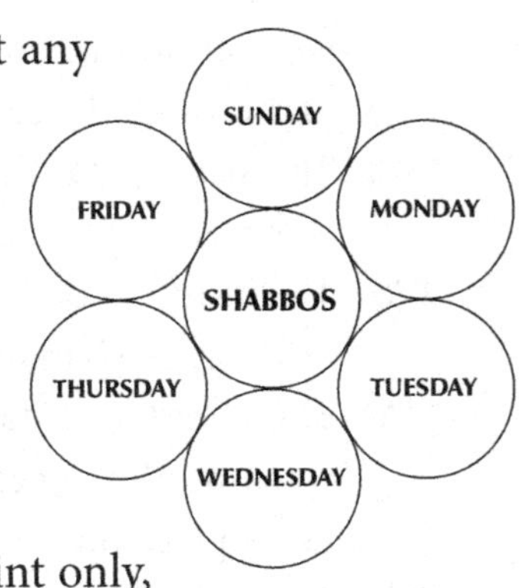


The At–Bash method also connects Shabbos with all the Jewish festivals. In *Vayikra* (ch. 23) we are commanded regarding the different festivals of the Jewish year. As a prologue, the commandment to observe Shabbos is mentioned first, and only then are the various festivals enumerated. Rashi explains that this juxtaposition comes to teach us that whoever desecrates the festivals is considered to have desecrated Shabbos. Likewise, whoever observes the festivals is considered to have upheld Shabbos as well. Their correct observance is as important as that of Shabbos.

Just as the At–Bash funnel shape connects Shabbos observance with the ultimate declaration of ה' ימלך, the At–Bash structure in its alphabetic pairs connects the physical dates of the Jewish festivals to the days on which they occur in the Jewish calendar.

The *Shulchan Aruch* (*Orach Chayim* 428:3) writes as follows:

> A characteristic sign to remember the dates of the Jewish holidays is by using the At–Bash alphabetic transformation method:
>
> **א"ת**: The *first* (**'א**) day of Pesach is always on the same day of the week as Tishah b'Av (**ת**שעה באב). This is alluded to in the *pasuk* that

we mention in the Pesach Haggadah: "You shall eat…matzah together with bitter herbs."

**ב"ש**: The *second* (ב') day of Pesach is always on the same day of the week as Shavuos (**שבועות**).

**ג"ר**: The *third* (ג') day of Pesach is always on the same day of the week as Rosh Hashanah (**ראש השנה**).

**ד"ק**: The *fourth* (ד') day of Pesach is always on the same day of the week as the special Reading of the Torah (**קריאת התורה**) that takes place on Simchas Torah.

**ה"צ**: The *fifth* (ה') day of Pesach is always on the same day of the week as the fast day of Yom Kippur (**צום כפור**).

**ו"פ**: The *sixth* (ו') day of Pesach is always on the same day of the week as Purim (**פורים**) of the previous year.

Therefore, we can understand why the Torah introduces the Jewish festivals with Shabbos, since they are connected through the At–Bash alphabetic structure.

In the Havdalah prayer after the conclusion of Shabbos, we underscore the contrasts between the light and dark, between the Jewish People and the other nations, and between Shabbos and weekdays. Just as the Shabbos is so vividly displayed by the contrast of the At–Bash formation, so, too, its termination is portrayed by mentioning these various contrasts.

◈ ◈ ◈

It is interesting to note that there are three places in Scripture where the At–Bash transformation is used in order to explain the meaning of a word. In all three places we would not know the meaning of the word were it not for the At–Bash alphabetic structure.

The first occurs in *Yirmeyahu* 25:26: **ואת כל מלכי הצפון הקרבים והרחקים איש אל אחיו ואת כל הממלכות הארץ אשר על פני האדמה ומלך ששך ישתה אחריהם** — "…and all the kings of the North, both near and far, one after the other, and all the kingdoms of the earth that are on the face of the earth, and the king of Sheshach shall drink after them." It should be noted that there is no such place as Sheshach. Rashi points out that by using the At–Bash formula, the word ששך (Sheshach) transforms into the word בבל (Bavel). Thus the king of Sheshach refers to the king of Bavel (Babylon).

*Yirmeyahu* 51:41 also refers to Sheshach: איך נלכדה ששך ותתפש תהלת כל הארץ איך היתה לשמה בבל בגוים — "How was Sheshach captured and fallen, he who was universally praised, how he has become lower than all the nations." Here again the name ששך transforms to בבל using the At–Bash formula. This refers to Nevuchadnetzar, the mighty king of the Babylonian Empire. The At–Bash transformation method is used on both occasions to portray Nevuchadnetzar.

This alphabetic structure is composed from contrasting letters from both ends of the *alef-beis*. Haughty King Nevuchadnetzar fell to a great depth, as we are told in the passage: ואתה אמרת בלבבך השמים אעלה ממעל לכוכבי אל ארים כסאי ואשב בהר מועד בירכתי צפון אעלה על במתי עב אדמה לעליון אך אל שאול תורד אל ירכתי בור — "And you said to yourself, 'To the heavens will I ascend, above God's stars will I raise my throne, and I will sit at the head of the assembly in the farthest end of the north. I will ascend above the heights of the clouds; I will compare myself to the Most High.' But into the nether world you shall be brought down, to the bottom of the pit" (*Yeshayahu* 14:13–15). Appropriately, this contrast is represented by the At–Bash transformation.

Moreover, the numerical value of the word ששך is 620, the same as that of the word כתר, a reference to the royal crown that Nevuchadnetzar was so proud of possessing. In contrast, the numerical value of the word בבל is thirty-four, the same as that of the word דל, the poor pauper that he eventually became.

The third instance where the At–Bash formula is used to explain a word in Scripture also occurs in *Yirmeyahu*, in the same chapter in fact: כה אמר ה' הנני מעיר על בבל ואל ישבי לב קמי רוח משחית — "So says Hashem, 'I will arouse against Babylon and against the inhabitants of Lev-Kamai a spirit of destruction'" (*Yirmeyahu* 51:1). Using At–Bash, the words לב קמי (Lev-Kamai) transforms into the word כשדים (Kasdim), the people of Chaldea (see Rashi). We see that they were also destined to be destroyed as a result of their haughtiness.

The Rokeach gives an example of how the At–Bash formula is used to explain the meaning of an entire *pasuk*. *Tehillim* 62:12 states: אחת דבר א-להים שתים זו שמעתי — "One thing Hashem spoke; these two I heard" (*Tehillim* 62:12). The Rokeach expounds upon the connection between the number one and the Name of Elokim, and his explanation clarifies the wording of this *pasuk*.

In At–Bash, the letters of Hashem's Name, א-להים, become ת'כ'צ'מ'י', which have a total numerical value of 560 — the equivalent to the letters ת'ק'ס'. By converting these letters again using At–Bash, we obtain the word אחד, which represents the Unity of Hashem. Thus, converting the word Elokim using the At–Bash method twice, produces the word *echad*. Therefore we can interpret the *pasuk* to mean: **אחת** דבר **א-להים שתים** זו שמעתי — "I understood (*shamati*) that [the word] *achas* (*echad*) [is derived from] the word Elokim [when converted through the At–Bash transformation method] *twice*.

### ◈ The Al–Bam (א"ל ב"מ) Method

Another alphabetic structure is known as the Al–Bam (א"ל ב"מ) method. The twenty-two letters of the *alef-beis* are divided into two halves of eleven letters each, as illustrated below:

**א ב ג ד ה ו ז ח ט י כ** transforms into
**ל מ נ ס ע פ צ ק ר ש ת**

In Al–Bam, both halves of the *alef-beis* progress in an ascending order. We have already explained that when the letters of the *alef-beis* follow an ascending order they represent the attribute of kindness. Therefore, the Al–Bam alphabetic structure displays a double portion of kindness, which represents a more powerful level of kindness.

This alphabetic structure is referred to as the "Alphabet of Torah." The first set of letters, א'ל', spells out the Name of Hashem that denotes His ultimate kindness, as חסד א-ל כל היום — "The kindness of Hashem is all day long" (*Tehillim* 52:3). The second set, ב'ם', represents the entire Torah, as the Written Torah begins with the letter ב (בראשית) and the Oral Torah with the letter מ (מאימתי). Also, the Oral Torah ends with the word בשלום — the final letter corresponding to the ם in ב"ם. Moreover, the combined numerical values of the words בכתב (the Written [Torah]) and בעל פה (the Oral [Law]) is 611, equal to that of the word תורה, Torah. The Al–Bam alphabetic structure represents Hashem's wisdom that is incorporated into both the Written and Oral Torahs.

By the use of the Al–Bam method, we can reveal the depth of wisdom that is contained in the Torah. By its acronym, the opening set א"ל hints at this wisdom. The letter א represents the חכמה (wisdom) of the Torah, as we find embedded in the *pasuk*: ואאלפך חכמה — "I will teach you wisdom" (*Iyov* 33:33). The letter ל represents the understanding of the Torah, as suggested by the words of our prayers: מלמד לאנוש בינה — "He teaches understanding to mankind." These two letters, the א and ל, are therefore the appropriate acronym with which to introduce the "Alphabet of Torah."

Only by Torah learning does one become closer to Hashem. This is signified in the name of this method, א"ל ב"מ, which in Aramaic means: "Hashem is with them (i.e. those who learn Torah)." Appropriately, this alphabetic structure also displays the double portion of kindness that Hashem gives to those who study His Torah.

As with all the other alphabetic structures, the Al–Bam structure derives it name from the first two pairs of letters in its sequencing. The numerical value of the letters א'ל'ב'מ' is seventy-three, the same as for the word חכמה, "wisdom," which is also equal to the numerical value of the word ובינה, "with understanding."

The Rokeach writes that the source for interpreting the Torah using the Al–Bam method is the *pasuk*: ראשית חכמה יראת ה' שכל טוב לכל עשיהם — "The beginning of wisdom is fear of Hashem; good understanding is given to all who practice it" (*Tehillim* 111:10). We can derive from this *pasuk* that ראשית חכמה (i.e. the deepest understanding of the Torah) is unearthed by using the Al–Bam method.

◆ ◆ ◆

Each letter of the Hebrew alphabet is shaped in a unique form. The Radvaz, in his *sefer Magen David*, explains that the composition of four of them — א'ל'ס'מ' — symbolize Hashem in a direct way. The letter א is composed of two *yud*s and a diagonal letter ו, which together have a total numerical value of twenty-six, the same as that of Hashem's Name of י-ה-ו-ה. The letter ל is composed of a letter כ as the base and a letter ו that forms its neck and head. These also have a total numerical value of twenty-six. The combination of these two letters, the א and the ל — the first set of the Al–Bam alphabetic structure — represent the *beginning of wisdom* that *Hashem* (א-ל) has incorporated into His Torah.

The other two letters of the *alef-beis* that symbolize Hashem in a direct way are the letters מ and ס, which are both formed by joining the letters כ and ו. The Chasam Sofer points out that because Torah study is so vital for the continued existence of the universe, the *Satan* will try its utmost to prevent and distract a person from his Torah learning.

The *Satan* is known by the name סמאל — a word which incorporates all of the above four letters. It can also be read as סמ + א-ל — the poison that kills the spiritual power of Torah. Thus, the letters that symbolize Hashem, the optimum spiritual power, also make up the name סמאל, attracting an opposing power of evil from the *Satan*.

◆ ◆ ◆

As we said, Hashem's Name of א-ל, meaning Almighty, represents the knowledge that Hashem has incorporated into His Torah. Each letter of the *alef-beis* has a fulfillment — those letters which are used to articulate the name of that letter (see p. 157). The fulfillment of Hashem's Name of א-ל is **אלף למד**, which has a total numerical value of 185, the same as the word הקף, a protective fence. Torah-learning guarantees our full protection and security, as explicitly stated in the Gemara: תורה מגנא ומצלא — "Torah learning protects a person and ensures his success" (*Sotah* 21a).

The Torah was given to us using the *alef-beis*. The numerical value of all twenty-seven letters of this alphabet is 4,995. This averages out to a value of 185 for each letter, the same as the numerical value of the word הקף. Every letter of Torah learning incorporates this unique power of protection. The word הקף also means "circumference," which is measured by a line that completely surrounds a circle.

As we have said, the entire *alef-beis* proclaims the aim of Creation, for humanity to acknowledge Hashem as the universal King. This will be accomplished at the end of the cycle of time, with the arrival of Mashiach. Each letter of the *alef-beis* acts as a component cog in the wheel of time. They therefore have an average numerical value of הקף, as each letter contributes towards the movement in time that will lead us to the final declaration of Hashem's rulership forever and ever.

The Rokeach points out that the letters of the acronym formed from the phrase **תורה צוה לנו משה** — "Moshe instructed us with the Torah" (*Devarim* 33:4) can spell out the word **מצלת**, which means "saves." This unique protection is given to all who learn and obey the commandments of the Torah. Hashem alone shelters and protects a person at all times, as the *pasuk* states: אתה סתר לי מצר תצרני — "You are a shelter for me from distress; You preserve me" (*Tehillim* 32:7). The acronym of the first four words — **אתה סתר לי מצר** — are the same letters used to compose the word **סמאל**.

Hashem, Who is represented in the format of these four letters, provides shelter and protection from the *Satan*.

By using the Al–Bam formula, we can convert the first letter of the Torah ב, written out as בית, into the word משך, which means "to draw near" and has a numerical value of 360 — corresponding to the 360 degrees of a complete circle. The meaning of the word משך incorporates the vital pulling forces of gravity and magnetism that are essential for life to exist. This number also equals the numerical value of the word ש"ס, which is the acronym of the words **ששה סדרים**, the Six Orders of Mishnayos that make up the complete Oral Torah.

The last set of letters in this structure are כ"ת, which is the acronym of the words of **כתר תורה**, the Crown of Torah, an appropriate way with which to complete the "Alphabet of Torah."

Rabbi Yosef Giktalia, author of *Ginas Eigoz*, also finds similarities between the Al–Bam method and that of the Aiy–Bak, which is discussed further on under a separate heading.

### ◈ The At–Bach (א"ט ב"ח) Method

Rabbeinu Chananel in his commentary to the Gemara (*Sukkah* 52b) explains that the At–Bach alphabetic structure is composed from eleven sets of two letters each.

The letters in the first four sets all have numerical values in the integers, and the combined value of each set adds up to ten.

The second four sets contain letters whose numerical values are in the tens, with the numerical value of each pair totaling one hundred.

The next two sets are composed from letters whose numerical values are in the hundreds, and the combined value of each set is five hundred.

The final set is composed of the remaining letters — ה and נ — both of which do not conform to the above pattern.

### *The At-Bach Structure According to Rabbeinu Chananel*

| | |
|---|---|
| א ב ג ד | transforms into |
| ט ח ז ו | with the letter ה having no partner.<br>Each set has a numerical value of 10 |
| י כ ל מ | transforms into |
| צ פ ע ס | with the letter נ having no partner.<br>Each set has a numerical value of 100 |
| ק ר | transforms into |
| ש ת | Each set has a numerical value of 500. |
| ה | transforms into |
| נ | |

The Gemara uses the At-Bach transformation to explain the meaning of the *pasuk*: מפנק מנער עבדו ואחריתו יהיה מנון — "If one pampers his evil inclination from childhood, it will later testify against him" (*Mishlei* 29:21). The Gemara explains that the last word in the *pasuk*, מנון, can only be explained using the At-Bach method. It transforms into סהדה, which is Aramaic for "witness."

Another example is found in the *Midrash Yalkut Shimoni* (*Parashas Balak* 768) which demonstrates the use of this alphabetic transformation with the *pasuk*: הן עם לבדד ישכן ובגוים לא יתחשב — "They are a people who dwell alone, and amongst the nations they are not reckoned" (*Bemidbar* 23:9).

In the At-Bach alphabetic transformation method, the letters ה and נ have no partners to pair with, and are therefore appropriately used to express the uniqueness of the Jewish People. (This idea is further explained in Chapter 6, in the section dealing with the letter ה, p. 254.)

The Aruch explains the At-Bach alphabetic transformation method by including all the twenty-seven letters of the alphabet. He also divides them into groups, which are similar to those of

Rabbeinu Chananel, but uses the higher numerical values of the final letters, such that the last sets add up to one thousand.

***The At-Bach Structure According to the Aruch***

| | |
|---|---|
| א ב ג ד | transforms into |
| ט ח ז ו | with the letter ה having no partner.<br>Each set has a numerical value of 10 |
| י כ ל מ | transforms into |
| צ פ ע ס | with the letter נ having no partner.<br>Each set has a numerical value of 100 |
| ק ר ש ת | transforms into |
| ץ ף ן ם | with the letter ך having no partner.<br>Each set has a numerical value of 1000. |
| ה נ ך | are interchangeable |

### ◈ The Av-Gad (א"ב ג"ד) Method

The Av-Gad method is composed of eleven pairs of adjacent letters, as illustrated below:

| | |
|---|---|
| א ג ה ז ט כ מ ס פ ק ש | transforms into |
| ב ד ו ח י ל נ ע צ ר ת | |

The Ginas Egos gives as an example of the use of the Av-Gad alphabetic structure. He explains that the evil power of Amalek distorted the spiritual light that is represented in the letters of the *alef-beis*. Amalek was the first nation that had the arrogance to wage war against the Jewish People after the latter's miraculous departure from Egyptian bondage. As a result of this battle, we are told: ויאמר כי יד על כס י-ה מלחמה לה' בעמלק מדר דר — "And He said, 'For there is a hand on Hashem's throne, Hashem maintains a war against Amalek from generation to generation'" (*Shemos* 17:16). The spelling of Hashem's Name in the *pasuk* is incomplete, using only the first two letters (י'ה'). His throne, too, is spelled without the last letter א. Rashi explains that Hashem swore that both His Name and His throne will remain incomplete until Amalek will be totally eradicated.

The Av–Gad alphabetic structure is, in a sense, a distortion of the *alef-beis,* as the second letter of each set is a refraction of the first. Thus, it represents the distortion of the spiritual light by Amalek, as seen by the fact that the words על and כס that appear in the phrase כי יד על כס י-ה are interchangeable using the Av–Gad transformation method.

Moreover, the hidden fulfillments (see p. 166ff) of the letters י'ה' add up to eleven (יוד הא), corresponding to the last two letters of Hashem's Name (ו'ה'), as their numerical values also total eleven. Thus, in the *pasuk* these last two letters are hidden within the י-ה.

The numerical value of eleven alludes to the eleven sets of the Av–Gad alphabetic structure.

### ◈ The Achas–Beta (אח"ס בט"ע) Method

In this alphabetic structure, the twenty-two-letter *alef-beis* is divided into groups of three, as illustrated below. The final letter ת is appended to the last set, making it a four-letter set, זנש"ת.

א = ח = ס
ב = ט = ע
ג = י = פ
ד = כ = צ
ה = ל = ק
ו = מ = ר
ז = נ = ש = ת

The Gemara in *Shabbos* (104) discusses this alphabetic structure. An example of the use of the Achas–Beta transformation method is found in the Gemara's explanation of the *pasuk*: שבעת ימים מצות תאכלו אך ביום הראשון תשביתו שאר מבתיכם — "For a seven-day period you shall eat matzos, but on the first day you shall eliminate leaven from your homes" (*Shemos* 12:15).

The Gemara (*Pesachim* 5) expounds on the meaning of the *pasuk*, explaining that the word אך teaches us that leaven has to be removed *half* a day *before* Pesach itself — meaning, on the 14th of Nisan. The Gemara explains that the word אך is a diminutive word, denoting half.

Rashi explains that the above interpretation is alluded to in the word itself; by using the Achas–Beta method, אך converts to the word חץ, "half." Thus, the Gemara says that the day is divided into two halves — during the first part one can eat leaven yet during the second half of the day, it is forbidden.

Moreover, the Ginas Eigoz points out that since the letter כ, as the eleventh letter of the twenty-two-letter *alef-beis*, appears half way through, the word אך naturally represents the division of the entire *alef-beis* from the beginning to the middle — from א through כ.

### ◈ The Ayik–Bekar (אי"ק בכ"ר) Method

In this alphabetic structure, the full twenty-seven-letter *alef-beis* is divided into nine sets, each containing three letters. The five final letters are placed at the end of the regular alphabet.

This alphabetic structure is unique in that the letters of each set all have an equivalent value for their *mispar katan* (the single-digit integer that is the sum of all the digits of a number — see p. 142ff for clarification).

For example, in the אי"ק set: א has a numerical value of one and that is also its *mispar katan*; the numerical value of י is ten, so י also has a *mispar katan* of one (1 + 0 = 1); the numerical value of ק is one hundred and thus it, too, has a *mispar katan* of one (1 + 0 + 0 = 1), as well.

Using the higher numerical values for the five final letters, the structure and progression are as follows:

| SET | NUMERICAL VALUE OF SET | MISPAR KATAN OF EACH LETTER |
|---|---|---|
| א = י = ק | 111 | 1 |
| ב = כ = ר | 222 | 2 |
| ג = ל = ש | 333 | 3 |
| ד = מ = ת | 444 | 4 |
| ה = נ = ך | 555 | 5 |
| ו = ס = ם | 666 | 6 |
| ז = ע = ן | 777 | 7 |
| ח = פ = ף | 888 | 8 |
| ט = צ = ץ | 999 | 9 |

In the number progression, each number is one more than the previous one. In order to create a starting point for this progression, we need to begin from the number one, to which another one is added, to create the number two. To the number two another one is added, to produce the number three. This symbolizes the unity of the number system.

In a similar way, אי"ק בכ"ר represents the Unity of Hashem that is encapsulated in the letters of the entire *alef-beis*. Each group has a numerical value that is 111 more than the previous set. One hundred and eleven is the numerical value of the first letter א in its expanded form — אלף (א = 1, ל = 30, פ = 80).

Rabbi Zvi Elimelech of Dinov, in his book *Igro d'Pirko*, points out that the factors of the number 111 are three and thirty-seven.

In the total numerical values for the complete Ayik–Bekar structure, the factor of thirty-seven is repeated 135 times.

| SET | NUMERICAL VALUE OF SET | FACTORS |
|---|---|---|
| א = י = ק | 111 | 3 x 37 |
| ב = כ = ר | 222 | 6 x 37 |
| ג = ל = ש | 333 | 9 x 37 |
| ד = מ = ת | 444 | 12 x 37 |
| ה = נ = ך | 555 | 15 x 37 |
| ו = ס = ם | 666 | 18 x 37 |
| ז = ע = ן | 777 | 21 x 37 |
| ח = פ = ף | 888 | 24 x 37 |
| ט = צ = ץ | 999 | 27 x 37 |
| **Total** | **4,995** | **135 x 37** |

He points out that thirty-seven is the numerical value of the word הבל, "a breath of air," and that 135 is the numerical value of the word קול, a "voice." Sound is produced when air passes through the following *three* organs: the trachea (wind pipe), larynx (voice box) and the pharynx (mouth and nose). Sound production is symbolized in the triplicate nature of the sets of this alphabetic structure. Furthermore the voice itself is composed from *three* components: sound, resonance and articulation.

The Shlah, in his commentary to *Shevuos*, points out that this alphabetic structure can be mapped out in three mathematical squares, according to their digits, i.e. ones, tens and hundreds. The sum of the numerical values of the letters in each row/column — vertically, horizontally, as well as diagonally — will always produce a *mispar katan* of fifteen:

| SINGLES | | | TENS | | | HUNDREDS | | |
|---|---|---|---|---|---|---|---|---|
| ד | ט | ב | מ | צ | כ | ר | ץ | ת |
| ג | ה | ז | ל | נ | ע | ש | ך | ן |
| ח | א | ו | פ | י | ס | ף | ק | ם |

| | | | | | | | | |
|---|---|---|---|---|---|---|---|---|
| 4 | 9 | 2 | 40 | 90 | 20 | 400 | 900 | 200 |
| 3 | 5 | 7 | 30 | 50 | 70 | 300 | 500 | 700 |
| 8 | 1 | 6 | 80 | 10 | 60 | 800 | 100 | 600 |

The number fifteen corresponds to the numerical value of י and ה, the first two letters of Hashem's Name — the Name from which these letters derive their spiritual power.

At the end of each book of Tanach, *Chazal* list the total number of *pesukim* contained therein. Also mentioned is a *pasuk* from that book which contains a *siman* (sign), a word which has the numerical equivalent of the total number of *pesukim*. This is meant to serve as a mnemonic to remember how many *pesukim* there are.

The book of *Koheles* contains a total of 222 *pesukim*. The *pasuk* that hints at this number is the 112th *pasuk*, which states מה שהיה **כבר** נקרא שמו, "What has been was already named" (*Koheles* 6:10). This is the only time in Tanach that the word used as the mnemonic falls in the middle *pasuk* of the book. (Since the penultimate *pasuk* is repeated at the end, there are actually a total of 223 *pesukim*, and thus the 112th *pasuk* is the middle one.)

The word כבר, "already," has a numerical value of 222, representing the blessings that are signified by the Ayik–Bekar alphabetic structure. The first set (אי"ק), with a numerical value of 111, signifies the midpoint. The second set (בכ"ר), with a numerical value of 222, signifies the complete book of *Koheles* and alludes to those blessings that this second set represents. The book of *Koheles* is read in public during the joyous festival of Sukkos, in order to remind the entire nation of the vanity of our physical lives and to stress the importance of spiritual enhancement as the greatest source of blessing.

◈ ◈ ◈

The Shlah brings down that this alphabetic structure is referred to as the "Alphabet of Charity and Tithes." The correct order for tithing produce — that is applicable to our discussion on the *alef-beis* — is that a farmer would initially separate *terumah gedolah* and give it to the *Kohen*. Although there is no minimum quantity that one must give, *Chazal* suggested that the farmer allocate two percent of his produce for this purpose. From the remaining produce, the farmer deducts ten percent and gives it to the *Levi* — this is called *ma'aser rishon*. The *Levi* then deducts ten percent of that *ma'aser rishon* and gives it a *Kohen*. This is known as *terumas ma'aser*.

Let us illustrate this by way of example:

After having deducted the *terumah gedolah*, a farmer is left with one hundred sacks of produce. From these he gives ten sacks to the *Levi*, who gives one of these to the *Kohen*. This exact pattern of 100–10–1 is represented by the numerical values of the first set (א-י-ק) of the Ayik–Bekar alphabetic structure.

The numerical value of the second set of this sequence (בכ"ר) is not only 111 more than the first set, but is, in this case, double that of the first set. The letters of the second set spell out the word ברך, the blessing that Hashem bestows upon those who separate their tithes correctly. It is through the merit of giving charity that Hashem repays the donor with His blessing. This bountiful blessing is also displayed by the fact that each letter of the אי"ק בכ"ר acronym is double in numerical value to its respective counterpart. The first letter ב is double that of the previous letter א, the second letter כ is double that of second letter י, and the third letter ר is double that of the third letter ק.

Thus the alphabetic structure of Ayik–Bekar is representative of the way the *berachos* are channeled down through the Jewish nation: from the *Kohen* with the assistance of the *Levi* and then to the *Yisrael*.

Just before Yaakov left home he received the blessings from his father which began: ויתן לך הא-להים מטל השמים ומשמני הארץ — "And May Hashem give you of the dew of the heavens and of the fatness of the earth..." (*Bereishis* 27:28). The numerical value of the word טל is thirty-nine, a tenth of that of the word שמים, which is 390. Yaakov realized that he would receive this "heavenly dew" as a direct reward for separating tithes. He therefore undertook to be scrupulous in separating the correct tithe from all his income. He declared: וכל אשר תתן לי עשר אעשרנו לך — "And whatever You will give me, I shall surely tithe for you" (*Bereishis* 28:22).

The Chasam Sofer points out the interrelationship between the words כל and לך in the above *pasuk*. They are both composed from the same two letters, but in the reverse order. Thus signifying that if you are scrupulous in separating tithes, then Hashem will fully recompense you (לך), i.e. you will get back everything (כל) you have separated as a tithe.

Yaakov's vow to separate tithes from *all* his possessions included his twelve children. In "tithing" his children, one would have expected that Yaakov would have consecrated his tenth son to the service of Hashem. However, it was the third child, Levi (לוי), who was chosen to serve in the *Beis haMikdash*. The tribe of Levi also includes Aharon, the *Kohen* (כהן). The acronym of these two words (כהן לוי) forms the word כל. Thus, the word כל in the above *pasuk* hints to this tithe, as well.

The third and fourth sets of this alphabetic structure also display the benefits that are gained by performing acts of charity. The fourth set, דמ"ת, represents the four different types of capital punishments (enumerated by the Mishnah in the seventh chapter of *Sanhedrin*) which can be averted by giving charity. This is alluded to in the letters themselves דמ"ת, which can be read as ד' + מת, the four types of death sentences. The letters of the third set, גל"ש, spell out שלג, "snow." Snowfall produces a white blanket that protects and covers everything in a spectacular way. Each snowflake is a six-sided star, which represents the six physical directions. Similarly, acts of charity produce a protective shield that guard a person from impending danger, which we know from the *pasuk*: צדקה תציל ממות — "Charity saves a person from death" (*Mishlei* 11:4).

The concept that "charity saves from death" is reinforced by an explanation given by the Vilna Gaon. Every Jewish person was obliged to contribute half a *shekel*, *machatzis ha-shekel* (מחצית השקל) to the *Mishkan*. The middle letter of the word מחצית is צ, which symbolizes צדקה, *tzedakah*, the giving of charitable contributions. In the word *machatzis* the צ is surrounded by the letters ח and י, which together mean "life." The letters on the outer edges of the word *machatzis* (**מ**חצי**ת**) spell out מת, "death." The juxtaposition of the letters in this word reinforce the teaching that charity brings one closer to life thus distancing him from death.

The Ben Ish Chai points out that the letters of the word צדקה, when transformed using the At–Bash formula, will produce the letters ה'ק'ד'צ', which also spell out the word צדקה, in reverse order. The fact that the word צדקה remains the same word, even when transformed in At–Bash, reinforces the concept that acts of *tzedakah* will literally remain forever, as in the *pasuk*: פזר נתן לאביונים צדקתו עמדת לעד — "He distributed widely by giving to the poor, his righteousness endures forever" (*Tehillim* 112:9).

This same sentiment is also indicated in the *pasuk*: רודף צדקה וחסד ימצא חיים צדקה וכבוד — "He who pursues charity and kindness will find life, charity and honor" (*Mishlei* 21:21). Again, since the At–Bash conversion of the word צדקה is also צדקה, it follows that if one pursues *tzedakah*, one will also find *tzedakah*.

In teaching us the importance of charity, the Torah states (*Devarim* 15:10–11):

> נתן תתן לו ולא ירע לבבך בתתך לו כי בגלל הדבר הזה יברכך ה' א-להיך בכל מעשך ובכל משלח ידך. כי לא יחדל אביון מקרב הארץ על כן אנכי מצוך לאמר פתח תפתח את ידך לאחיך לעניך ולאבינך בארצך — Giving, you shall give him, and let your heart not feel bad when you give him, for because of this, Hashem, your God, will bless you in all deeds and in every undertaking. For poor people will not cease to exist within the land, because of this I command you, saying, "You shall surely open your hand to your brother, to your poor one, and to your destitute in your land."

According to this passage, Hashem sends His blessings *as a result of* performing acts of charity. This is what is meant by the phrase: **בגלל הדבר הזה**, "for because of this." As the wheel of fortune is always turning, appropriate acts of charity ensure that one remains at the upper segment of this wheel. This is clearly indicated in the way the word **צדקה** remains unchanged even when transformed with the At–Bash formula.

This same idea is mentioned by the Ba'al HaTurim on *Shemos* 30:12. There, the word **ונתנו**, "and you shall give," is a palindrome — it reads the same backwards and forwards. This alludes to the idea that one does not lose out by giving charity. Whatever you give away to charity, Hashem ensures that you get repaid.

There are four standard ways of expanding the Name of Hashem of **י-ה-ו-ה**. One of these expansions — **יוד הה וו הה** — is referred to as the "expansion of kindness." The numerical value of the hidden fulfillment is the same as the original Name. This duality symbolizes the hidden power of charity to fully recompense the donor.

Therefore, there is a custom by pious people to give a fifth of their income to charity. By allocating double the obligatory tenth, such people emulate Yaakov Avinu's example: **וכל אשר תתן לי עשר**

אעשרנו לך — "And whatever You will give me, I shall surely tithe for you." The double wording of עשר אעשרנו, which hints at a double tithing of one tenth, alludes to the Hashem's Name of kindness, for in its open and the hidden fulfillment — **יוד הה וו הה** — there is also a doubling of its numerical value. Those who keep this custom do not separate one fifth of their income; rather they separate one tenth twice, as hinted at by the double expression of עשר אעשרנו and also by the format of the fulfillment of Hashem's Name of kindness.

The Ayik–Bekar alphabetic structure ends with the letter ץ. We have previously explained, in the name of *Pirkei d'Rabbi Eliezer*, that the Final Redemption is symbolized by the final letter ץ.

Furthermore, the Ben Ish Chai points out that one of the expansions of the word צדקה is **צדי דלת קוף הה**. The second letters of each of these words have a total numerical value of forty-five, the same as for the word גאולה, "redemption." Thus the inherent power of charity will bring the redemption closer. This is the literal meaning of the teaching: גדולה צדקה שמקרבת את הגאולה — "Charitable acts are great because they bring the Final Redemption nearer" (*Bava Basra* 10).

In summary, the alphabetic structure of Ayik–Bekar incorporates two salient features:

(1) The three letters that compose each of its nine sets all have the same *mispar katan*.
(2) This structure represents the blessings that the donor receives as a reward for his acts of charity.

These two features are closely connected and teach us that a donor should treat his recipient as his equal — just as in any given set of the Ayik–Bekar formula, the *mispar katan* of the letters that make up that set are equal. This is alluded to in the passage from *Devarim* quoted earlier: פתח תפתח את ידך לאחיך — "You shall surely open your hand to your brother." In other words, you should view the recipient like a brother — this approach will guarantee Hashem's blessings.

### ◈ The Avag-Beged (אב"ג בג"ד) Method

First listed in the Ohr Zaruah, this alphabetic method is composed of twenty-two sets, each containing three letters, in the following sequence:

| אבג | בגד | גדה | דהו | הוז | וזח | זחט | חטי | טיך | יכל | כלם |
|---|---|---|---|---|---|---|---|---|---|---|
| למן | מנס | נסע | סעף | עפץ | פצק | צקר | קרש | רשת | שתא | תאב |

In this alphabetic method any given letter can be exchanged for either of its neighboring letters in the alphabetic order.

The best example of this method's implementation is on the back of a *mezuzah*, where the names "Hashem *Elokeinu* Hashem" are transformed into Names that are spelled from the letters that follow in the alphabetic sequence:

י ה ו ה א ל ה י נ ו י ה ו ה transforms into
כ ו ז ו ב מ ו כ ס ז כ ו ז ו

It is brought down in Kabbalah that these names have a protective power.

The Vilna Gaon gives another example of the use of the Avag-Beged alphabetic transformation with reference to the meaning of the word כסף, which means "silver" or "money." In Avag-Beged, the letters before those of כ'ס'ף' spell out the word עני (when written as a mirror image). Furthermore, these same letters are found in the *pasuk*: והכסף יענה את הכל — "and money answers everything" (*Koheles* 10:19).

The Chasam Sofer points out that in the *Beis haMikdash* the *Levi'im* played a large number of musical instruments during the *avodah*. He explains that music has a protective power. The Hebrew word for music and song is זמר. Using the Avag-Beged method, those letters can be exchanged for the letters that follow them, transforming them into the word נחש, "snake." The Chasam Sofer explains that through the appropriate use of music and song, a person is kept away from being influenced by the "Snake" — a reference to the Serpent who was the initial cause of human sin in the Garden of Eden — which, in our case, refers to the *yetzer ha-ra.*

Another example of the use of this alphabetic structure, is found in *Bereishis* 7:9: שנים שנים באו אל נח אל התבה זכר ונקבה — "Two by two they came to Noach into the ark, male and female...." Rashi explains that the *pasuk* uses the word "came" because they were not brought in; they came in by themselves. Using the Avag–Beged method, we can see that this is indicated in the wording of the text itself: The word שנים, "two," can also be translated as "second." Therefore, if we take the phrase שנים שנים and interpret it by taking the second letters that follow the word שנים — as literally implied in the phrase שנים שנים — we end up with the letters ת'ס'כ'נ'. When rearranged, they spell out the word תכנס, the *active* form of the verb that means "to enter," implying that they entered on their own accord.

Another similar example where adjacent letters are used to illustrate a point in question is in the phrase from *Koheles* (4:9): טובים השנים מן האחד — "...a pair of two is better than one." Again interpreting the word השנים to mean "second," and transforming the word האחד with its adjacent letters of the *alef-beis*, we obtain the letters ו'ב'ט'ה', which spell out the word טובה, which brings us to a literal understanding of the entire phrase: טובים השנים מן האחד — "a pair of *two* is *better* than *one*."

The above *pasuk* can also be taken as a reference to marriage, interpreting it to mean that a pair together is better than two single people. The Rokeach points out that the numerical value of the words השנים מן האחד is 513, which is equal to the sum of the numerical values of the words חתן and כלה, the bride and bridegroom, who join together in marriage.

### ◈ The Aiy–Bak (אי״ בכ״) Method

The Aiy–Bak alphabetic structure is perhaps one of the more obscure ones. In this structure the first nine letters of the *alef-beis* are paired off with the second set of nine letters. The final four letters form two further sets. These sets are listed below, with their combined numerical values.

| ש | ק | ט | ח | ז | ו | ה | ד | ג | ב | א |
|---|---|---|---|---|---|---|---|---|---|---|
| ת | ר | צ | פ | ע | ס | נ | מ | ל | כ | י |
| 700 | 300 | 99 | 88 | 77 | 66 | 55 | 44 | 33 | 22 | 11 |

In the decimal system, everything revolves around the first ten numbers. These represent a full circle, the wheel and the planetary orbits. The number ten itself symbolizes a return to the starting point in this numeric circle.

The Ginas Eigoz explains that since ten represents a full circle, the number eleven represents the next stage, the movement of that circle — the turning of a wheel. The triangular value of eleven is sixty-six (1 + 2 + 3 + 4 + 5 + 6 + 7 + 8 + 9 + 10 + 11 = 66), the same as the numerical value of the word גלגל, "wheel."

In the Aiy–Bak alphabetic structure, the first nine sets are progressive multiples of eleven, representing regular and continuous movement. However, upon closer analysis, these sets correspond to a wheel as well. The total numerical value of the first two sets is equal to the numeric value of the third set (11 + 22 = 33). The sum total of all these three equals sixty-six (11 + 22 + 33 = 66), which, as stated above, is the numerical value for גלגל, "wheel." The total of the numerical values of the fourth and fifth set (55 + 44 = 99) is the same as that of the סגול vowel, which also represents a complete cycle. (This will be discussed in greater detail in Chapter 7.) The sixth set has a numerical value of sixty-six, again representing the גלגל. Therefore, we can say that these first six sets of the Aiy–Bak alphabetic structure symbolize two wheels that are transporting the סגול vowel.

The continuous cyclical movement that the Aiy–Bak alphabetic structure represents includes all of the cycles in nature (i.e. the food chain, water cycle, nitrogen cycle) as well as the astronomical orbits.

In the above explanation, the complete wheel (גלגל) is formed by the first three sets of Aiy–Bak. The first two pairs, א"י ב"כ, have a total numerical value of thirty-three, and that of the third set, ג"ל, is also thirty-three. The Ginas Eigoz points out that the sun, in its daily orbit around the earth, is visible during the day and remains below the horizon at night. The visual part of the orbit is represented by the third set of letters, ג"ל, whereas night time — the obscure part of the orbit — is represented by the first two pairs of Aiy–Bak, because that half of the wheel (גל) is apparent only when the numerical values of those sets are combined. Together, they complete the daily cycle, as represented by the whole wheel (גלגל).

The combined numerical value of the final two sets, ק"ר ש"ת, is one thousand. We have previously pointed out how the numerical values of the twenty-seven letters of the *alef-beis* complete a cycle, starting with the number one — symbolized by the אָלֶף — and ending at 900 (ץ), which brings us to אֶלֶף, one thousand — a complete revolution.

## ◈ The Ach–Bi (א"כ ב"י) Method

In the Ach–Bi method the *alef-beis* is divided into two equal groups, each with eleven letters. Within each group, the letters pair reflectively, the first with the last, the second with the penultimate, etc.:

א ב ג ד ה ו transforms into
כ י ט ח ז ו

ל מ נ ס ע פ transforms into
ת ש ר ק צ פ

The three alphabetic structures of Al–Bam, At–Bash and Ach–Bi are closely connected. They form a "triangular transformation ring," which means that the results of transforming letters using any two of the above alphabetic structures will result in the third one. For example, the letter א transforms in Al–Bam into to letter ל. The letter ל transforms in At–Bash into the letter כ, which transforms back to the original א using the Ach–Bi transformation. This is true for any letter transformed using all three alphabetic structures.

## ◈ The Gemara's Explanation of the Alphabetic Structures

Previously we cited the Gemara (*Shabbos* 104a), which gives an explanation for the alphabetic order. The continuation of that passage explains some of the alphabetic structures.

### At–Bash

In the At–Bash structure, the first two sets represent the remarks that Hashem makes regarding the wicked.

**א"ת ב"ש אותי תעב אתאוה לו ב"ש בי לא חשק שמו יחול עליו — *"At–Bash"*: Me, you abominated, shall I desire him? Me, he did not want; should My Name rest on him?**

Rashi explains this passage in the Gemara as a question. As the wicked have rejected Hashem, should they then expect Him to like them? However, the Maharsha explains it as a statement: Despite the wicked having rejected Hashem, He still looks forward to accepting their repentance.

**ג"ר גופו טומא ארחם עליו — *"Gar"*: His body he defiled, shall I have mercy on him?**

**ד"ק דלתותי נעל קרניו לא אגדע — *"Dak"*: My doors he locked, shall I not cut down his pride?**

**עד כאן מדת רשעים אבל מדות צדיקים — Up to this point** [we can interpret the At-Bash alphabet] **with regard to wicked people, but with regard to righteous people** [a different interpretation is given].

Rashi explains that the following letters of ה"ו, correspond to letters of Hashem's Name. It would be inappropriate to continue to expound the At-Bash alphabet with reference to wicked people, who have turned their backs away from listening to Hashem.

We have already explained that the At-Bash structure represents repentance. Appropriately, the Gemara initially explains it with reference to the wicked, and then returns to explain its significance with regard to the righteous:

**א"ת ב"ש אם אתה בוש—*"At-Bash"*: If you are embarrassed to sin,**

**ג"ר ד"ק אם אתה עושה כן גור בדוק—*"Gar-Dak"*: If you do this then you will dwell in the heavenly spheres.**

These first four sets of the At-Bash sequence, refer to righteous people who are embarrassed to sin and will be rewarded in the World to Come, by occupying the heavenly spheres. The Toras Chayim explains that this is the source of the saying in the Mishnah that states: ובשת פנים לגן עדן—"Those who are shamefaced will go to *Gan Eden*" (*Avos* 5:24).

Those people who feel a sense of disgrace when thinking about sin, will not habitually transgress and will therefore merit the reward of *Gan Eden*.

**ה"ץ ו"פ חציצה הוי בינך לאף—*"Hatz-Vaf"*: There will be a barrier between you and anger.**

The letters ה and ח are interchangeable as they both belong to the Gutturals group (see p. 88), transforming the ה"ץ into ח"ץ, thereby forming the first part of the word **חציצה**, a "barrier."

The Gemara explains that the ו"פ set is a reference to אף, "anger."

(This is another example of when the last letter of a word is used to represent it, as explained earlier [see p. 52]. In the alphabetic order the letter ף appears later than the א, and since the ף is needed to complete the word אף, it is used to represent it.)

The Toras Chayim explains that there are a total of six expressions used to represent anger, corresponding to the numerical value of the letter ו. These six expressions — **זעף קצף שצף נשף נגף אף** — all end with a final letter ף, which in At–Bash converts to a ו. Moreover, the numerical value of ו"פ, eighty-six, equates to the Name of א-להים, symbolizing strict justice, which is a manifestation of Divine anger. The following are examples of the usage of each of these six expressions of anger:

ויבא אליהם יוסף בבקר וירא אתם והנם **זעפים** — "Yosef came to them in the morning. He saw them and behold! They were aggrieved" (*Bereishis* 40:6).

ולא יהיה **קצף** על עדת בני ישראל — "And there shall be no wrath on the assembly of the children of Israel" (*Bemidbar* 1:53).

**בשצף** קצף הסתרתי פני — "With a little wrath did I hide My countenance" (*Yeshayahu* 54:8).

ובטרם יתנגפו רגליכם על הרי **נשף** — "Before your feet stumble on the dark mountains" (*Yirmeyahu* 13:15).

ולא יהיה בהם **נגף** בפקד אתם — "And there will be no plague among them when counting them" (*Shemos* 30:12).

ויחר **אף** יעקב — "Yaakov's anger flared up...." (*Bereishis* 30:2).

The full force of Hashem's anger is displayed by these six expressions, each ending with the letter ף, that has a numerical value of eighty. A full expression of anger, therefore, corresponds to the number four hundred and eighty (6 x 80 = 480), which is the numerical value of the word שקף. Rashi comments, in his commentary to the *pasuk*: **וישקפו** על פני סדום — "And they gazed towards

Sodom" (*Bereishis* 18:16), that every time the Torah uses the word **השקפה**, it is used detrimentally, as it represents the full extent of Hashem's anger.

**ז"ע ח"ס ט"ן ואין אתה מזדעזע מן השטן** — *"Za–Chas–Tan"*: **And you will not** [need to] **be afraid from the Satan.**

Since righteous people are embarrassed to sin, they receive Divine protection, and thus have no need to fear from the evil slander of the *Satan*.

**י"ם כ"ל אמר שר של גיהנם לפני הקב"ה רבונו של עולם לים כל** — *"Yam–Kol"*: **The minister of *Gehinnom* said before Hashem: Master of the Universe, all sinners should be thrown into the sea.**

Rashi explains that the sea refers to *Gehinnom*, into which all sinners, including the Jewish ones, should enter.

**Achas–Beta**

**אמר הקב"ה** — **Hashem responded** [to the previously quoted accusations, by using the Achas–Beta alphabetic structure]:

**אח"ס בט"ע גי"ף אני חס עליהם מפני שבעטו בגי"ף** — *"Achas–Beta–Gif"*: **I have pity on them** (i.e. the Jewish People) **because they have rejected adultery.**

**דכ"ץ דכים הם כנים הם צדיקים הם** — *"Decatz"*: **They are innocent, upright and righteous.**

**הל"ק אין לך חלק בהן** — *"Helek"*: **You** [*Gehinnom*] **have no share with them.**

**ומרז"ן ש"ת אמר גיהנם לפניו רבונו של עולם מרי זניני מזרעו של שת** — *"Vemarzan–Shes"*: ***Gehinnom* said before Hashem, Master of the Universe, My Master, feed me from all the descendants of Shes.**

A reference to the human race is expressed by the phrase "the descendants of Shes" rather than as the descendants of Adam, who was, in fact, the first member of the human race. The reason for this is provided in Rashi's explanation of the *pasuk*: ולשת גם הוא ילד בן ויקרא את שמו אנוש אז הוחל לקרא בשם ה' — "And also to Shes a son was born, and he named him Enosh. They then began to call in the Name of Hashem" (*Bereishis* 4:26). Rashi cites the Midrash (*Bereishis Rabbah* 23:7) which states that this refers to Shes's introduction of idol worship into the world.

As explained earlier, the Gemara states that the letter ש represents שקר, "falsehood," and ת represents אמת, "truth." These two letters spell out the name שת, Shes. Moreover, the juxtaposition of the letters of Shes's name indicates that he promoted idol worship. The ש — representing falsehood, and in this case idolatry — is placed before the ת — representing truth, which is, of course, Hashem — just as Shes placed idol worship before his service of Hashem.

**Al-Bam**

The response that Hashem provided, uses the alphabetic form of the Al-Bam transformation, as the alphabet of Torah learning:

> **א"ל ב"ם ג"ן ד"ס להיכן אוליכן לגן הדס — *"Al-Bam-Gan-Das"*: To where will I lead them** (i.e. the Jewish People) **to a garden of myrtle** (i.e. the Garden of Eden).
>
> **ה"ע ו"ף אמר גיהנם לפני הקב"ה רבונו של עולם עיף אנכי — *"Ha-Vaf"*: *Gehinnom* said before Hashem, Master of the Universe, I am hungry** [for victims].
>
> **ז"ץ ח"ק הללו זרעו של יצחק — *"Zatz-Chak"*: These are the descendants of Yitzchak** [and you cannot have them].
>
> **ט"ר י"ש כ"ת טר יש לי כיתות כיתות של עובדי כוכבים שאני נתן לך — *"Tar-Yesh-Cat"*: Wait! I have many groups of idolaters that I will give you.**

This concludes the narrative of the Gemara.

## PHONETIC GROUPING OF THE LETTERS

The *Sefer Yetzirah* (2:3) divides the twenty-two letters of the *alef-beis* into five phonetic groups, classifying the letters according to the speech organs used in their pronunciation. These are grouped in a progression, in the same order that sound emanates, starting from the throat and ending with the lips. They are:

| LETTERS | NAME OF GROUP | FORMED BY |
|---|---|---|
| א ח ה ע | Gutturals | the throat (גרון) |
| ג י כ ק | Palatals | the palate (חיך) |
| ד ט ל נ ת | Linguals | the tongue (לשון) |
| ז ס ש ר צ | Dentals | the teeth (שיניים) |
| ב ו מ פ | Labials | the lips (שפה) |

In his commentary to *Vayikra* 19:16, Rashi explains that all letters formed by the same speech organ are interchangeable with one another. He provides an example as to how the interchangeable letters of each group also have a similarity in their meanings. The *pasuk* there states: לא תלך רכיל בעמיך — "You shall not go about gossiping among your people."

Rashi's commentary states:

> It is an expression of "going to spy," as the letter כ interchanges with the letter ג. All letters that have their source from the same organ of speech are interchangeable with one another.

In other words, the letter כ in the word רכיל can be exchanged for the letter ג, as they both originate from the Palatals group. This produces the word רגיל, which means to "go and seek out" fresh information that will provide a new agenda for gossip.

Another example is given by Rashi in his commentary to *Nachum* 3:18, where it says: נפשו עמך על ההרים — "Your people are scattered on the mountains." Without Rashi's explanation one might think that this *pasuk* means: "Your people are with you on the mountains." However, Rashi explains that the letter ש in the word נפשו interchanges with the letter צ — both belonging to the Dentals group — such that the word should be read as נפצו, "scattered." This substitution provides us with the correct meaning.

It is interesting to note that in his commentary to *Shemos* 3:15, Ibn Ezra is of the opinion that the inter-changeability of the letters within each of the five phonetic groups applies only when they are articulated with the *patach* vowel. In other words, the letter א, for example, belongs to the Gutturals group only when it is pronounced as "ah." However, most other commentators are not of this opinion and use these substitutions without regard for the vowels.

The Yoel Ohr points out that the middle of these five phonetic groups is the Linguals — the one that emanates from the לשון, which in this case means "tongue" but it is often used to mean "speech" in general. Moreover, the middle letter of this group (ד ט ל נ ת) is the ל, which is also the tallest of all the letters, symbolizing a prominent, important stature. The articulated name of this letter is למד, meaning to learn and/or teach. Thus, all these factors allude to the lesson to be gleamed here — that a person has to learn the importance and the power of correct speech.

The Rokeach points out that there is a significant lesson that can be learned from the relative position of the letters in these phonetic groups. He gives the following example: We know that the letter א symbolizes the all-encompassing power of Hashem. The articulated name of the א (אלף) is composed from the first, middle and last letters of these five phonetic groups. The א is the first letter of the first group (Gutturals), ל is the middle letter of the middle group (Linguals), and ף is the final letter of the last group (Labials). Appropriately, the letter א represents the all–encompassing power of Hashem, as its fulfillment spans the gamut of these letter groupings.

◈ ◈ ◈

Special significance is attached to words that are composed of letters taken from each of the five phonetic groups, as they represent a complete symphony of possible sounds. One such example is the word ישתבח, used to sing eternal praises to Hashem in our daily prayers. By its very structure, the word ישתבח encapsulates an entire symphony of praise to Hashem. By using this word to sing His praises, we are using all of the tools of speech that Hashem has bestowed upon us.

CHAPTER 3

# The Uniqueness of the Torah Script

THERE ARE TWO MAIN traditions for the shape of the Hebrew letters used in Torah scrolls, *tefillin*, *mezuzos* and *megillos*. The first one, used mainly by Jews of Ashkenazic decent, is known as the Beis Yosef script as it is based on the rulings of Rabbi Yosef Karo (1488–1575)—author of the famous *Shulchan Aruch*, the most authoritative code of Jewish Law. The laws pertaining to the writing of each letter is codified in the *Shulchan Aruch*, *Orach Chaim* 36.

The second script is known as the *Arizal*'s script, which is essentially the same as the Beis Yosef's, with some minor changes in the letters א'ו'ח'י'ע'צ'ש'. This particular script follows the teachings of *Arizal*—Rabbi Yitzchak Luria Ashkenazi (1534–1572), famed kabbalist—who instituted these changes in the form of letters based on Kabbalah.

It appears that the *Arizal* script was initially used only for *tefillin* and *mezuzos*, where the written text is encased and cannot be seen during daily use. In later generations it became more widespread, and is now used even for writing *sifrei Torah* and *megillos*, where the text is visible and read. Most Chassidim and Jews of Sephardic decent use this style script.

Moreover, there are variations in how specific letters in certain words are formed. One such example is the second ה in Hashem's Name of י-ה-ו-ה. They are differing opinions as to how the second ה should be written. The Beis Yosef maintains that both *hei*s are composed from a ד with a י as its foot; the *Arizal* maintains that the second ה is composed from a ד and a ו.

This book is based primarily on the Beis Yosef script, although reference has been made to the *Arizal*'s script, as well. (A chart of *alef-beis* according to the Beis Yosef script appears on p. 343.)

## Large and Small Letters

In the Hebrew language, there are no capital letters. However, use is made of both larger and smaller letters to teach specific lessons. The large letters are written twice as large as the normal lettering, while the small letters are half the normal size. The entire alphabet is found scattered throughout Scripture, written in both the larger and smaller sizes.

At the beginning of *Bereishis* and again in *Divrei HaYamim*, the Mesorah lists all the places where large letters are found throughout Scripture, and a list of all the places where small letters are used appears in the Mesorah at the beginning of *Vayikra*.

The following is a combined list in alphabetic order, with the large letters first, followed by their corresponding small ones, and if applicable, by the final letters, as mentioned in the Mesorah. Depending upon the source, there may be slight variations to this list.

(An asterisk next to the entry indicates that it appears only in some editions of the Mesorah.)

| | | |
|---|---|---|
| א | אדם | *Divrei HaYamim* 1:1 |
| | ויקרא | *Vayikra* 1:1 |
| ב | בראשית | *Bereishis* 1:1 |
| | שתי בנות הב | *Mishlei* 30:15 |
| ג | והתגלח | Vayikra 13:33 |
| | לבש בשרי רמה וגוש | *Iyov* 7:5 |
| ד | אחד | *Devarim* 6:4 |
| | אדם עשק בדם | *Mishlei* 28:17 |
| ה | ה לי-ה-ו-ה תגמלו | *Devarim* 32:6 |
| | בהבראם | *Bereishis* 2:4 |
| ו | כל הולך על גחון | *Vayikra* 11:42 |
| | ויזתא | *Esther* 9:9 |
| | ולא נשא לשוא | *Tehillim* 24:4 |
| ז | זכרו תורת משה עבדי | *Malachi* 3:22 |
| | ויזתא | *Esther* 9:9 |
| ח | חור כרפס | *Esther* 1:6 |
| | חף אנכי | *Iyov* 33:9 |
| ט | יסר מעלי שבטו | *Iyov* 9:34 |
| | טוב שם משמן טוב | *Koheles* 7:1 |
| | טבעו בארץ | *Eichah* 2:9 |
| י | ועתה יגדל נא כח | *Bemidbar* 14:17 |
| | צור ילדך תשי | *Devarim* 32:18 |
| כ | וכנה אשר נטעה | *Tehillim* 80:16 |
| | ולבכתה | *Bereishis* 23:2 |

| | | |
|---|---|---|
| ל | וישלכם | *Devarim* 29:27 |
| | ליני הלילה | *Rus* 3:13* |
| | לוא אליכם | *Eichah* 1:12 |
| מ | משלי שלמה | *Mishlei* 1:1 |
| | ממרים הייתם | *Devarim* 9:24* |
| | על מוקדה | *Vayikra* 6:2 |
| נ | נצר חסד | *Shemos* 34:7 |
| | ליני הלילה | *Rus* 3:13* |
| | ונבושזבן רב סריס | *Yirmeyahu* 39:13 |
| | את משפטן | *Bemidbar* 27:5 |
| | נטע ארן וגשם יגדל | *Yeshayahu* 44:14 |
| | ונרגן מפריד | *Mishlei* 16:28 |
| ס | סוף דבר | *Koheles* 12:13 |
| | יצפונני בסכה | *Tehillim* 27:5 |
| | בסופה ובשערה | *Nachum* 1:3 |
| ע | שמע ישראל | *Devarim* 6:4* |
| | לעות אדם בריבו | *Eichah* 3:36 |
| פ | בשפרפרא | *Daniel* 6:20 |
| | בשפרפרא | *Daniel* 6:20 |
| | ובהעטיף הצאן | *Bereishis* 30:42 |
| צ | צפו עורים כלם לא ידעו | *Yeshayahu* 56:10 |
| | וצוחת ירושלם | *Yirmeyahu* 14:2 |
| | על פני פרץ | *Iyov* 16:14 |
| ק | קן לה | *Tehillim* 84:4 |
| | קצתי בחיי | *Bereishis* 27:46 |

| | | |
|---|---|---|
| ר | לאל אחר | *Shemos* 34:14 |
| | יערי אורגים | *Shemuel* II 21:19 |
| ש | שמע ישראל | *Devarim* 6:4* |
| | שיר השירים | *Shir HaShirim* 1:1 |
| | פרשנדתא | *Esther* 9:7 |
| | פרמשתא | *Esther* 9:9 |
| ת | תמים תהיה עם | *Devarim* 18:13* |
| | ותכתוב אסתר | *Esther* 9:29 |
| | פרמשתא | *Esther* 9:9 |
| | פרשנדתא | *Esther* 9:7 |

A slightly different list is enumerated in the Machzor Vitri, who quotes from a contemporary of his known as Rabbeinu Yossi Tov Olam. He writes that all of the letters of the twenty-seven-letter *alef-beis* appear as large letters in the Chumash, and that all of the letters of the twenty-two-letter *alef-beis* are also found in the Prophets. Each of these letters appears at least once at the beginning of a word, with the exception of the letter פ.

The list quoted by the Machzor Vitri varies slightly from the one found in our version of the Mesorah. *Minchas Shai* confirms that ancient manuscripts did contain the list quoted by the Machzor Vitri, although our custom is to follow the teachings of the Mesorah. Again, there might be slight variations of this list.

The following is a listing of the large letters found in the Chumash as quoted by the Machzor Vitri.

(It is interesting to note that he includes the final letters as well, with the exception of the final ך. I have not found an explanation for this exclusion, but nevertheless found it of relevance to point it out.)

| | | |
|---|---|---|
| א | אשריך ישראל | *Devarim* 33:29 |
| ב | בראשית | *Bereishis* 1:1 |
| ג | והתגלח | *Vayikra* 13:33 |
| ד | אחד | *Devarim* 6:4 |
| ה | ה לה' תגמלו | *Devarim* 32:6 |
| ו | כל הולך על גחון | *Vayikra* 11:42 |
| ז | הכזונה | *Bereishis* 34:31 |
| ח | חכלילי | *Bereishis* 49:12 |
| ט | ותרא אתו כי טוב הוא | *Shemos* 2:2 |
| י | ועתה יגדל נא כח | *Bemidbar* 14:17 |
| כ | והתמכרתם | *Devarim* 28:68 |
| ל | וישלכם | *Devarim* 29:27 |
| מ | מה טובו אהלך יעקב | *Bemidbar* 24:5 |
| ם | לאפרים בני שלשים | *Bereishis* 50:23 |
| נ | נצר חסד | *Shemos* 34:7 |
| ן | את משפטן | *Bemidbar* 27:5 |
| ס | ויהס כלב את העם | *Bemidbar* 13:30 |
| ע | שמע ישראל | *Devarim* 6:4 |
| פ | ופתלתל | *Devarim* 32:5 |
| ף | ובהעטיף | *Bereishis* 30:42 |
| צ | צא אתה וכל העם | *Shemos* 11:8 |
| ץ | ועשית ציץ | *Shemos* 28:36 |
| ק | קן לה | *Tehillim* 84:4 |
| ר | אל אחר | *Shemos* 34:14 |
| ש | ערש ברזל | *Devarim* 3:11 |
| ת | תמים תהיה עם | *Devarim* 18:13 |

The large letters found in the Prophets, as quoted by the Machzor Vitri, are:

| | | |
|---|---|---|
| *Divrei HaYamim* I 1:1 | אדם | א |
| *Shir HaShirim* 8:14 | ברח דודי | ב |
| *Shir HaShirim* 4:12 | גן נעול | ג |
| *Koheles* 1:1 | דברי קהלת | ד |
| *Tehillim* 77:8 | הלעולמים יזנח | ה |
| *Esther* 9:9 | ויזתא | ו |
| *Malachi* 3:22 | זכרו תורת משה עבדי | ז |
| *Esther* 1:6 | חור כרפס | ח |
| *Koheles* 7:1 | טוב שם משמן טוב | ט |
| *Mishlei* 11:26 | מנע בר יקבהו לאום | י |
| *Tehillim* 80:16 | וכנה אשר נטעה | כ |
| *Yeshayahu* 9:6 | לםרבה המשרה | ל |
| *Mishlei* 1:1 | משלי שלמה | מ |
| *Yeshayahu* 40:1 | נחמו נחמו | נ |
| *Koheles* 12:13 | סוף דבר | ס |
| *Tehillim* 18:50 | על כן אודך בגוים | ע |
| *Daniel* 6:20 | בשפרפרא | פ |
| *Yeshayahu* 56:10 | צפו עורים כלם לא ידעו | צ |
| *Tehillim* 84:4 | קן לה | ק |
| *Mishlei* 8:22 | ראשית דרכו | ר |
| *Shir HaShirim* 1:1 | שיר השירים | ש |
| *Esther* 9:29 | ותכתוב אסתר | ת |

According to the Machzor Vitri, the small letters found throughout Scripture are:

|  |  |  |
|---|---|---|
| *Vayikra* 1:1 | ויקרא | א |
| *Mishlei* 30:15 | שתי בנות הב | ב |
| *Iyov* 7:5 | לבש בשרי רמה וגוש | ג |
| *Mishlei* 28:17 | אדם עשק בדם | ד |
| *Bereishis* 2:4 | בהבראם | ה |
| *Tehillim* 22:30 | בנפשו לא חיה | ו |
| *Esther* 9:9 | ויזאתא | ז |
| *Iyov* 33:9 | חף אנכי | ח |
| *Eichah* 2:9 | טבעו בארץ | ט |
| *Devarim* 32:18 | צור ילדך תשי | י |
| *Bereishis* 23:2 | ולבכתה | כ |
| *Eichah* 1:12 | לוא אליכם | ל |
| *Devarim* 9:24* | ממרים הייתם | מ |
| *Eichah* 4:14 | נעו עורים | נ |
| *Mishlei* 18:8 | דברי נרגן | ן |
| *Nachum* 1:3 | בסופה ובשערה | ס |
| *Eichah* 3:36 | לעות אדם בריבו | ע |
| *Daniel* 6:20 | בשפרפרא | פ |
| *Yirmeyahu* 11:13 | חצות ירושלים | צ |
| *Iyov* 16:14 | יפרצני פרץ | ץ |
| *Bereishis* 27:46 | קצתי בחיי | ק |
| *Shmuel* II 21:19 | יערי ארגים | ר |
| *Esther* 9:9 | פרמשתא | ש |
| *Esther* 9:9 | פרמשתא | ת |

## ◈ The Correlation Among the ב, א, מ and ש

From all of the twenty-four books of Scripture, only four begin with a large letter:

*Chumash Bereishis* begins with a large ב in the word בראשית
*Divrei HaYamim* begins with a large א in the word אדם
*Mishlei* begins with a large מ in the word משלי
*Shir HaShirim* begins with a large ש in the word שיר

The fulfillment of the first of these letters, the letter ב, is בית. Using the At–Bash method, these letters transform into ש'מ'א', which correspond to the large letters that appear in the remaining three instances — in *Shir HaShirim*, *Mishlei* and *Divrei HaYamim*. These three books of Tanach describe the ultimate accomplishment of the aim of Creation.

However, of the three, the book of *Shir HaShirim* is the one most overtly represented in the large ב since its first letter, the large letter ש, is the direct transformation of the letter ב in At–Bash. In the *Midrash Tanchuma* on *Shir HaShirim* 1:1 (as quoted by Rashi, there) we find an explicit reference to this connection: גדול יום שניתן בו שיר השירים כיום שנברא בו שמים וארץ — "The day that the book of *Shir HaShirim* was given to us is as great as the day of the creation of heavens and earth."

There are also hints to this connection in the letters themselves. The fulfillment of the large letter ש is שין; these letters also spell שני, second, which translates as "two," corresponding to the numerical value of the letter ב, the first letter of *Bereishis*.

In the Mishnah there are also instances where these four letters correlate. At the end of the first chapter of *Pirkei Avos*, for example, the Mishnah states:

> רבי שמעון בן גמליאל אומר על שלשה דברים העולם קים על הדין ועל האמת ועל השלום שנאמר אמת ומשפט שלום שפטו בשעריכם — Rabbi Shimon Ben Gamliel said, "By the virtue of three things does the world endure: by

truth, by justice and through the pursuit of peace, as it is said: 'Judge with truth, justice and peace in your gates' (*Zechariah* 8:16)."

The three things that guarantee the endurance of the world are אמת משפט שלום, whose acronym spell out the word אמש. As we explained earlier, these letters correspond to the inaugural letter of the Torah, the letter ב. Therefore, the ב in the first word of the Torah incorporates these three important requirements that guarantee the endurance of the world, as they are the foundations on which it was established.

Another Mishnah (*Bava Kama* 2a) begins by spelling out the four principle causes of damage: בור (damage caused by a pit being dug in the ground), אש (damage to another person's property caused by fire), מבעה (damage that is caused by an animal eating another person's produce), and שור (damage that is caused by an animal trampling over a neighbor's field). The acronym of these four causes of damage corresponds to that of the four books of Scripture mentioned earlier:

| | | |
|---|---|---|
| בור | corresponds to | בראשית |
| אש | corresponds to | אדם |
| מבעה | corresponds to | משלי |
| שור | corresponds to | שיר השירים |

Thus, there appears to be a connection between the four large letters that begin the books of Tanach and the four main causes of damage, known as the ארבעה אבות נזיקים.

Moreover, these principle causes of damage can be compared to a growing plant. Just as a plant has its roots anchored within the earth, while its main stem, flowers and leaves are all above ground, the damage from the first of the four principal causes is below ground, while the other three are caused above ground level. Similarly, the ב of בראשית is the root of the other three letters, אמש, which are formed through the At–Bash transformation of the letter's fulfillment (בית).

A further example of the connection among the letters of ב, א, מ and ש is found in the Chumash where we are told of the order of the construction of the vessels for the *Mishkan*, the dwelling-place for the *Shechinah* in the desert. In *Shemos* (ch. 25), when Moshe Rabbeinu was commanded to build the *Mishkan*, he was told to first build the Ark (ארון), then the golden Menorah (מנרת זהב), and then the Table (שלחן). Eventually, these vessels were transferred to the *Beis haMikdash*. These first three objects that Moshe was instructed to build for the *Mishkan* — **א**רון, **מ**נרה and **ש**לחן — have the acronym of אמש.

The first letter of the Torah represents the בית, the House of Hashem, the *Beis haMikdash*, where the *Shechinah* would dwell. Using the At–Bash method, בית transforms into שמא, the same letters as אמש, representing the first three objects that were made for the *Mishkan*.

A further connection between these letters is found in *Sefer Yetzirah* (1:10), which divides the twenty-two letters of the *alef-beis* into three groups. The first group contains the letters א'מ'ש'. The second group consists of the letters ב'ג'ד'כ'פ'ר'ת', and the third is comprised of the letters ה'ו'ז'ח'ט'י'ל'נ'ס'ע'צ'ק'. These three groupings have a grammatical significance as well, as explained in *Sefer Yetzirah*.

## ◈ The Large and Small Letters in the Torah

Rabbi Yaakov Rinitz explains that according to all opinions there are seventeen large and small letters which appear in the Chumash. The seventeen letters, in the order in which they appear in the Torah, are:

| | |
|---|---|
| *Bereishis* 1:1 | בראשית |
| *Bereishis* 2:4 | בהבראם |
| *Bereishis* 23:2 | ולבכתה |
| *Bereishis* 27:46 | קצתי בחיי |
| *Shemos* 34:7 | נצר חסד |

| | |
|---|---|
| *Shemos* 34:14 | אל אחר |
| *Vayikra* 1:1 | ויקרא |
| *Vayikra* 6:2 | על מוקדה |
| *Vayikra* 11:42 | כל הולך על גחון |
| *Vayikra* 13:33 | והתגלח |
| *Bemidbar* 14:17 | ועתה יגדל נא כח |
| *Bemidbar* 27:5 | משפטן |
| *Devarim* 6:4 | שמע ישראל |
| *Devarim* 6:4 | אחד |
| *Devarim* 29:27 | וישלכם |
| *Devarim* 32:6 | ה לה' תגמלו |
| *Devarim* 32:18 | צור ילדך תשי |

An in-depth explanation of all the large and small letters found in the entire Tanach, would require a separate book, so we will concentrate in providing a sample explanation only for those that appear in the Torah itself. This will provide a guideline as to how large/small letters can be explained elsewhere, as well.

We must preface our examples by explaining that there are three methods used to interpret the significance of the appearance of the large and small letters within the specific context of the passage.[1] The source of these three approaches can be traced to *Midrash Osios Ketanos*, as quoted by the Ba'al HaTurim.

The three approaches are:

(A) **Letter Interpretation:** Interpreting a word based on the meaning or significance of the letter itself.

1. I am very grateful to Mr. J. Pearlman of London, who provided the concepts that explain and classify these letters.

(B) **Magnification/Diminution.** Interpreting a large letter as having a "magnifying" effect and, likewise, a small one as having a "reducing" effect, with regard to the meaning of the word in which it appears.

(C) **Addition/Omission.** In the case of a large letter, interpreting the word as if that letter were duplicated, i.e. that it appears twice; or, alternatively, interpreting the text vis-à-vis the expansion (fulfillment) of that letter. In the case of a small letter, interpreting the word as if that letter separates between that which comes before it and that which comes after, or as if the letter is omitted from it altogether.

Rabbeinu Bechaye points out that there is a connection between the letters, with each large letter being connected to its corresponding small letter. Therefore, these letters are to be considered as one linked alphabetic structure, and not as two distinct ones. Moreover, the Megalleh Amukos states that the large letters represent the attribute of mercy, whereas the corresponding smaller ones represent the attribute of justice.

The seventeen instances of large and small letters that appear in the Torah are presented here in alphabetic order. The method being implemented to explain the letter's usage is indicated in parenthesis.

### The Small א in *Vayikra* 1:1 — ויקרא

In the book of *Shemos*, Moshe becomes the leader of the Jewish People. He brings them out of Egypt and teaches them the Torah. In contrast, in the book of *Vayikra* Moshe's brother Aharon takes on a leading role as *Kohen Gadol*, responsible for the service in the *Mishkan* and the only person privileged to enter the Holy of Holies on Yom Kippur. It is at the juncture between these two books that this small letter א appears, in the *pasuk*: ויקרא אל משה וידבר ה' אליו מאהל מועד לאמר — "He called to Moshe, and Hashem spoke to him from the Tent of Meeting, saying" (*Vayikra* 1:1).

The Megalleh Amukos provides a fascinating insight that includes all three methods to explain the use of the small letter which, at the same time, explains why it is placed just at this juncture between these two books of the Torah.

The letter א represents Torah wisdom (Method A), as in the phrase אאלפך חכמה — "I will teach you wisdom" (*Iyov* 33:33), while the virtues of the Torah are described as being יקרה היא מפניים — "even more valuable than diamonds" (*Mishlei* 3:15). Omitting the letter א from the word ויקרא (Method C), results in the word ויקר, which describes the great value of Torah. Through the use of the small א, Hashem is emphasizing to Moshe that even a small amount of Torah learning (Method B) is still considered more important and valuable than the privilege of entering the Holy of Holies on Yom Kippur.

The Megalleh Amukos wrote a complete book containing one thousand different explanations for the use of the small letter א in the first word of the book of *Vayikra*. This is no longer available, but eighty-five of these explanations can be found in his Torah commentary to this *pasuk*. They are all expounded through the three methods mentioned above.

The Ba'al HaTurim explains that the small א in the word ויקרא represents Moshe Rabbeinu's humbleness. Due to his humility Moshe Rabbeinu wanted to write the word ויקרא in the above *pasuk* as ויקר — without the א — the same expression used when Hashem addressed the gentile prophet Bilaam (see Rashi on *Bemidbar* 23:4). (Method C) However, Hashem insisted that Moshe write the complete word, so he wrote it as a small letter — its minimal size signifying his humility. (Method B)

Although Moshe was fully aware of his own qualities and greatness as the leader of the Jewish People, his humility resulted from the fact that he was convinced that his personal elevated status was bestowed on him solely in the merit of the Jewish People.

The Minchas Shai points out that the Machzor Vitri's list of large and small letters includes a large letter א, in the words אשריך ישראל — "Fortunate are you, O Israel" (*Devarim* 33:29), as it was only in their merit that Moshe rose to greatness. This explanation concurs with the general rule of Rabbeinu Bechaye that large letters connect with their corresponding small ones.

### The Large ב in *Bereishis* 1:1 — בראשית

The Ba'al HaTurim, in his commentary on the first *pasuk* of *Bereishis*, explains why the Torah chose to begin with the letter ב, the second letter of the *alef-beis*, rather than with the first letter, א. He quotes the *Talmud Yerushalmi* (*Chagigah* 2:1) which states that the letter ב represents blessing (ברכה), in contrast to the letter א which denotes a curse (ארור). The Torah wants to begin on a pleasant note, as it states in *Mishlei* (3:17): דרכיה דרכי נעם וכל נתיבותיה שלום — "Its ways are ways of pleasantness and all its paths are peace." (Method A)

The Rokeach adds that not only does the first letter ב represent the blessings found in the Torah, but in fact the first two letters of the word ברכה are the same as the first two letters of the first two words — בראשית and ברא — of the Torah, as it provides bountiful blessings to all those who adhere to its teachings. (Method B)

Not only does the Torah begin with blessing, but we also find it in the last *parashah* of the Torah, *VeZos HaBerachah* (וזאת הברכה). In a similar fashion, the Oral law begins with the Tractate of *Berachos* (ברכות), and the final Mishnah ends with the words ה' יברך את עמו בשלום — "Hashem Blesses His people with peace." Thus both the Written and Oral Torah begin and end with the subject of blessing, as the entire Torah encapsulates blessing.

The Ba'al HaTurim points out that the ב signifies a duality in creation, being that it is the first letter of the Torah yet the second letter of the *alef-beis*. One of the main purposes for the creation of this physical world was to enable us to earn our reward in the spiritual World to Come. Therefore, this world should be treated as secondary — as it is only a means to achieve an end — rather than be viewed as the end itself.

The duality of this first ב is alluded to in the letter itself as well. The numerical value of ב is two, a reference to the fact that the physical world was created in such a way that the continuity of every human being or animal — as well as some vegetation — is dependent upon the duality of the species, i.e. male and female. (Methods A and C)

This duality can be seen in inanimate objects, as well. We find corresponding objects of creation complementing each other in a natural way, such as the moon and the sun. Similarly, every molecule is composed of positive and negative polarities, and magnetic and electrical forces contain positive and negative poles which complement and balance each other. This is all represented in the large ב of *Bereishis.* (Method C)

The Rokeach points out that this duality of creation is alluded to in the word בראשית itself. The letters of this word spell out ברא שתי, which refers to the creation that functions through sets of twos.

This large ב also alludes to the both the First and Second Temples (Method A) which is elaborated on in the section on letter fulfillments (see p. 163).

**The Large ג in *Vayikra* 13:33 — והתגלח**

*Vayikra* 13:33 states: והתגלח את הנתק — "And the *nesek* shall shave himself." The Ba'al HaTurim explains that the word והתגלח (to shave) is written with a large letter ג — which has the numerical value of three — indicating that there are three types of people who are required to have their hair shaved off. They are: a *nazir*, a *Levi*, and a *metzora.* (Method A)

A *nazir* is a person who undertakes, for a minimum period of thirty days, to abstain from drinking wine, taking a haircut, and from defiling himself by coming in contact with a dead body. If he inadvertently was unable to honor this undertaking for the complete period, he shaves off all his hair and commences a new period of abstinence for thirty days. The *Levi'im*, when they were inaugurated into the service of the *Mishkan*, had to shave off their hair. A *metzora* is a person suffering from the affliction of *tzara'as* (a punishment for speaking *lashon ha-ra*). *Tzara'as* renders a person ritually unclean and as a part of the person's purification process, he is required to shave off all his hair.

There are actually several types of *tzara'as*, which can affect one's house, clothes, skin or hair. If a person had a blemish which might be *tzara'as*, he must go to the *Kohen* to have it evaluated. In the case of suspected *tzara'as* of the hair (*nesek*), the person is first required to shave off all of his hair, *except* for hair which surrounds the suspected area of blemish. The blemish is then checked periodically to determine whether the person is indeed afflicted.

The *pasuk* in which the large ג appears is specifically discussing the case of one who is suspected of having *tzara'as* of the hair (*nesek*). Why is the large letter written in this particular chapter?

The *Arizal* provides an answer. The haircut given to a *metzora*, *nazir* or *Levi* is performed while those individuals are in a state of ritual impurity, and it is part of their purification process. However, in the case of a suspected *nesek*, where it needs to be established whether the blemish is *tzara'as*, the person is still ritually clean. His haircut is a method through which to establish the true identity of the blemish. The requirement to shave in the case of a *nesek* is unique in that it is the only time the person is still ritually clean while having his hair shaved off. In order to differentiate between them, the Torah uses the large letter ג when issuing the command that the hair of the *nesek* be shaved. (Method A)

It is a widespread custom that a boy has his first haircut at the age of three. This corresponds to the numerical value of the letter ג in the word והתגלח, used concerning a *nesek*. It is appropriate to use this ג to indicate the age of the child when he receives his first haircut, when he is still pure and innocent from sin.

### The Large ד in *Devarim* 6:4 — אחד

It is well-known that the letter ד in the first *pasuk* of the *Shema* is written as a large letter: שמע ישראל ה' א-להינו ה' אחד — "Hear O Israel, Hashem is our G-d, Hashem is One" (*Devarim* 6:4). In his commentary on this *pasuk*, the Ba'al HaTurim cites another *pasuk*: כי לא תשתחוה לאל אחר — "You shall not prostrate yourself to an alien god" (*Shemos* 34:14). He explains that the last word אחר — a reference to idolatry — is written with a large ר to emphasize that letter, so that it will not be confused with the contrasting word אחד — referring to Hashem — that ends with a large letter ד in the first *pasuk* of the *Shema*.

When the Jewish People sinned through idol worship, in essence they exchanged these two letters. This is indicated in the rebuke that Moshe gave shortly before his death in the *pasuk*: כי דור תהפכת המה בנים לא אמן בם — "You are a generation that reverses things, children without trust (*Devarim* 32:20). The expression דור תהפכת, "a generation that reverses things," refers to a generation that reverses their correct allegiance, by replacing the אחד (Hashem) with אחר (idolatry). Appropriately, the word דור incorporates both of these letters. (Method A)

This large letter is explained in further detail below with reference to the large letter ר of אחר, and the large letter ע of שמע.

### The Large ה in *Devarim* 32:6 — ה לה'

In Moshe Rabbeinu's rebuke to the Jewish People for having sinned and rebelled against Hashem, he says: ה לה' תגמלו זאת עם נבל ולא חכם הלוא הוא אביך קנך הוא עשך ויכננך — "Is this how you repay Hashem, O vile and unwise people? Is He not your Father, Who acquired you? He made and established you!" (*Devarim* 32:6).

The letter ה alludes to the Chumash, as the numerical value of ה is five — representing the Five Books of the Torah. The large letter ה in this *pasuk* comes to stress the greatness of the Torah. In essence,

Moshe's rebuke is that they seem to have forgotten this; for if they had an appreciation of how valuable a treasure the Torah is, they would not have abandoned it. (Methods A and B)

Moreover, the use of the large letter ה is meant to convey the message that Hashem remains unaffected by their rebellious actions. It portrays the fact that He remains as great after their rebellion as He was previously. (Method B)

◈ ◈ ◈

This large letter ה is unique, as it is the only instance where a letter in the Torah stands alone, written detached from the remainder of the word. This word is the first word of the sixth *pasuk* in *Parashas Ha'azinu*. The total numerical value of the first letters of the first six *pesukim* total 345, the same numerical value as Moshe (משה). Being that this large letter completes the numerical value of Moshe's name, Moshe felt it inappropriate to join his name with Hashem's and therefore distanced this letter ה from Hashem's Name.

The Minchas Shai quotes the *midrash* (*Shemos Rabbah* 24) which states that for this same reason the ה should actually be written lower than the rest of the word.

◈ ◈ ◈

Logic would dictate that when a person transgresses Hashem's will, he should be punished. However, Hashem has created the concept of repentance, whereby the sinner can gain full atonement for his wrongdoings. Thus, repentance is a special Divine gift that overrides normal human logic. Earlier we mentioned that the letter ה represents repentance. The Ben Ish Chai quotes a Gemara (*Talmud Yerushalmi, Makkos* 2:6) to explain that הלה' should be understood as "repentance emanates from Hashem." When Moshe introduced his rebuke with the large ה, he alluded to this great divine gift of repentance which emanates from Hashem Himself.

Moshe is castigating them for rejecting the Torah's teachings and admonishing them to repent and return to the ways of Hashem. He therefore prefixes his rebuke by using the large letter ה. (Method A)

Moshe's message was: Hashem created the possibility of repentance and you, foolish people, do not utilize the opportunity to return to Him. (Methods A and B)

**The Small ה in *Bereishis* 2:4 — בהבראם**

After the narrative of Creation, the second chapter of *Sefer Bereishis* begins with the *pasuk*: אלה תולדות השמים והארץ בהבראם — "These are the products of the heavens and the earth when they were created." The word בהבראם is spelled with a small letter ה, which is interpreted by the Midrash as a reference to Avraham Avinu, in whose merit the world was created. Avraham was to be the first person to make as his life goal the mission to proclaim and publicize the Divine Presence to mankind. At birth, Avraham was named Avram (אברם); half way through his life Hashem added the letter ה to his name, after which he was known as Avraham (אברהם). Being that this letter was incorporated for only a part of his lifetime, it is written as a small letter. In this way, the word בהבראם accurately represents his name during his lifespan. (Method B)

The Gemara in *Menachos* (29b) states that the physical world was created by the use of the letter ה. The Me'or V'Shemesh explains that the small letter 'ה in the word בהבראם teaches us that a person needs to view the physical world from a perspective of minimizing his indulgence in its transient pleasures and luxuries. (Method B)

Furthermore, the letter ה represents repentance. This is reflected in the actual shape of the letter. The Gemara explains that the shape of the ה represents a sinner falling through the wide opening at the bottom of the letter. However, if the sinner repents, and wants earnestly to return to Hashem, a special entrance is available to him, at the side of the letter.

Avraham was the first person who actively encouraged repentance, as we learned from the *pasuk*: ואת הנפש אשר עשו בחרן — "...with the souls that they had made in Charan" (*Bereishis* 12:5). These are the people that they converted into believers in Hashem. Thus, we can also say that the additional small letter ה here represents the first *ba'al teshuvah* movement, which was started by Avraham. (Method A)

### The Large ו in *Vayikra* 11:42 — גחון

The Gemara in *Kiddushin* (30a) writes that the earlier *chachamim* were known as סופרים, "counters," obtaining this "nickname" because they used to count the number of letters in the Torah and derive significance from their totals (see *Divrei HaYamim* I 2:55). They said that the middle letter of the Torah is the large letter ו of the word גחון in the *pasuk*: כל הולך על גחון — "Everything that creeps on its belly" (*Vayikra* 11:42). Rabbi Rinitz, in his *sefer Dikdukei Torah*, discussed this *gemara* at length. He writes that the Gemara's statement is initially difficult to understand, being that the letter ו of the word גחון is the 157,237th letter of the entire Torah. Mathematically, the middle letter should be the 152,403th letter, which is the letter ו of the word הוא found in *Vayikra* 8:28.

However, Rabbi Rinitz points out that this large letter ו in the word גחון is the ninth and middle instance of large and small letters appearing in the Torah, as enumerated earlier (see pp. 101–102 for a list of the seventeen instances). Thus, the Gemara's statement that it is the middle letter of the Torah appears to refer to the fact that it is middle letter of the listing of large and small letters. Its large size emphasizes this central position in the Torah. (Method B)

Rabbeinu Efrayim explains that the words כל הולך על גחון, "all that goes on its belly," refer to the Serpent that enticed Adam ha-Rishon and Chavah to transgress. Initially the Serpent was created with feet, and part of its punishment was that it would be forced to crawl on its belly (see *Bereishis* 3:14).

Rabbeinu Efrayim cites a Midrash (*Bereishis Rabbah* 12:6) that specifies six items that were taken from Adam after this transgression, all of which will eventually be returned to him with the arrival of Mashiach. Three of these items affected Adams physicality: His spirituality was radically reduced, his life was shortened, and his height was minimized. The other three affected the world around him: Vegetation lost much of its unique taste, some fruit trees stopped producing fruit, and the moonlight was diminished. These six items are alluded to by the use of the large letter ו, which has a numerical value of six. (Method A)

Moreover, the Rokeach explains that this large letter ו alludes to another group of six that pertains to the Serpent. (Method C) He points out that the Torah specifies *six* curses that the Serpent received for having been the cause of this initial sin. These are indicated in the translation of the relevant passage (*Bereishis* 3:14–15):

> And Hashem Elokim said to the Serpent, "Because you have done this, *you are cursed* (1) more than all the animals and beasts of the field. *You shall go on your belly* (2), and *dust you shall eat* (3) your entire life. I will put *enmity between you and the woman* (4), and between *your offspring and hers* (5). He will *pound you on the head* (6), and you will hiss at his feet."

### The Large י in *Bemidbar* 14:17 — יגדל

*Bemidbar* 14:17 states: ועתה יגדל נא כח ה' — "And now may Hashem's strength be magnified." The Ba'al HaTurim explains that Moshe Rabbeinu's use of a large letter י, which has a numerical value of ten, alludes to the ten trials that Avraham Avinu successfully withstood, as mentioned in the fifth chapter of *Avos*. Moshe Rabbeinu was *davening* to Hashem not to destroy the Jewish People and he wanted to invoke the righteous merits of Avraham Avinu in having successfully withstood his trials. Moshe prayed that, in this merit, the Jewish People should be spared annihilation. (Method A)

The Pane'ach Raza explains that the usage of the large letter י hints at the fact that when the Jewish People observe the Torah's commandments, Hashem's Name, which begins with a letter י, becomes magnified and publicized to the world. This is alluded to in the actual spelling of the word יגדל; it can also be read as גדל + י, "the *yud* (i.e. Hashem's Name) becomes glorified." (Method B)

Furthermore, in the expansion of the letter י into יוד, both the original letter and the hidden fulfillment have the same numerical value of ten. As we have said, when a letter is written larger it can be interpreted as being doubled. Thus we have a doubling of the י, as well as a doubling in its expansion, which together represent a manifold increase. This represents the magnification of the manifestation of Hashem's Divine glory in this world when the Jewish People adhere to the Torah. (Method C)

### The Small י in *Devarim* 32:18 — תשי

The converse of the explanation given by the Pane'ach Raza on the large letter י of יגדל above, is true for the corresponding small letter י found in the *pasuk*: צור ילדך תשי — "You ignored the Rock Who gave birth to you" (*Devarim* 32:18). When Torah commandments are transgressed, it causes a decrease in the manifestation of His Glory in this world. Here, too, the word תשי can be read as תש + י, a decrease or weakening in our appreciation of His Divine power. (Method B) All Torah commandments are encapsulated in the Ten Commandments and are represented by the small letter י. Alternatively, since the letter י represents the יצר טוב, the good inclination, the fact that it is written as a small letter here alludes to the weakening of the influence of the good inclination due to sin. (Method A and B)

The Rokeach points out that the passage which precedes the above *pasuk* lists ten wrongdoings that the Jewish People transgressed (see ibid. 32:15–17). These ten transgressions weakened the possibility of any Divine benefits being allotted to the Jewish People. (Method C)

### The Small כ in *Bereishis* 23:2 — ולבכתה

When Sarah died, the *pasuk* relates: ויבא אברהם לספד לשרה ולבכתה — "And Avraham came to eulogize Sarah and cried for her" (*Bereishis* 23:2). The word ולבכתה ("and [he] cried for her") is written with a small letter כ. The Ba'al HaTurim explains that it is written with a small letter because Avraham minimized his outward display of sorrow at her funeral since she died after having lived a full and successful life. Another possible explanation might be that because Sarah died as a result of hearing the news of the *Akeidah* (the Binding of Yitzchak), onlookers at the funeral might think that Avraham's weeping was brought on by feelings of regret for having indirectly caused her death. (Method B)

The Rokeach offers a different explanation for the small letter, citing the Gemara in *Bava Basra* (16b) which debates whether or not Avraham had a daughter. In order to reconcile both opinions, the Rokeach explains that this daughter died during her parents' lifetime. Thus Avraham was eulogizing his wife and daughter at the same time. When spelled without the small letter כ, the word ולבכתה becomes ולבתה, "for his daughter." (Method C)

Sarah died at the age of 127, and Avraham at the age of 175. Being that Avraham was ten years older than his wife, this means that he lived thirty-eight years after her death. This state of loneliness as a widower was another upsetting factor, which we find indicated in the word ולבכתה, as well. The small letter divides the word into two parts. In the first part, we have the letters ו'ל'ב', which have a combined numerical value of thirty-eight. This signifies the additional reason for Avraham's weeping and sorrow at her funeral — for his years of widowhood. (Method C)

In addition, the fulfillment of the letter כ is כף, which translates as the palm [of the hand]. Both Rashi and *Metzudas David* explain that the phrase והך כף אל כף, "strike your hands together" (*Yechezkel* 21:19), is a reference to mourning. (Method A)

### The Large ל in *Devarim* 29:27— וישלכם

The letter ל represents Torah study. The fulfillment ל (למד) literally means "to learn."

In *Devarim* 29:27 the ל is written as a large letter (וישלכם — "and

He cast them away") to emphasize the importance of Torah learning at all times. This *pasuk* refers to times of exile and persecution, when Hashem will cast the Jewish People out of their homeland. The message of this ל is that despite the exile, the Jewish People will remain a nation as long as they continue learning Torah. (Methods A and B)

This same lesson prompted Rabbi Yochanan ben Zakkai to negotiate with the Roman general Vespasian, at the time of the destruction of the Second *Beis haMikdash*, to spare the Torah Academy of Yavneh and its scholars from destruction. For as long as there is Torah study, the Jewish nation retains its unique identity despite their exiles.

Furthermore, the large ל alludes to the destruction of the First *Beis haMikdash*, denoting that this "casting" would take place during the *thirtieth* generation after Avraham Avinu — thirty being the numerical value of the letter ל. This corresponds to the Mesorah (according the the Minchas Shai) which states that the word ליני in *Rus* 3:13 uses a large letter ל, when Boaz says to Ruth: ליני הלילה — "Stay the night." Boaz was telling Ruth, as the ancestress of Mashiach, to have patience and that her descendants should continue learning throughout the extended long night of exile, as Mashiach would eventually redeem her descendants when the morning of redemption arrives. (Method A)

(It should be noted that in the Mesorah according to Machzor Vitri, it is the נ that is written as a large letter in that *pasuk*. He explains that the reckoning of the generations begins from Creation — fifty generations before the destruction of the First *Beis haMikdash*, corresponding to the numerical value of נ, which is fifty.)

The Gemara (*Kiddushin* 40b) teaches us that Torah learning is more important than performing good deeds, since learning results in people observing its commandments. This priority is stressed by the use of the large letter ל as the letter fulfills as למד — to learn. (Method B)

The Pane'ach Raza explains that the word וישלכם in the above *pasuk* is spelled with a large letter, but it lacks a second י — because it should be written as וישליכם. The י represents the ten tribes (the numerical value of י is ten), who were lost after being cast into exile as stated in *Sanhedrin* 94. (Method B)

The continuation of *Devarim* 29:27 reads: "And Hashem removed them from their soil, with anger, wrath and great fury (אף), and He cast them to another land, as this very day." When Torah is studied in abundance — represented by the large letter ל — then it (meaning the letter itself) can be "cast" into the midst of the word אף, mitigating this Divine anger by becoming the word אלף, a letter that represents Torah knowledge, as previously explained. (Method C)

The letter ל has a numerical value of thirty. Its expansion is למד, and thus its second fulfillment is **למד מם דלת**, which has a *mispar katan* of thirty (when adding together the *mispar katan* of each individual letter), the same as the numerical value of the original letter. (Method C)

### The Small מ in *Devarim* 9:24 — ממרים

We find a small letter מ in *Devarim* 9:24: ממרים הייתם עם ה' מיום דעתי אתכם — "You have been rebels against Hashem from the day that I knew you." The word **ממרים** is written with a small letter מ. In his *sefer Pardes Yosef*, Rabbi Yosef Baumgarten, *zt"l*, explains this by citing the Gemara which states that the evil inclination entices a person to rebel against Hashem and His commandments in small stages, continuously until eventually it succeeds in bringing him to serve idols (see *Shabbos* 105b). This rebellion begins with small deviations from the correct path, which is indicated by the small מ in **ממרים**. (Method B)

These deviations result in bitter consequences, which are alluded to when omitting the small מ, for then the word read as מרים, "bitterness." (Method C)

Moreover, this *pasuk* begins and ends with a letter מ — the first one being small and the final one being normal size. This lends extra significance to the letter and at the same time duplicates the lesson taught by the above-mentioned *gemara*. (Methods A and C)

The small letter מ in ממרים corresponds to the large letter מ of משלי, the first word of *Sefer Mishlei*. This small letter מ represents rebellion against Hashem, while the large מ introduces *Mishlei* — the ethical teachings that ensure that a person keeps within the correct Torah guidelines, so that he will not want to rebel against Hashem.

### The Small מ in *Vayikra* 6:2 — מוקדה

Rabbeinu Bechaye explains that this phrase alludes to the greatness of the human intellect that can assist a person to reach spiritual heights far beyond those of angels. The intellect, known as the נפש משכלת (Method A), occupies a minimal amount of physical space in the body. The small letter מ in *Vayikra* 6:2, הוא העולה על מוקדה — "It is the *olah*-offering that stays on the flame," represents this small physical space. (Method B)

The simple interpretation of this *pasuk* refers to the *olah* sacrifice, which atones for a person's impure thoughts. However, the word *olah* can also be translated as "height," alluding to a person's haughtiness, when he considers himself higher and better than others. The Ramban writes that haughty people are punished with many different types of fires that exist in *Gehinnom*. This idea is alluded to in this *pasuk*. By translating *olah* as "haughty," the above *pasuk* can be interpreted as: "one who is haughty [will be punished by being] placed on the flame."

The Gemara (*Sanhedrin* 38a) states: "A person who wishes to combat his haughtiness should bear in mind that at the time of Creation, even a small fly was created *before* mankind. So what is there to be haughty about?" This advice is hinted at in the word מוקדה, whose letters spell out the word קודמה, "*before* you." (Method C)

However, a person is permitted to possess a minimal amount of pride in order to retain his own self-esteem. (Method B)

### The Large נ in *Shemos* 34:7 — נצר

Hashem wanted to destroy the Jewish People after they had served the Golden Calf, but Moshe Rabbeinu prayed on their behalf. Immediately preceding this prayer, we find a listing of the Thirteen Attributes of Mercy. Moshe Rabbeinu incorporated in his prayer one of those attributes, the praise of נצר חסד, "Preserver of kindness" (*Shemos* 34:7), which is written with a large letter נ. The Shlah explains the large נ alludes to the two *nuns* in the phrase נעשה ונשמע, "We will do and we will obey" (ibid. 24:7). The Jewish People had previously proclaimed their willingness to accept the Torah with the use of these two words. In his prayer, Moshe wanted to stress the Jewish People's merits. (Methods A and C)

The large נ alludes also to the נחש, the Serpent that enticed Adam to sin, thereby introducing the evil inclination into the world. At the time of the Golden Calf the evil inclination's power had become so great that it was able to influence the Jewish People to perform such a blatant act of idol worship. (Method B)

### The Large ן in *Bemidbar* 27:5 — משפטן

Rashi explains that Moshe Rabbeinu forgot the correct law regarding the inheritance due to the daughters of Tzelofchad: ויקרב משה את משפטן לפני ה׳ — "And Moshe brought their claim before Hashem" (*Bemidbar* 27:5), meaning that he did not know how to rule in their case. This was a punishment for having assumed too much authority when he said to the Jewish People: "Whatever is too difficult for you, you shall bring to me" (*Devarim* 1:17). Part of his punishment was that he had to publicly admit that he had forgotten the correct law. The letter נ, with a numerical value of fifty, alludes to the fifty gates of understanding, of which Moshe was only able to grasp forty-nine. The word משפטן stresses this, as it can be read as משפט + ן, which can be interpreted to mean that the judgment impeded him from attaining the fiftieth level of understanding. (Method A)

Alternatively, it alludes to the laws pertaining to women inheriting land, and is interpreted as the acronym for משפט + נשים, the law concerning women.

The Gemara (*Temurah* 16a) relates that just before Moshe died, he asked his successor, Yehoshua, if there were any points in the Torah that still needed clarification. The latter replied that since he never failed to be at Moshe side, he could not have missed any of his teachings, and therefore nothing extra needed explaining. After Moshe passed away, seven hundred doubtful matters cropped up, to which they could find no resolution. The higher numerical value of the final letter ן is seven hundred. Yehoshua was punished in a similar way that Moshe was, for being too confident, which is alluded to by the use of the large letter ן. (Methods B and C)

### The Large ע in *Devarim* 6:4 — שמע

In some editions of the Chumash the letter ע is written as a large letter in the *pasuk*: שמע ישראל ה' א-להינו ה' אחד — "Hear O Israel, Hashem is our G-d, Hashem is One!"

The Ba'al HaTurim (*Bemidbar* 11:16) enumerates seventy descriptive Names of Hashem, as well as seventy Names by which the Jewish People are referred to throughout the Torah. Seventy is the numerical value of the letter ע. In the above *pasuk* from *Devarim*, the large letter ע is immediately followed by the words "Yisrael" and "Hashem," alluding to the fact that each is referred to by seventy different names. We find this idea hinted at in the actually text, which can be read as: שמ + ע ישראל ה' — "the seventy names that Yisrael and Hashem [are known by]." (Methods A, B and C)

The letter ע expands as עין, with a numerical value of 130. This first *pasuk* of the *Shema* is followed by another five that together form its first chapter. Those five *pesukim* all begin with a letter ו and end with a letter כ, the total numerical value of which is twenty-six, the same as that of Hashem's Name. Therefore, Hashem's Name is referred to a total of five times in those *pesukim*. This produces a total value of one hundred and thirty (5 x 26 = 130) — the numerical value of the fulfillment of the large ע. (Method C)

Rabbeinu Efrayim quotes the Midrash which says that each of the following four are called by seventy different names: Hashem, Yisrael, Jerusalem and the Torah. These are alluded to in the large letters ע (seventy) and ד (four) in the first *pasuk* in *Shema*. (Method A)

The Ba'al HaTurim mentions that in some editions the letter ש of the word שמע is written as a large letter and not the ע. In this case, it is the ש and ד which are large, a reference to the first chapter of *Shema* (as represented by the ש) which is recited four (the numerical value of ד) times daily — twice in the morning prayers, once in the evening one, and once at bedtime.

**The Small ק in *Bereishis* 27:46 — קצתי**

At the end of *Parashas Toldos* Rivka Imeinu says: קצתי בחיי מפני בנות חת — "I am disgusted with my life on account of the daughters of Ches" (*Bereishis* 27:46). She was upset because Eisav had married a Canaanite woman, a non-believer, and she was distressed at the prospect of her son Yaakov also "marrying out," so to speak.

However, Rivkah used this argument as an excuse to send Yaakov away. Yaakov had obtained the blessings from his father, as a result of which Esav hated him and intended to kill him. Rivkah's main concern was to ensure that her two sons would be separated from each other, for a real danger existed that a mortal fight would be fatal to both of them, as she expresses in the previous *pasuk* (ibid. 27:45). (Method B)

Rabbeinu Bechaye comments on this *pasuk*:

> The word קצתי (I am disgusted) is written with a small letter ק. This alludes to the fact that Rivkah saw, through *ruach ha-kadosh*, the eventual destruction of the *Beis haMikdash* and the *Heichal*. The *Kodesh haKodashim* was one hundred *amos* high, corresponding to the nu-

merical value of the letter ק. This destruction would be a direct result of the Jewish People intermarrying with gentile nations.

The [corresponding] large letter ק appears in *Tehillim* 84:4, in reference to the building of the *Beis haMikdash*: גם צפור מצאה בית ודרור קן לה — "Even the bird finds its home and the free bird her nest."

The Megalleh Amukos reinforces Rabbeinu Bechaye's explanation by interpreting the words קצתי as קץ ת"י, "the end [of] 410," meaning that the *Beis haMikdash* would be destroyed after 410 years of existence.

The *Beis haMikdash* is symbolized by the large letter ק and its destruction by the corresponding small letter. In other words, one has an effect on the other. This connection between a large letter and its corresponding small one is true for all the letters of the *alef-beis*.

The Megalleh Amukos points out that the letter ק, with a numerical value of one hundred, alludes also to the *Mishkan*, which was one hundred *amos* long. It was fifty *amos* wide, and had an entrance on the eastern side that was twenty *amos* wide. Moreover, the *Mishkan* incorporated the *Heichal* that was thirty *amos* long. These measurements are alluded to in the *pasuk*: שמחתי באמרים לי בית ה' נלך — "I rejoiced when they said to me, 'To Hashem's House let us go'" (*Tehillim* 122:1). The last word נלך has a total numerical value of one hundred, corresponding to the dimensions of both and *Mishkan* and the *Beis haMikdash* and the numerical value of its letters are fifty, thirty and twenty, corresponding to those of the *Mishkan*, as described above.

The Shlah points out that the letter ק expands as קוף, with a numerical value of 186, which equates to the value of the word מקום, "place," representing the *Beis haMikdash*, where the *Shechinah* rested. It also translates as a "monkey," alluding to the fact that immoral conduct displays animal-like behavior. (Method A)

By omitting the small letter from **קצתי**, the word reads as **צתי**, an expression used regarding the destruction of the *Beis haMikdash* by fire, as in the *pasuk*: **ויצת** אש בציון — "[Hashem] kindled a fire in Tzion" (*Eichah* 4:11). The numerical value of **צתי** is five hundred, alluding to the size of *Har haBayis* (which is 500x500 *amos*) upon which the *Beis haMikdash* was built (see Mishnah *Tamid* 2:1). (Method C)

**The Large ר in *Shemos* 34:14 — אחר**

As mentioned above, the Ba'al HaTurim (on *Devarim* 6:4) points out that the large letter ר in the *pasuk*, כי לא תשתחוה לאל **אחר** — "For you shall not prostrate yourself to an alien god" (*Shemos* 34:14), is meant to emphasize this letter (Method A) so that it should not be confused with the similar but contrasting word **אחד**. The large letter ר refers to idol worship, while the large letter ד refers to Hashem.

The combination of these two letters form the word רד, "descend." After the Jewish nation had served the Golden Calf, Hashem used this word when He told Moshe to go and rejoin the people at the foot of Mount Sinai. Hashem said: לך רד כי שחת עמך — "Go, descend for your nation has degenerated..." (*Shemos* 32:7).

The word רד also signifies a person who has lost his wealth and has fallen from his previous financial status, as the Gemara states: "When a person becomes poor in this world below, he also finds disfavor with Hashem above" (*Sanhedrin* 103a). One of the fulfillments of the letter ר is רֵישׁ (*reish*); when read as רָשׁ (*rash*), it means "poor" or "destitute." The large ר serves to emphasize that the person is doubly poor — both in this world below and in the eyes of Hashem above. This is an example of a large letter having a duplicating effect. (Method C)

**The Large ת in *Devarim* 18:13 — תמים**

In some editions of the Mesorah the letter ת is written as a large letter in the *pasuk*: **ת**מים תהיה עם ה' א-להיך — "You shall be wholehearted with Hashem" (*Devarim* 18:13). The Ba'al HaTurim explains that the large letter indicates that if a person is wholehearted in his trust in Hashem, then Hashem reckons it as if he has kept the entire Torah from beginning to end, as symbolized by the ת, the last letter of the *alef-beis*. (Method B)

◆ ◆ ◆

When the numerical value of each individual letter in Hashem's Name is multiplied by the sum of the numerical values of the remaining three, the sum of the products totals 490.

| | | | | | |
|---|---|---|---|---|---|
| 10 x 16 | = | 160 | י | x | הוה |
| 5 x 21 | = | 105 | ה | x | יוה |
| 6 x 20 | = | 120 | ו | x | יהה |
| 5 x 21 | = | 105 | ה | x | יהו |
| **Total** | = | **490** | | | |

The Megalleh Amukos points out that the above figure is the same as that of the numerical value of the word תמים. This connection signifies the extent of our trust in Hashem. In other words, in whatever situation we find ourselves, our trust in Hashem must be steadfast and wholehearted. (Method C)

◆ ◆ ◆

The above *pasuk* appears in a chapter that deals with various abominations, including that of דרש אל המתים — the prohibition against consulting spirits of departed people. In contrast, we are instructed to place our complete trust in Hashem and be תמים with Him. Both words, מתים and תמים, are composed from the same letters. To stress the correct alternative that should be chosen, the ת in תמים is written as a large letter. (Methods A and C)

◆ ◆ ◆

The *Shulchan Aruch* (*Orach Chayim* 603) states that during the Ten Days of Repentance a person should be more stringent than the rest of the year; for example, being particular only to eat bread that has been baked by a Jewish baker. Although he might not be able to keep up this extra stringency during the rest of the year, it is still important to be more careful during this period, as a person is judged by Hashem on Rosh Hashanah according to his current level. Rabbeinu Efrayim explains that these extra stringencies are alluded to in *Devarim* 18:13 as the numerical value of the words תמים תהיה is the same as that of the word תשרי, the month of Tishrei, which also begins with the letter ת. (Methods A and C)

## SUSPENDED LETTERS

In the above section, we have dealt with the large and small letters that appear in Tanach. As we explained, the large letters are twice the normal size, while the smaller letters are written as half the size of the rest of the text.

There are, however, four occasions when normal-sized letters are written higher than the rest of the text, in a raised position, giving them a suspended appearance. These are referred to as the ארבע אותיות תלויות, the "four suspended letters."

The first instance where we find a suspended letter is in the *pasuk*: ויהונתן בן גרשם בן מ׳נשה הוא ובניו היו כהנים — "And Yonasan, the son of Gershom, the son of Menashe, he and his sons were priests" (*Shoftim* 18:30). The above *pasuk* is in contrast to the one in *Divrei HaYamim* I 26:24 that refers to that same Gershom as the son of Moshe, which, in fact, he was. However, here in *Shoftim* he is referred to as the son of Menashe because of their similar life histories. Both Gershom and Menashe were sinners in the earlier part of their lives and later repented. This comparison is indicated by the addition of the suspended letter נ to the word משה, so that it reads מנשה. From this explanation, we can deduce that the suspended letters should not actually be in the text at all, and that when removed, we find the correct meaning of the *pasuk*. Gershom was the biological son of Moshe and not of Menashe. This suspended letter is only inserted to reveal an extra dimension to the subject in question. In this case, it teaches us that Gershom pursued a similarly wicked lifestyle to that of Menashe.

◈ ◈ ◈

The second instance is the raised ע in *Tehillim* 80:14: יכרסמנה חזיר מיער וכו' — "The boar of the forest ravages it...." This *pasuk* is explained as referring to the savage behavior of Esav and his descendants towards the Jewish People. The "boar" refers to Esav himself, who spent his entire life trying to kill his brother Yaakov. The word מיער, with the suspended letter ע, is said to refer to the Roman Empire, a nation which descended from Esav. They have both pursued a similar history of persecuting the Jewish nation. The Rokeach points out that when reading the word מיער without the suspended letter, as מיר, the letters spell out the word רמי, the Hebrew equivalent to "Rome." In this case, too, removing the suspended letter gives us the correct interpretation.

The word מיער describes a wild boar, attacking and endangering both people and property. These animals are sent as a punishment when the Jewish People disobey Hashem and His commandments. The Midrash in *Vayikra Rabbah* 13 and in *Avos d'Rabbi Nasan* 34:3 interpret this suspended letter by replacing the word with its homonym מיאר, which is accomplished by substituting an א for the ע. מיאר refers to a tame boar that comes up from the river and causes no harm at all. It will ascend only when the Jewish People obey Hashem and His commandments.

The other suspended letters are interpreted by actually removing them from their context in order to gain their true meaning. The word מיער, however, is the exception as it can also interpreted by replacing the ע with the א.

The Gemara in *Kiddushin* 30a states that the letter ע in this *pasuk* is the midpoint in *Sefer Tehillim*. Essentially, it acts as a pivot that will allow two alternative meanings, depending on the obedience of the Jewish People. The Maharsha writes that he spent a long time counting the number of *pesukim*, words and letters contained in *Sefer Tehillim* to confirm that the letter ע is the middle letter.

◆ ◆ ◆

The third and fourth occurrences of a suspended letter are in *Iyov* (ch. 38), both being a suspended letter ע. In *pasuk* 13 it states: לאחוז בכנפות הארץ וינערו רשעים ממנה — "To grasp the corners of the earth, so that the wicked shall be shaken from it."

*Minchas Shai* points out that the letters of the word רשעים, also spell the word עשרים, rich people. The wicked referred to here are those who become rich through devious means and use their wealth to adversely influence others. Here again, the suspended letter should be removed in order to understand the *pasuk* correctly: the word רשעים becomes רשים, poor. Wealth that is gained by devious means does not last, and these wicked people will become poor again and lose their influence.

Then, in *pasuk* 15, we find the same word also with a suspended letter: וימנע מרשעים אורם וזרוע רמה תשבר — "And their light shall be withheld from the wicked, and the high arm shall be broken." Rashi, in his explanation to the fourth *pasuk* of *Bereishis*, quotes the Midrash which states that Hashem saw that the wicked people did not deserve to use the initial light of Creation, so He set it aside for the righteous to use in the future. The letter ע is written out as עין, which means "eye." Thus, the suspended letter ע in the above *pasuk* alludes to the withholding of the initial light of Creation from the eyes of the wicked people.

As we have said, removing the suspended letter from רשעים forms the word רשים. Rashi (commenting on the Gemara in *Sanhedrin* 103b) points out that this word is in the plural form, implying that such people are doubly poor — both in this world below and in the eyes of Hashem above. In this case, as well, removing the suspended letter reveals the word's true interpretation.

## Full/Deficient Spellings

There are numerous occasions when certain words are spelled with an additional ו, י or ה, or when words that normally include those letters are spelled without them. For example, the name David (דוד) is usually spelled with three letters, but there are occasions when it is spelled as דויד, as found in *Divrei HaYamim* (I 29:10) in the phrase ויברך דויד — "and David blessed." The same word will appear a number of times in a passage spelled in its usual form, and the instance where the word is spelled differently alludes to an additional insight on the relevant topic.

Normally the addition of one of these letters denotes an extra degree of holiness, as these three letters are the ones that compose Hashem's Name. However, each specific occurrence needs to be explained within the context that it appears.

Conversely, when a word that normally includes one of these letters is written with that letter missing, it denotes a decrease in holiness or that something is lacking in the protagonist's behavior.

The name Efron is spelled as עפרון, with one exception — in the *pasuk*: וישמע אברהם אל עפרון וישקל אברהם **לעפרן** את הכסף אשר דבר באזני בני חת ארבע מאות שקל כסף עבר לסחר — "Avraham listened to Efron, and Avraham weighed out to Efron the money that he had mentioned in the presence of the children of Ches, four hundred silver shekalim, in negotiable currency" (*Bereishis* 23:16). The first time Efron is mentioned in this *pasuk*, the name is spelled with the ו; yet a few words later it is spelled without it. Rashi explains that Efron is spelled without the ו to point out that he promised a lot but did not even do a little. Initially he wanted to give the field to Avraham for free, but then he demanded its full price — to be paid in a currency that was universally acceptable. The missing letter represents his stinginess and, at the same time, alludes to the price of four hundred shekalim — four hundred being the numerical value of עפרן.

Another example of a word spelled deficiently is in *Devarim* (22:15–16) where the word נערה, referring to a woman, is written as נער (i.e. without a ה). In that passage, the woman is suspected of immoral behavior, and thus she is referred to without the ה, alluding to a decline in her spirituality.

## CROWNS

In the Torah script, certain letters of the *alef-beis* are adorned by תגים (*tagim*), "crowns," placed on top of those letters. Each crown takes the form of a thin vertical line, similar to a letter ז.

*Midrash Talpios* writes, in the name of *Sefer Hapliyah*, that with regard to the "crowns" the letters of the *alef-beis* are divided into three groups. The letters that form the acronym מלאכת סופר are written without any crowns, the letters of the acronym בדה חקי possess one crown each, while those of שעטנז גץ, each have three crowns on them (this last acronym translates as "the strength of the *Satan* shall be crushed").

The Magen David explains that the use of crowns on these letters serve the same function as the roots of a plant. Roots extract nourishment from the soil enabling them to grow. In the reverse order, these crowns, act as filters through which spirituality descends, via the Ten *Sefiros*, into the body of the letters themselves.

◆ ◆ ◆

The Gemara (*Eruvin* 21b) tells us that Rabbi Akiva was capable of expounding "heaps and heaps of laws from each crown that adorns the top of these letters" in the *sefer Torah* script. The Maharsha points out that this does not refer to hidden explanations, but rather to the revealed sections of the Torah. The source of this double expression "heaps and heaps" (תלין תלין) is explained by the Rokeach in the introduction to his commentary on the Chumash.

These words are hinted at the beginning and at the end of the Torah. In the second *pasuk* of the Torah we read: **ורוח א-להים מרחפת על פני המים** — "And the spirit of Hashem was hovering over the surface of the waters." The final letters of the last four words spell out the word **תלים**, which is the Hebrew equivalent of the Aramaic **תלין**. The vertical space above each letter created by the crown allows the spirit of Hashem — that is contained within the letters — to "hover" over the top of letters. *Devarim* 33:3 states: **והם תכו לרגלך ישא מדברתיך** — "They follow Your footsteps and uphold your word." The acronym of four of these words also spells out **תלים**.

The following true story, which I read many years ago, may help us to comprehend how so much information can be contained within each and every crown.

> During World War II, a soldier undertook a dangerous espionage mission to go behind enemy lines, posing as a German citizen, so that he could gather secret information about the enemy and their planned maneuvers.
>
> This spy went about his work discreetly, and managed to gather many secret documents. Then, in the attic of his home, he would carefully photograph these documents using a high resolution camera, develop the film, and then proceed to photograph the negative. Each negative is much smaller than the original document that was photographed. This process was repeated several times, each time reducing further the original document size. Eventually, the secret document was reduced to the size of a pin head.
>
> The spy would then type a general letter to his mother living in England, informing her about his family and any other local news.
>
> At the time, the standard mechanical typewriter worked in such a way that when one pressed a key on the keyboard, an arm containing the typeface of that letter would strike against a printing ribbon and make the appropriate impression on the paper. This worked well for most letters. It was only when one reached the end of a sentence and wanted to type a "period" that, more often than not, one actually

made a small hole in the paper, because the small typeface simply cut through the paper.

And so it was that into each "period" in his letters, the spy would carefully place this small piece of film containing a secret document and cover it with the original small circle of paper that had been cut out by his typewriter. The end result of this meticulous work was what appeared to be a normal social letter. He would then mail it to his mother's home, where it would be later collected by the secret services. They would then carefully remove each "period" containing the secret film. With the use of suitable enlarging equipment, they magnified the film until they could read the required information.

This correspondence continued throughout the war and provided the Allies with a valuable source of information.

Today mechanical typewriters are a thing of the past and have been superseded by computers and word-processing equipment. The mechanical typewriter was replaced by the daisy wheel and, later, a dot-matrix printer. The latter prints by using a substantial number of dots to form each letter, being effectively composed from a large number of periods. If every period could physically contain secret information, a complete letter of the *alef-beis*, printed as a series of dots contains a substantial amount. Ever since the invention, some thirty years ago, of the silicon chip there has been a tremendous development in its miniaturization. It is common for modern computers to contain silicon chips of half a micron (one micron = one millionth of a meter) in dimension, each containing the equivalent to ten million transistors with the ability to store a phenomenal amount of information.

If every "period" can contain such a wealth of information, we can appreciate the vast knowledge that Rabbi Akiva could glean from each crown on the letters of the Torah.

## CHAPTER 4

# Numerical Methods for Interpreting the Torah

EACH LETTER OF THE *alef-beis* possesses an intrinsic numerical value — commonly referred to as its *gematria* — from one, for the first letter א, to four hundred, for the final letter ת. Furthermore, the five final letters continue this numeric sequence with values from five hundred to nine hundred. The complete *alef-beis* is listed below, including the five final letters, together with their appropriate numerical values.

| ת | ש | ר | ק | צ | פ | ע | ס | נ | מ | ל | כ | י | ט | ח | ז | ו | ה | ד | ג | ב | א |
|---|---|---|---|---|---|---|---|---|---|---|---|---|---|---|---|---|---|---|---|---|---|
| 400 | 300 | 200 | 100 | 90 | 80 | 70 | 60 | 50 | 40 | 30 | 20 | 10 | 9 | 8 | 7 | 6 | 5 | 4 | 3 | 2 | 1 |

| ץ | ף | ן | ם | ך |
|---|---|---|---|---|
| 900 | 800 | 700 | 600 | 500 |

Numerical values are used to attach added meaning to letters, words, phrases and even complete sentences. It is part of the wisdom of the Torah that such a connection exists. The Ba'al HaTurim in his commentary to the Chumash makes frequent use of the numerical values of words and phrases to explain the text.

Moreover, the Torah can be expounded by equating different subjects by their respective numerical values. The source for this is found in *Devarim* 32:47: כי לא דבר רק הוא מכם כי הוא חייכם וכו' — "For it is not an empty thing from you, for it is your life..." The Ba'al HaTurim and the Rokeach both point out that the numerical value of the first part of this *pasuk* (כי לא דבר רק הוא מכם) is 679, which equals the numerical value of the word גימטריות, *gematrios*. Through the use of *gematrios* one can gain an appreciation as to the depth of the Torah. Since every letter has its own individual numerical value, we can say that there are no superfluous or meaningless words in the Torah. This is explicit in the literal translation of the phrase: כי לא דבר רק, "for there are no empty words."

The following example illustrates how the numerical value of a complete sentence provides additional meaning. *Tehillim* 119:91 states: למשפטיך עמדו היום כי הכל עבדיך — "In judgment they stand [before] You today, for they are all Your servants." This entire *pasuk* has a numerical value of 861, which equates to the words ראש השנה, Rosh Hashanah, when the entire universe stands in judgment before Hashem. This is the only *pasuk* in all of Scripture that has this numerical value.

## Gematrios

The Rokeach explains that there are actually two values contained within the concept of *gematrios*, and it is for this reason that it is referred to in the plural (*gematrios*, as opposed to *gematria*).

The first value is the standard numerical value, referred to as the external, or exposed, value. In this format, the word "*gematria*" originates from the same source as the word "geometry." Using this method, two words that have the same numerical value are connected to each other, just as two similar triangles are connected in geometry.

The second value is called the internal, or hidden, value, and reveals a latent power concealed within each word. The Rokeach explains that in this case the word "*gematria*" is derived from Aramaic, being composed from the word גיא (*gey*), meaning "valley," and the word טוריא (*turia*), meaning "mountain." If a mountain could be uprooted and then be placed upside-down into a valley, the result would be an even surface. In this "mountain and valley" concept, the words do not have equal numerical values, rather they equate via the values produced by summing the numerical values of the letters of the words in something similar to a "building block" structure. This process is referred to as the *generation* or *degeneration* of a word.

Rabbi Akiva, who was able to appreciate the hidden powers in embedded within a word, is referred to as an *oker harim* — one who was capable of "uprooting mountains"; he was capable of interpreting each word using the generative and degenerative processes.

### ◈ The Generative and Degenerative Values

One of the unique features of the *alef-beis* is the way the Hebrew words are formed. Many *Rishonim* discuss the concept of the generation and degeneration of words. Just like a seed will develop and grow into a full plant, so every word is seen as growing from the first letter until the complete word is formed. This process also takes place in the reverse order, when the word degenerates. It decreases until we are left with only the final letter. This is a difficult concept to grasp; the following examples will help to explain this more clearly.

The word אחד, *echad*, has a numerical value of thirteen. Its three Hebrew letters have the following numerical equivalents: א = 1, ח = 8 and ד = 4. In order to simplify the following explanation, I shall use only the numerical value of the letters, rather than the letters themselves. Numerically, the word אחד will thus be written as 4 + 8 + 1, each number representing the numerical value of the appropriate letter.

When generating, a word develops in the following manner:

| | | |
|---|---|---|
| 1 | = | 1 |
| 8 + 1 | = | 9 |
| 4 + 8 + 1 | = | 13 |
| **Total** | = | **23** |

The *generative* value of the word אחד is twenty-three.

In its degenerative form, the word forms the pattern:

| | | |
|---|---|---|
| 4 + 8 + 1 | = | 13 |
| 4 + 8 | = | 12 |
| 4 | = | 4 |
| **Total** | = | **29** |

The *degenerative* value of the word אחד is twenty-nine.

Together the generative and degenerative values total fifty-two (23 + 29 = 52). This is the *internal gematria.*

It is interesting to note that the internal value of a word always equals the product of the external value (i.e. the standard numerical value) of the word multiplied by one more than the number of letters in that word. Using the above example, the word אחד has three letters; by adding one to the number of letters in this word (n + 1), we get four. Now, we multiply the numerical value of the word — in this case thirteen — by four, and the product is fifty-two (4 x 13 = 52).

When using the generative and degenerative forms, this formula works for every word in the Hebrew language, as this phenomenon is a natural property of the decimal number system. Since the letters of the *alef-beis* incorporate a numerical value based in the decimal number system, therefore these properties are also inherent in the letters themselves.

The first time that the word אחד appears in the Torah is at the end of the first day of Creation — יום אחד, "one day" (*Bereishis* 1:5). It is the fifty-second word of the Torah. Of these first fifty-two words, twenty-nine of them are used only once in the passage. The latter number corresponds to degenerative value of the word אחד (29). The remaining twenty-three words are repeated within the passage, corresponding to the generative value of this word (23).

These three numbers — 13, 23 and 29 — are all prime numbers, which represent the singularity and unity that is expressed by the word אחד. Fifty-two is also the numerical value of אליהו, Eliyahu haNavi, who is destined to announce the arrival of Mashiach, and the universal proclamation to all mankind of ה' אחד — Hashem is One!

In *Parashas Bereishis*, the word אחד is used three times. The first time, as mentioned above, is in *Bereishis* 1:5, ending with the words יום אחד, "one day." Here, the word אחד refers to the concept of time. The second time it appears is in the ninth *pasuk*, in conjunction with the gathering of the waters: יקוו המים מתחת השמים אל מקום אחד וכו' — "and the waters under the heavens were gathered to one place…"; here it is used with reference to the concept of space. (Note that *Bereishis* 1:9 also contains a total of fifty-two letters.) The third occasion is in reference to marriage: על כן יעזב איש את אביו ואת אמו ודבק באשתו והיו לבשר אחד — "And therefore a man shall leave his father and his mother and cling to his wife, and they shall become one flesh" (ibid. 2:24), where it refers to the soul. Each of these three *pesukim* are composed from thirteen words, the same as the numerical value of the of the word אחד.

◆ ◆ ◆

Let us now look at the word אהבה, which also has a numerical value of thirteen, the same as the word אחד. This example illustrates how two words with the same external *gematria* can have different internal *gematrios.*

Its generative and degenerative forms are:

| | | | | | | |
|---|---|---|---|---|---|---|
| | 13 | = אהבה | | א | = | 1 |
| | 12 | = הבה | | אה | = | 6 |
| | 7 | = בה | | אהב | = | 8 |
| | 5 | = ה | | אהבה | = | 13 |
| **Totals** | **37** | | | | | **28** |

Together these total sixty-five (28 + 37 = 65). Again, by implementing the above formula, we see that the external value equates with this internal value. The numerical value of אהבה is thirteen; there are four letters in the word, with one more for a total of five ([n + 1] = 5; 5 x 13 = 65).

◆ ◆ ◆

The generation and degeneration of a word can be used to gain a greater understanding of a *pasuk. Bereishis* 6:8 states: ונח מצא חן בעיני י-ה-ו-ה — "And Noach found favor in the eyes of Hashem." One might ask why this phrased is used specifically with regard to Noach. A connection can be seen by analyzing the Name of Hashem, י-ה-ו-ה.

The generative and degenerative processes produce:

| | | | | | | |
|---|---|---|---|---|---|---|
| | 26 | = י-ה-ו-ה | | י | = | 10 |
| | 16 | = ה-ו-ה | | י-ה | = | 15 |
| | 11 | = ו-ה | | י-ה-ו | = | 21 |
| | 5 | = ה | | י-ה-ו-ה | = | 26 |
| **Totals** | **58** | | | | | **72** |

The result of the generative process here represents the seventy-two sets of letters that compose the *Shem haMeforash*, Hashem's complete Name. It is also the numerical value of the fulfilled spelling of Hashem's Name (יוד הי ויו הי = 72). The value produced by the degenerative process is the same as the numerical value of the name נח, Noach, and also of the word חן, "favor." The total of the generative and degenerative values equals 130, the same as the numerical value of the word עין, "eye," a number that equates to five times the numerical value of Hashem's Name. All of these words appear in the *pasuk* quoted above: **ונח מצא חן בעיני י-ה-ו-ה**.

◆ ◆ ◆

Another example is found in the *pasuk*: וכתבת על האבנים את כל דברי התורה הזאת באר היטב — "You shall inscribe on the stones all the words of this Torah, well clarified" (*Devarim* 27:8).

Rashi explains the phrase of "well clarified" to mean that the Torah was to be inscribed in seventy languages, deriving this from the fact that the generative value of the word היטב, "well," is seventy.

| | | |
|---|---|---|
| ה | = | 5 |
| הי | = | 15 |
| היט | = | 24 |
| היטב | = | 26 |
| **Total** | **=** | **70** |

◆ ◆ ◆

The Gemara (*Yoma* 84a) teaches us the greatness of sincere repentance: גדולה תשובה שמגעת עד כסא הכבוד — "Repentance has the potential to reach [Hashem's] Throne of Glory." This statement is substantiated by the fact that the words תשובה and כסא הכבוד are connected.

We know that one of the principles for understanding the Torah is the concept that there is a connection between words that have equal values. The numerical value of the word תשובה, "repentance," is 713, which is equal to the generative value of the words כסא הכבוד.

| | | |
|---|---|---|
| כ | = | 20 |
| כס | = | 80 |
| כסא | = | 81 |
| כסא ה | = | 86 |
| כסא הכ | = | 106 |
| כסא הכב | = | 108 |
| כסא הכבו | = | 114 |
| כסא הכבוד | = | 118 |
| **Total** | = | **713** |

### ◈ Further Classification of Gematrios

At the beginning of this chapter we explained that the term *gematrios* is in the plural form because it refers to the normal numerical value (external) as well as the generative and degenerative one (internal).

Perhaps another explanation for the word being in the plural form can be found in the words of Rabbi Moshe Cordovero (Ramak), in his work *Pardes Rimonim* (30:8), who categorizes the numerical values of *pairs* of words into three different groups. In all three groups, the two comparative words themselves have an equal numerical value.

A member of the highest group is a pair of words that have the same number of letters. He gives an example of this first group by pointing out the similarity between the name of the angel רזיאל and the name אברהם, whose numerical values equal 248, and each word contains five letters. Similarly, Rashi explains that the word גרתי in *Bereishis* 32:5 (אם לבן גרתי — "I have sojourned with Lavan") has the same *gematria* as תריג, a reference to the 613 Torah commandments — the implication being that Yaakov kept the mitzvos even while living with Lavan. This combination forms the highest class of *gematria*.

The Ramak explains that an example of the second group would be when the sum of the numerical values of two letters in a four-letter word equals that of one of the letters of a three-letter word *and* the remaining letters in each word are identical. For example, the words חיים, "life," and חכם, "wise," both have the equivalent numerical value of sixty-eight. The numerical value of the two *yuds* in חיים equals that of the letter כ in חכם, leaving the letters ח and ם, which are the remaining letters in both words.

The third group in the classification are words that have equal numerical values only after one of them has been transformed by using one of the alphabetic transformation methods, such as At–Bash. For example, Rashi (*Bemidbar* 7:20) explains that the word קטרת, "incense," has a numerical value of 613, corresponding to the total number of commandments. This is achieved by substituting the letter ק of קטרת with the letter ד, using the At–Bash transformation. Another example of this third category is illustrated by transforming Hashem's Name of י-ה-ו-ה — the Name that denotes mercy — using the At–Bash formula, resulting in the letters מ'צ'פ'צ'. Combined, these letters have a total numerical value of three hundred, the same as that of the word ברחמים, "with mercy."

### ◈ The Kollel

When dealing with *gematrios*, one sometimes comes across an explanation where two numbers are said to be equal in their numerical values, but in fact one of these two numbers is actually off by one. The extra digit is referred to as the כולל, *kollel*. This concept is difficult to understand, as no mathematics student would expect to get a correct mark on his exam if each answer were to be incorrect by one digit. The Torah is a Torah of Truth, however, and therefore there must be a reason that such an anomaly is used.

The source of the concept of the *kollel* is traced to the *pasuk*: אפרים ומנשה כראובן ושמעון יהיו לי — "Efrayim and Menashe shall be to me like Reuven and Shimon" (*Bereishis* 48:5). In other words, taken literally, the combined numerical value of names of Yosef's sons, Efrayim and Menashe, is equal to that of the names of Reuven and Shimon. Reuven and Shimon equal 731 while Menashe and Efrayim equal 732. The Torah equates these two pairs despite the disparity in their numerical values. Thus Menashe and Efrayim, who were the grandchildren of Yaakov, were given the blessing that they should be considered equal to his own children.

The Shlah cites the Gemara (*Bava Basra* 16a) that compares the Serpent (נחש) — the cause of the initial sin — with the *Satan* (שטן). The numerical value of the former is 358 while that of the latter is 359. In this case, too, their numerical values differ by one, despite the fact that the Gemara equates them. The Shlah explains that the initial transgression instigated by the Serpent created the force known as the *Satan*. Thus it can be said that the Serpent produced the concept of *Satan*. This is borne out by the progression in the numerical values of these words: נחש (358) and שטן (359) — the result (שטן) being one more than the cause (נחש). This difference of one in the numerical values is called the "*kollel*." The *kollel* represents a cause and effect situation.

This concept is actually intrinsic to the numerical progression: in order to get to the next higher number, we add one to the number preceding it. The higher number is in a sense built onto the lower one; thus, we can say that the lower number "produces" the high one. In this way, when two words which have numerical values that differ by one are equated, it indicates that there is some sort of progression from the context of one of them to the context of the other.

## Composite Numerical Value

The *Arizal* often makes use of a numerical value known as the *composite numerical value* of a letter, the total numerical value of the letters from which that letter is composed (see "Composite Letters," p. 13). The composite numerical value is used to add further meaning and understanding to a letter or a word. The letter א, for example, has a composite value of twenty-six, as it is made up from the letters י'ו'י'. Thus Hashem's Name אדנ-י has a composite numerical value of ninety (26 + 4 + 50 + 10 = 90), a number that equals the numerical value of the word מלך, "King." The composite letters of the word מלך are כ'ו'כ'ו'ך', which have a total numerical value of seventy-two. This number corresponds to the seventy-two sets which make up the *Shem haMeforash* (Hashem's complete Name), to the generative value of Hashem's Name (see above, p. 136), and also to the numerical value of the fulfillment of His Name (יוד הי ויו הי).

There are four letters in the standard *alef-beis* whose fulfillment incorporate two letters that each have composite values of twenty-six. They are: אלף, למד, מם, and סמך. The combined numerical values of all these letters totals 385, the same as the numerical value of the word שכינה, Hashem's holy *Shechinah*.

## Ordinal Value

There is another type of numerical value that is assigned to each letter based on the order in which it appears in the *alef-beis*. This is known as its *ordinal* value:

| | | | | | |
|---|---|---|---|---|---|
| 12 | = | ל | 1 | = | א |
| 13 | = | מ | 2 | = | ב |
| 14 | = | נ | 3 | = | ג |
| 15 | = | ס | 4 | = | ד |
| 16 | = | ע | 5 | = | ה |
| 17 | = | פ | 6 | = | ו |
| 18 | = | צ | 7 | = | ז |
| 19 | = | ק | 8 | = | ח |
| 20 | = | ר | 9 | = | ט |
| 21 | = | ש | 10 | = | י |
| 22 | = | ת | 11 | = | כ |

The following is an example of how the ordinal value may be used in expounding a Torah thought. Marriage is a bond between a man (איש) and a woman (אשה). The letters that are unique within these two Hebrew words are the י and ה, which form Hashem's Name and have a total numerical value of fifteen. The letter ס has an ordinal value of fifteen, and its shape resembles that of a wedding ring. A marriage is solemnized through the act of a man placing a ring on the woman's finger. The Kli Yakar points out that the first time the letter ס appears in the Torah in the context of Creation is in *Bereishis* 2:21: ויסגר בשר תחתנה — "And He closed the flesh below it," which refers of the creation of Chavah, the first woman, as the suitable marriage partner for Adam.

## MISPAR KATAN—SUM OF THE DIGITS

In addition to the above values, each letter has a numerical value known as its "*mispar katan.*" *Mispar katan* is a concept by which we drop all the zeros of the numerical value of a letter and remain with a basic integer ranging from one to nine. For example, the letter ד has a numerical value of four, which is also its *mispar katan*. The letters מ (40) and ת (400) also have a *mispar katan* of four. Although these letters have different numerical values, they are in fact of the same essence. Letters with the same *mispar katan* equate because they represent a "contraction" in Creation. In order to understand this, we first need to explain the concept of "contraction" vis-à-vis the creation of the universe.

### ◈ Mispar Katan vis-à-vis the Ten Sefiros

The *Sefer Yetzirah* writes that there are Ten *Sefiros* that were used in creating the universe. Rabbi Aryeh Kaplan explains that the *Sefiros* are the most basic modes of Hashem's creative power. It is through the *Sefiros* that Hashem interacts with the universe, as they act as bridges between Hashem and His Creation. Everything in the world takes place through the medium of the *Sefiros*. They act as filters to dilute the powerful effect of the *Shechinah* itself, so that it can be used effectively. These filters are essential to enable mankind to benefit from these powerful sources. (This can be compared to the light of the sun when reflected off the moon. Although the rays emanating from the sun are too powerful and harmful to look at directly, once they are reflected by the moon, their intensity is greatly diminished and they can be viewed safely.)

Each of these filters is known as a *tzimtzum* (צמצם), a "contraction" of Hashem's initial light of Creation. There is a large degree of concealment that develops on a scale of descending magnitude, and each *tzimtzum* capitalizes on the previous degree of concealment and merely serves to further attenuate this light. The creative process unfolds downwards, involving at each stage a greater diminution of light. This results in a greater concealment and separation from the Divine at each level. Because of these filters, we are able to maintain a closeness to Hashem without being obliterated by His infinite light.

In *Adon Olam*, which stresses that Hashem is timeless, we say: והוא היה והוא הוה והוא יהיה בתפארה — "It is He Who was, He Who is, and He Who shall remain in splendor." Using the At–Bash transformation method, the word יהיה converts into the word צמצם. Only as a result of these "contractions" are we able to appreciate Hashem in His splendor.

The word עולם can be translated as "universe," and is derived from the same root as the word עלם, which means "to be concealed and hidden." Whenever we make a *berachah* we say: ברוך אתה ה' א-להינו מלך העולם וכו' — "Blessed are You Hashem, our God, King of the universe...," proclaiming the fact that Hashem is the King of the universe. At the same time, we are acknowledging that He is the King Who hides Himself in His world, through the medium of the Ten *Sefiros*.

Hashem has an infinite desire to do kindness with His creations. At the time of Creation, the universe was in a process of continuous expansion in order to create more opportunities for acts of kindness to be performed. Ultimately, however, Hashem declared that this expansion was sufficient. The Gemara in *Chagigah* (12a) explains that Hashem is known by the Name of ש-די, which signifies that it was Hashem Who said to the expanding universe "Enough (די)!" As we said above, Creation was achieved by a process of contraction via the Ten *Sefiros*. If we constrict the letters די — in other words, push them together — they form the letter ה (with the י forming the foot of the letter ה), the letter through which the physical world was created (see Rashi on *Bereishis* 2:4).

Each *Sefirah* is a specific power through which Hashem governs and sustains the universe. At the same time, each *Sefirah* functions in perfect harmony with every other *Sefirah* and contains within itself aspects of all the other *Sefiros* as well. Due to the constriction afforded by the *Sefiros* of Hashem's light, man has the ability to receive from Hashem the ultimate gift of existence. The last *Sefirah* — called *Malchus* — contains extracts from all the other *Sefiros*. This final concealment of the Divine, for the purpose of interacting with creation itself, is represented numerically by the *mispar katan*.

To clarify this, let's go back to the example that we started with: the numerical value of the letter ת is four hundred, that of the letter מ is forty, and that of ד is four. The numerical value of each letter is contracted — similar to the concealment of the original light of the *Shechinah*, which has been hidden through the filtering process of the Ten *Sefiros* — and the result is the *mispar katan*, which in this case is four, the number which has been filtered down.

Thus, the *mispar katan* represents the final speck of Divine power that has been filtered through the final *Sefirah* of *Malchus*.

## ◈ The Inherent Properties of the Number Nine

Each letter of the *alef-beis* can be written out in its fully articulated form. For example, the first letter א is spelled out as אלף, the second letter ב as בית, and so forth. This is called the letter's "fulfillment" (this concept will be explained in the next chapter).

Rabbi Yonasan Eibeshitz points out that by using the concepts of *gematria*, *mispar katan*, and "fulfillment" for each of the letters of the *alef-beis* we arrive at a remarkable result.

Let us use, for example, the letter א: the three letters of its fulfillment (אלף) have a combined numerical value of 111 (1 + 30 + 80). The total of those letters' *mispar katan* is twelve (1 + 3 + 8). If we deduct the *mispar katan* from the numerical value, the result is ninety-nine (111-12 = 99). The difference between these two numbers will always be a multiple of nine. This is true for all the letters of the *alef-beis*, as shown below:

| | כף | יוד | טית | חית | זין | ואו | היא | דלת | גימל | בית | אלף |
|---|---|---|---|---|---|---|---|---|---|---|---|
| GEMATRIA | 100 | 20 | 419 | 418 | 67 | 13 | 16 | 434 | 83 | 412 | 111 |
| MISPAR KATAN | 10 | 2 | 14 | 13 | 13 | 4 | 7 | 11 | 11 | 7 | 12 |
| DIFFERENCE | 90 | 18 | 405 | 405 | 54 | 9 | 9 | 423 | 72 | 405 | 99 |

| | תיו | שין | ריש | קוף | צדיק | פה | עין | סמך | נן | מם | למד |
|---|---|---|---|---|---|---|---|---|---|---|---|
| GEMATRIA | 416 | 360 | 510 | 186 | 204 | 85 | 130 | 120 | 100 | 80 | 74 |
| MISPAR KATAN | 11 | 9 | 6 | 15 | 6 | 13 | 13 | 12 | 10 | 8 | 11 |
| DIFFERENCE | 405 | 351 | 504 | 171 | 198 | 72 | 117 | 108 | 90 | 72 | 63 |

This is a mathematically inherent property of the decimal system, and not of the *alef-beis* itself. However, since every letter possesses a numerical value as well, this numeric property is transferred to the letters of the *alef-beis*.

A further unique feature of the number nine is that the integers of the multiples of nine will always add up to nine as well — for example, the number eighteen is composed of the numbers one and eight, which together add up to nine. The numerical value of the word אמת, "truth," is 441, which is also a multiple of nine (4 + 4 + 1 = 9). All multiples of nine are, in a sense, indestructible because the sum of their digits will always be nine, alluding to the eternal and indestructible power of truth that is contained in the Torah's letters.

The concept of indestructibility represents the infinite power of Hashem as the אין סוף, the limitless Power. The words אין סוף have a numerical value of 207 — a multiple of nine — and a final *mispar katan* of nine. This reinforces the infinite truth that is to be found in the twenty-seven letters of the *alef-beis*, as the digits that make up the number twenty-seven also add up to nine. All letters of the *alef-beis* incorporate the truth that Hashem has hidden within them.

The Ibn Ezra, in his book entitled *Sefer Echad*, points out that the number nine — and its multiples — correspond to the combined attributes of mercy and justice, whose integration was essential in the creation of the universe. The double-digit multiples of nine contain both tens and units. Placing them in order in columns, the left-hand column (containing the tens) progresses in an ascending order, while the right-hand column (containing the units) decreases in a descending order. The ascending order of the left-hand column represents the attribute of mercy while the descending right-hand column represents the attribute of justice.

| A | | | | B | C |
|---|---|---|---|---|---|
| 1 | x | 9 | = | 0 | 9 |
| 2 | x | 9 | = | 1 | 8 |
| 3 | x | 9 | = | 2 | 7 |
| 4 | x | 9 | = | 3 | 6 |
| 5 | x | 9 | = | 4 | 5 |
| 6 | x | 9 | = | 5 | 4 |
| 7 | x | 9 | = | 6 | 3 |
| 8 | x | 9 | = | 7 | 2 |
| 9 | x | 9 | = | 8 | 1 |
| 10 | x | 9 | = | 9 | 0 |

Furthermore, the first ten multiples of the number nine form a pattern. The first five products are composed of the same pairs of integers as the second five. For example, the multiples 45 and 54 both contain the same integers of five and four, but in reverse order. Moreover, the first five multiples are actually a mirror image of the second five, again in reverse order.

This reversal of integers in multiples also works when two numbers that add up to eleven are multiplied by nine; their products will have the same numbers in the reverse order. For example, the numbers seven and four total eleven. Multiplying each by nine, we obtain 63 and 36.

The Ibn Ezra also discusses the concept of the "Circle of Truth," in which the digits 0–9 are situated around the circumference of a circle. (This concept is also mentioned in the Ibn Ezra's commentary on *Shemos* 3:15.) The results of all the multiples of nine are composed from the numbers situated on the same horizontal level of this circle.

0 — 9
1 — 8
2 — 7
3 — 6
4 — 5

When placing these numbers around a sphere (i.e. a three-dimensional circle), the connection between the pairs forms a spherical helix shape — duplicating that of the DNA molecular structure, which is the basis of all living cells. We find an allusion to this in Scripture, in the phrase כלה זרע אמת — "all seed of truth" (*Yirmeyahu* 2:21). "Seed" is the basis from which all living matter develops — and, as we know, all matter is composed from DNA — "truth" is represented by the number nine. Moreover the first ten multiples of the number nine (Columns B and C, on the previous page) create a three-dimensional mathematical model which resembles the DNA molecular structure, as well.

Only through the attribute of truth can one attach himself to Hashem, as we find in the *pasuk*: ואתם הדבקים בי-ה-ו-ה א-להיכם חיים כלכם היום — "But you who cling to Hashem, your God, you are all alive today" (*Devarim* 4:4). The Torah says **ואתם** הדבקים, "but *you* who cling"; the word אתם, "you," also spells out the word אמת, truth. Only by a person being completely truthful and honest can he connect to Hashem.

Ibn Ezra provides a fundamental connection between the Name of Hashem, the concept of truth, and the wisdom that is incorporated into the twenty-two letters of the *alef-beis*. The Hebrew basic number system is made up from the numbers one to ten, from which all other higher numbers are composed. Let us take a closer look at the composition of the Name of Hashem of י-ה-ו-ה and these basic decimal numbers.

The first ten numbers are:

| 1 | 2 | 3 | 4 | 5 | 6 | 7 | 8 | 9 | 10 |
|---|---|---|---|---|---|---|---|---|---|
| א | ב | ג | ד | ה | ו | ז | ח | ט | י |

These ten digits correspond to the letter י, first letter of Hashem's Name, which has a numerical value of ten. Moving from the outside in, these numbers form five pairs, each one totaling eleven. These five groups are represented by the letter ה, which has a numerical value of five and is the second letter in Hashem's Name. This grouping of elevens corresponds to the last two letters of Hashem's Name of ו'ה', which have a combined numerical value of eleven. In this way, the Hebrew decimal number system that is used throughout the Torah is displayed in the Name of Hashem.

The three letters that make up the word אמת, incorporate the entire *alef-beis*, as it is composed from the first, middle and last letters of the alphabet. By extracting the first, last and middle two numbers of the numbers from one to ten, we retain the numbers one and ten at the extremities, and the numbers five and six are in the middle; added together they total twenty-two, corresponding to the number of letters in the *alef-beis*.

Ibn Ezra refers to these four numbers collectively as מספר עגול, the number that represents a circle. The numbers one and ten represent the circumference of the circle that is formed when the units complete the full number cycle and are about to begin the next cycle of tens, while the numbers five and six represent the center of this circle.

When discussing the letters that correspond to these numbers, the Ibn Ezra writes: ואלה ארבעתם א'ה'ו'י' הם הנכבדים — "These four, א'ה'ו'י', are the most prestigious ones." From all of the first ten numbers, these four display a unique property, which substantiates the eternal truth and wisdom that is incorporated in the letters of the *alef-beis*.

By way of example, let us analyze this unique property with regard to the number six. Any number that contains the number six as the final digit will likewise contain a six in the final digit when squared or cubed. For example:

**6** x **6** = 3**6**
**6** x **6** x **6** = 21**6**

11**6** x 11**6** = 13,45**6**
11**6** x 11**6** x 11**6** = 1,560,89**6**

This unique property applies only to multiples of the numbers, one, ten, five and six, which are symbolic of the Name of Hashem. This is to illustrate that however large the radius of the circle is, it always connects to the center. Similarly, Hashem remains at the center of the circle, attached to each Jewish soul — however far away the person might have wandered from Him.

## Triangular Values—Mispar HaKadmi

In addition to the numerical values presented above, every letter of the *alef-beis* possesses a triangular value, which is the the sum of all the numbers up to and including the letter's numerical value. For example, the letter ד has the numerical value of four, so the triangular value for this letter is ten (1 + 2 + 3 + 4 = 10). The triangular number is so-called because its components form a triangular shape when displayed graphically.

| | | |
|---|---|---|
| 1 | 1 | |
| 2 | 1 + 1 | |
| 3 | 1 + 1 + 1 | |
| 4 | 1 + 1 + 1 +1 | TOTAL 10 |

Triangular numbers are referred to by Rabbi Moshe Cordovero as מספר הקדמי (*mispar hakadmi*), the "original number," meaning a number that originates from its source. The letter א, with the numerical value of one, represents the Omnipresent power of Hashem. In forming triangular numbers, the number one is always at the apex of the triangle, a reference to the fact that everything emanates from Hashem.

The following is a list of the first ten numbers with their triangular values:

| | | |
|---|---|---|
| **1** | **1** | **1** |
| **2** | 1 + **2** | **3** |
| **3** | 1 + 2 + **3** | **6** |
| **4** | 1 + 2 + 3 + **4** | **10** |
| **5** | 1 + 2 + 3 + 4 + **5** | **15** |
| **6** | 1 + 2 + 3 + 4 + 5 + **6** | **21** |
| **7** | 1 + 2 + 3 + 4 + 5 + 6 + **7** | **28** |
| **8** | 1 + 2 + 3 + 4 + 5 + 6 + 7 + **8** | **36** |
| **9** | 1 + 2 + 3 + 4 + 5 + 6 + 7 + 8 + **9** | **45** |
| **10** | 1 + 2 + 3 + 4 + 5 + 6 + 7 + 8 + 9 + **10** | **55** |

The triangle formed by these values is narrow at the top and widens with each subsequent number — similar to the shape of a silo.

Rashi (on *Bereishis* 2:22), quoting the Gemara (*Berachos* 61a), points out that a silo of wheat is wide at the bottom and narrow at the top so that its burden should not weigh against its walls. The Chasam Sofer points out that the numerical value of חטה, "wheat" is twenty-two, representing the *alef-beis*. This number produces a triangular number of 253, equivalent to the word גרן, the granary that stores this wheat.

◆ ◆ ◆

The concept of using triangular numbers as a tool with which to expound the Torah is found in the first *pasuk* of *Bereishis*, as it contains seven words and twenty-eight letters, for the number twenty-eight is the seventh triangular number. *Targum Yerushalmi* translates the first *pasuk* of the Torah as: בחכמה ברה ה' — "With wisdom Hashem created." The numerical value of חכמה ("wisdom") is seventy-three; the seventy-third triangular number is 2,701, which is the numerical value of the entire *pasuk* בראשית ברא א-להים את השמים ואת הארץ.

◆ ◆ ◆

The *Arizal* states that the concept of triangular values represents the first dimension of length, which is pictorially displayed by a line.

The sum total of the triangular values of the four letters of Hashem's Name (י-ה-ו-ה) is 106, the same as the numerical value of the word קו (a "line"). This is arrived at in the following way:

| | NUMERICAL VALUE | TRIANGULAR VALUE |
|---|---|---|
| י | 10 | 55 |
| ה | 5 | 15 |
| ו | 6 | 21 |
| ה | 5 | 15 |
| | **Total** | **106** |

Conceptually, a line has no depth or breadth, as the Vilna Gaon explains, for it is purely a measurement of length. Therefore, a line does not really exist in a three-dimensional world and cannot be truly defined physically. Similarly, we cannot define or appreciate Hashem in a physical sense.

## Multiplication Method (Mispar Merubah)

The commentators use a variety of different methods which are all classified under the general term *mispar merubah* or "multiplication method." In this book we have used only a few of them. One approach is to multiply by itself the numerical value of each letter of a word, producing a squared numerical value to that word.

Alternatively, another multiplication method is to multiply the numerical values of each letter by that of the other letters of that word. This produces another type of multiplication value.

A further method is to divide the word in half and multiply the numerical values of each half together. There are numerous other applications of the multiplication method.

An example of the use of the most common multiplication method is given by the Shlah regarding the comparison made in the *pasuk*: כי האדם עץ השדה — "Is the tree of the field a man?" (*Devarim* 20:19). This analogy between a tree and man is easily understood using the multiplication method, as the product of the numerical values of the letters of the word אדם (1 x 4 x 40 = 160) equates to the numerical value of the word עץ, tree (70 + 90 =160).

### ◈ Squared Numbers

A number when multiplied by itself is called the "number square," so called because when represented by a matrix, the result creates a two-dimensional square.

```
x      xx     xxx     xxxx     xxxxx
       xx     xxx     xxxx     xxxxx
              xxx     xxxx     xxxxx
                      xxxx     xxxxx
                               xxxxx
```

$1^2$ $2^2$ $3^2$ $4^2$ $5^2$

This square represents "area."

Since each letter of the *alef-beis* has a numerical value, it is possible to square the letters. The result — the "squared value" of the letter — is the area that the latent power of the letter occupies.

To help us understand this concept, let's use the example of expanding the Name of Hashem. Summing the squares of the numerical values of the letters that make up Hashem's Name, results in the total squared-number value for His Name.

| | | | | |
|---|---|---|---|---|
| י x י | = | 10 x 10 | = | 100 |
| ה x ה | = | 5 x 5 | = | 25 |
| ו x ו | = | 6 x 6 | = | 36 |
| ה x ה | = | 5 x 5 | = | 25 |
| | | **Total** | **=** | **186** |

The number 186 is also the numerical value of the word מקום, the space and place where the *Shechinah* rests. We find this, for example, in the *pasuk*: ויאמר ה' הנה מקום אתי ונצבת על הצור — "And Hashem said, 'Behold, there is a place (מקום) with Me; and you will stand on the rock' (*Shemos* 33:21). Rashi explains that with regards to Hashem, we cannot speak of Him as being *in* a place, for that would imply that He is limited by the dimension of space; rather, we say that Hashem is *with* a place. For this reason, Hashem is sometimes referred to *haMakom*, as in the expression of ברוך המקום ברוך הוא, "Blessed is Hashem (*haMakom*), Blessed is He."

The Tosefos Yom-Tov, in his commentary on the final *mishnah* of *Middos*, explains that in order to remind us not to make the mistake of defining Hashem within a physical dimension of space, when saying ברוך המקום we always add the words ברוך הוא. This serves as a reminder that He remains the All-Encompassing Power of the world and is not confined to any physical, dimensional space.

The *Beis haMikdash* is the place where the *Shechinah* rested, as described in numerous places by the word מקום. For example: וקמת ועלית אל המקום — "And you shall rise and ascend to the place" (*Devarim* 17:8); and: ועשית על פי הדבר אשר יגידו לך מן המקום

ההוא — "You shall do according to the word that they will tell you, from that place" (ibid. 17:10).

### ◈ Pyramidial Values

As we have explained above, when the numerical value of a letter is squared, it represents the total area occupied by its latent power. Taking this concept further, the pyramidial value of a number is the sum of the squares of the numbers from one through that number (similar to how we derive the triangular value). This concept is best understood with an example.

The Gemara (*Sukkah* 4b) derives that the minimum height of a *sukkah* is ten *tefachim* because that was the height of the Ark that stood in the Holy of Holies. Hashem would speak to Moshe from above the lid of the Ark, as the *pasuk* states: ונועדתי לך שם ודברתי אתך מעל הכפרת — "It is there that I shall arrange an audience with you, and I shall speak with you from above the lid" (*Shemos* 25:22). This is because, as the Gemara explains, the *Shechinah* never descends below ten *tefachim* above ground level.

The total space represented by the number ten, is the sum of the total squared values of all the numbers between one and ten:

| | | | | | |
|---|---|---|---|---|---|
| 1 x 1 | = | 1 | 6 x 6 | = | 36 |
| 2 x 2 | = | 4 | 7 x 7 | = | 49 |
| 3 x 3 | = | 9 | 8 x 8 | = | 64 |
| 4 x 4 | = | 16 | 9 x 9 | = | 81 |
| 5 x 5 | = | 25 | 10 x 10 | = | 100 |
| | | | **Total** | **=** | **385** |

This number, 385, is the numerical value of the word שכינה, the Divine Presence, which, as we said, never descends below ten *tefachim*.

The total numerical value of the hidden fulfillment of the word שכינה (שין כף יוד נון הי) is 216. There are 216 letters in the *Shem haMeforash*, and the numerical value of the word גבורה, "strength," is 216, as well. Thus the hidden fulfillment of the word שכינה displays this Divine strength and power.

Furthermore, the numerical value of the word עשרה, "ten" is 575, which equates to that of the word להתפלל, "to pray." As we know, there must be ten adult males present to form a *minyan* for prayer. The *Shechinah* is present when ten men gather together, as the Gemara states (*Berachos* 6a): מנין לעשרה שמתפללין ששכינה עמהם שנאמר א-להים נצב בעדת א-ל — "From where is it derived that when ten people pray together that the Divine Presence is with them? [From the *pasuk*:] 'Hashem stands in the Divine assembly' (*Tehillim* 82:1)."

The Ben Ish Chai explains how we find the number ten in this *pasuk*. He points out that the triangular value of the number ten is fifty-five (1 + 2 + 3 + 4 + 5 + 6 + 7 + 8 + 9 + 10 = 55), a figure that is represented by the numerical value of the three last letters in א-להים, the Name of Hashem that is used in this *pasuk*. Thus, when ten people pray together to Hashem (א-ל), they all unite together to form the Name א-להים. He also points out that the minimum requirement of ten people to form a *minyan* is derived from the word עדה, "an assembly." Its fulfillment (עין דלת הא) has a numerical value of 570, the same as that of עשר, the representation of the number ten.

However, there is a *midrash* (*Midrash HaGadol Bereishis*, 32:3) that states: אין השכינה שורה בפחות משישים רבוא מישראל — "The Divine *Shechinah* does not rest with the Jewish nation unless there is a minimum of six hundred thousand Jews." This seeming contradiction can be reconciled by the fact that the number ten is the first number whose total permutations exceed the figure of six hundred thousand. The total number of permutations that can be made from the number nine are 362,880 (1 x 2 x 3 x 4 x 5 x 6 x 7 x 8 x 9 = 362,880) which is less that the required six hundred thousand; yet, the number ten will produce 3,628,800 permutations, higher than the required minimum.

By using the pyramidial values and the permutations of the number ten, we obtain the requirements for the Divine *Shechinah* to rest among the Jewish People, both on a communal and a national level.

◈ ◈ ◈

Another example of the significance that can be seen in pyramidial values is that of the number six, a number that represents the six physical dimensions. Its pyramidial value is ninety-one:

| | | |
|---|---|---|
| 1 x 1 | = | 1 |
| 2 x 2 | = | 4 |
| 3 x 3 | = | 9 |
| 4 x 4 | = | 16 |
| 5 x 5 | = | 25 |
| 6 x 6 | = | 36 |
| **Total** | **=** | **91** |

The word אחד, which represents unity, has a numerical value of thirteen, and therefore possesses a triangular value of ninety-one (1 + 2 + 3 + 4 + 5 + 6 + 7 + 8 + 9 + 10 + 11 + 12 + 13 = 91). The written and pronounced Names of Hashem — י-ה-ו-ה and אדנ-י — also have a combined numerical value of ninety-one, thereby displaying the Unity of Hashem and the six physical dimensions where He can be found.

CHAPTER 5

# Attributes of the Letters and Their Usage in Words

## LETTER FULFILLMENTS (MILLUI)

Each letter of the *alef-beis* expands into its articulated form, in other words, the name of the letter itself. This is called the letter's *millui*, "fulfillment." A letter's fulfillment can be used to uncover further insights which are latent within the letters. The following are the letters' expanded forms and alternate meanings depending upon how the word is vowelized:

| | | |
|---|---|---|
| prince; teaching; thousand | אלף | א |
| house | בית | ב |
| nourish; benevolence; camel; bridge | גימל | ג |
| door; poor man; elevation | דלת | ד |
| behold; to take seed; to be broken | הא | ה |
| hook | ואו | ו |
| weapon; sword; species; gender | זין | ז |
| grace of life; fear | חית | ח |

| | | |
|---|---|---|
| goodness | טית | ט |
| hand; possession | יוד | י |
| spoon; palm; power to suppress | כף | כ |
| to learn; to teach | למד | ל |
| water; blemish | מם | מ |
| fish; heir to the throne | נון | ן |
| support | סמך | ס |
| eye; color; fountain | עין | ע |
| mouth; here; present (tense) | פה | פ |
| righteous; hunting | צדיק | צ |
| monkey; surround; great strength | קוף | ק |
| destitute; head; beginning | ריש | ר |
| tooth; ivory; sleep; change | שין | ש |
| sign; musical notes | תיו | ת |

The Megalleh Amukos explains that the source for the use of fulfillments for each letter is alluded to at the beginning of the Torah, in the words בראשית ברא א-להים. The fulfillment of a letter builds it into a larger expansion. By interpreting the first three words of **בראשית ברא א-להים** to mean literally "the beginning of Creation [was the fulfillment of the Name] of א-להים." In other words, in the beginning, the expansion of Hashem's Name Elokim existed as: **אלף למד הי יוד מם**, which has a total numerical value of three hundred.

This connects to the next *pasuk*: רוח א-להים מרחפת על פני המים — "The Spirit of Elokim was hovering over the waters" (*Bereishis* 1:2). The numerical value of the words רוח א-להים is also three hundred. This hovering Spirit creates a dimension of height, similar to the concept of a letter's fulfillment, which expands that letter to give it additional meaning. The fulfillment of the Name of Elokim enabled His Spirit to hover over the waters.

It is interesting to point out that the word מרחפת in the above *pasuk* is the eighteenth word of the Torah. With a numerical value of 728, it is the first word in the Torah which is a multiple of twenty-six (26 x 28 = 728). The word מרחפת represents כח, "power" — the Divine power that hovers over the waters (the word כח has a numerical value of twenty-eight) and provides life (eighteen, "*chai*").

The fulfillment of each of the letters of the *alef-beis* is either a two-, three- or four-letter word. The letter equivalents of the numbers two, three and four, are ב'ג'ד', respectively. These letters spell out the word "*beged*," an article of clothing. The numerical value of the word בגד is nine, a number that symbolizes the absolute truth. Through the expansion of the letters into their fulfilled forms, the truth that is inherent within each letter is displayed.

This connection is hinted at in the Gemara in *Shabbos* (113a) in Rabbi Yochanan's statement: קרי למאניה מכבדותי — "...who named his clothes as his honor." The word כבוד (honor) has a numerical value of thirty-two, the combined numerical value of the first and last letters that appear in the Chumash, thereby representing the entire Torah.

Moreover, the word כבוד alludes to the thirty-two pathways of wisdom that are incorporated within the Torah. This wisdom is stored and hidden in the letters' fulfillments. Metaphorically, the letters conceal their fulfillments similar to the way that clothing camouflages the body that it covers.

It is important to point out that many letters fulfill with alternate spellings, each of which portrays a different message.

The following is a listing of those letters that have alternate spellings:

| | | | | |
|---|---|---|---|---|
| ג | גימל | גמל | | |
| ה | הא | הה | הי | היא |
| ו | ואו | וו | | |

| | | | |
|---|---|---|---|
| כ | כף | כוף | |
| מ | מם | מים | מום |
| נ | נון | נן | |
| פ | פה | פיא | פא |
| צ | צדיק | צדי | |

### ◈ Unique Properties of the Three-Letter Fulfillments

Taking into consideration these alternate spellings, we find that all of the letters have at least one fulfillment containing three letters. These have a special and unique property. If we expand each of the letters into its three-letter fulfillment, and continue to fulfill the middle letter of each of these fulfillments a total of five times, it will display an interesting unity among all the letters.

Let me illustrate this with the first three letters, although this unique property holds true for all the letters.

| | א | ב | ג |
|---|---|---|---|
| 1 | אלף | בית | גמל |
| 2 | למד | יוד | מים |
| 3 | מים | ואו | יוד |
| 4 | יוד | אלף | ואו |
| 5 | ואן | למד | אלף |

The middle letters of each of these five fulfillments all contain the letters א'ו'י'ל'מ'. There must be significance to the fact that all the letters of the *alef-beis* fulfill in this manner, with their backbone, so to speak, being formed by just the above five letters.

These five letters have a total numerical value of eighty–seven. (See p. 207 for an explanation of the connection between the numbers three and eighty-seven.) Eighty-seven is the numerical value of the words of אני י-ה-ו-ה, "I am Hashem."

Rabbeinu Yoel, in his *Sefer HaRemazim*, points out that the majority of the Torah's mitzvos are prefaced by one of the following two *pesukim*: וידבר י-ה-ו-ה אל משה לאמר or ויאמר י-ה-ו-ה אל משה לאמר, both of which have the acronym of ויאמ"ל, which is also made up of the above letters. By obeying Hashem's mitzvos, we are acknowledging "I am Hashem," Who commanded us regarding these specific commandments.

This unique property is only apparent when each individual letter is expanded five times. The fivefold expansion of the three-letter fulfillment incorporates a total of fifteen letters (3 x 5 = 15), and therefore corresponds to Hashem's Name of י-ה, which also has a numerical value of fifteen, and spells out the first half of the full Name of Hashem, י-ה-ו-ה.

The Chasam Sofer points out that the Torah was similarly given in a structure of five sets of threes, as we find in the text of the Gemara (*Shabbos* 88a):

> בריך רחמנא דיהב אוריאן תליתאי לעם תליתאי על ידי תליתאי ביום תליתאי בירחא תליתאי — Blessed is Hashem Who gave us the Torah in a triplicate form, to a Nation comprising of triplicates (i.e. *Kohen*, *Levi* and *Yisrael*), through the third oldest (i.e. Moshe Rabbeinu), after three days of abstention and purification, in the third month of the year.

The Aramaic word תליתאי (meaning, "three") is used five times in this passage. This corresponds to the fivefold fulfillments of each three-letter fulfillment of the *alef-beis*.

### ◈ Millui d'Millui

A unique feature of the Hebrew *alef-beis* is that not only can each letter be expanded, it can be magnified even further. For example, the fulfillment of the first letter א is אלף; as we said, this expansion is referred to as the *millui*, the "fulfillment" of that letter. Each of the letters of the word אלף can be expanded further to become **אלף**, **למד** and **פאי**. This process of expansion of continuous fulfillments is known as the מלוי דמלוי, the *millui d'millui*, and continues *ad infinitum*, providing a boundless source for delving into the Torah's wisdom and gaining new insights.

Each of the letters of the *alef-beis* has spiritual properties, through which Hashem channels certain powers into the world to bestow blessings upon us. Each expansion of these letters represents a further widening of these channels which allows greater benefit to be received.

The Ben Ish Chai illustrates this idea by the expanding the word ברכה, "blessing." The fulfillments of the letters of the word ברכה are **בית ריש כף הי**. The last letters of these words spell out שפתי, "my lips"; a person must use his lips to enunciate a *berachah***.** Thus, before beginning the prayers of the eighteen *berachos* of the *Amidah*, we say: אדנ-י שפתי תפתח ופי יגיד תהלתך — "Hashem, open my lips, so that my mouth can declare Your praise" (*Tehillim* 51:17).

◈ ◈ ◈

The universe was created through a combination of the attributes of kindness and judgment. In Rashi's commentary on the first pasuk in *Bereishis*, he makes the following comment, which is brought down by the Sages on the word **א-להים**:

> Initially, Hashem considered creating the universe with the attribute of strict justice; but when He saw that the world would not be able to endure, He gave precedence to the attribute of mercy, and joined it together with the attribute of justice. (*Bereishis Rabbah* 12:15)

The numerical value of the Hebrew word **מלוי**, "fulfillment," is eighty-six, the same as that of the Name of Elokim — the Name of justice. As we said earlier, the Megalleh Amukos explains that the letters of the *alef-beis* represent the attribute of mercy and that their fulfillments symbolize the attribute of justice. Since each expanded letter contains the original letter and those of the fulfillment, each *millui* displays both of these attributes together, while giving precedence to the attribute of mercy, as was done at Creation by Divine command.

Let's illustrate a practical example of the use of the *millui d'millui*. We learned previously that the large letter **ב** at the beginning of the Torah represents the *Beis haMikdash*, which is known as the **בית הגדול**, the "large house," the most important House that the Jewish People ever possessed. The fulfillment of the letter **ב** is **בית**. The hidden fulfillment — the **י** and the **ת** — have a numerical value of 410, which is equal to that of the word **קדוש**, "holy." Appropriately, the *Beis haMikdash* is referred to as **הבית הגדול והקדוש**, "the great and holy House."

The second fulfillment of the letter **ב** is **בית יוד תיו**. The hidden fulfillments of the hidden portion of this second expansion are the letters **ו**, **ד**, **י**, and **ו** (**יוד תיו**), which have a total numerical value of twenty-six, the same as that of Hashem's Name. This combination of expansions provides the exact expression that is used in the Grace After Meals: **ועל הבית הגדול והקדוש שנקרא שמך עליו** — "on the great and holy House upon which Your Name is called."

## ◈ Fulfillments That Contain the Letter ל

Only four letters contain the letter **ל** — the tallest of the letters — in their fulfillments; they are: **אלף**, **גימל**, **דלת** and **למד**. The acronym of these words spells out **אגדל** — "I will make you great." The expansion of the **למד** translates as "to learn and teach." It is only through Torah learning and teaching that true greatness can be achieved.

The Chasam Sofer points out that **למד** refers specifically to the teaching of Torah, which is the Word of Hashem, and not to the teaching of secular studies. This is alluded to in the *pasuk*: **מגיד דבריו ליעקב** — "He teaches His word to Yaakov" (*Tehillim* 147:19), as the letters of the acronym of these words spell out the word למד.

The Rokeach points out that the four letters that contain the letter ל in their fulfillment allude to the four types of students, which are enumerated in *Pirkei Avos* (5:15):

> There are four types of students: One who grasps quickly and forgets quickly: his gain is offset by his loss; one who grasps slowly and forgets slowly: his loss is offset by his gain; one who grasps quickly and forgets slowly — this is a good portion; and one who grasps slowly and forgets quickly — this is a bad portion.

By the way the Mishnah presents the list, these four types of students appear to be grouped into two sets. The four fulfillments that contain the letter ל can also be grouped into two sets: in אלף and דלת the letter ל is the middle letter, while in למד and גימל it appears at their extremities.

The *mishnah* (*Avos* 5:17) then states: ארבע מדות בהולכי בית המדרש — "There are four types of people who study in the *beis hamidrash*." The Mishnah continues to quantify four different types of students who sit before the sages to learn. These sets of four types of students have their root in the four letters of the *alef-beis* that contain the letter ל in their fulfillment.

The Gemara in the *Talmud Yerushalmi* (*Shabbos* 15b) states: "Shabbos was only given to enable us to learn Torah." This idea is reinforced by the fact that the above four fulfillments have a total numerical value of 702 (אלף [111], גימל [83], דלת [434] and למד [74]), the same as that of the word שבת, which was given to us to enable us to learn Torah.

The fact that only four letters of the *alef-beis* contain the letter ל in their fulfillments indicates that one must learn and review a new Torah concept a minimum of four times in order to begin to comprehend it. The Gemara (*Eruvin* 54b), which teaches us that the entire Oral Torah was taught to the Jewish nation a minimum of four times, has its source in the *alef-beis*:

Our Rabbis have learned the order by which the Oral Torah was taught to the Jewish People. Moshe was instructed directly by Hashem. When Aharon entered the room, Moshe learned with him what he himself had been taught, and upon completion, Aharon sat to the left side of Moshe. When Aharon's two sons, Elazar and Itamar, entered, Moshe taught them the complete Torah, and upon completing this, Elazar sat at the right of Moshe and Itamar to the left of his father, Aharon. Rabbi Yehudah maintains that Aharon always sat on the right side of Moshe.

Subsequently, the Elders entered the room and Moshe taught them the entire Torah, after which they sat on either side of Moshe and Aharon. Then the entire congregation entered and was taught the Oral Torah by Moshe. At this juncture, Moshe had taught the entire Torah four times to Aharon; the latter's two sons had listened to three teachings; the Elders to two lessons, while the entire congregation learned it only once.

Moshe then left the room, and Aharon taught the complete Oral Torah again. After this, Aharon left and his two sons taught the complete Torah again to the Elders and the entire congregation. Subsequently, they left and the Elders taught the entire congregation. In this way every single person had been taught the entire Torah a total of four times. From here we derive the ruling that a teacher should repeat and revise his lessons to his students a minimum of four times.

The importance of review of one's learning is pointed out by the Torah itself. The five books of the Chumash are divided into two parts; the first four contain new topics, while the final book, *Devarim*, is referred to as משנה תורה, a "review of the Torah," since it reiterates the Torah commandments that were previously given. The first time that the word למד appears in the Chumash with regard to teaching Torah is only in *Devarim* (5:1) — as true learning and understanding is only achieved by proper review.

In a more subtle way, this same lesson seems to be hinted at in the actual layout of the Vilna Gemara. On each page, before the text of the Gemara appears, there are four lines of explanation by Rashi and *Tosafos*. This parallels the idea that true understanding of the Gemara text requires an initial fourfold review.

### ◈ Fulfillments That Contain the Letter ד

Similarly, there are only four letters that use the letter ד — which itself has a numerical value of four — in their fulfillments: **דלת**, **יוד**, **למד** and **צדי**. The total numerical value of these expansions is 632, which is equivalent to the total numerical value of the first and last letters of each of the first words of the five books of the Chumash.

| | | | |
|---|---|---|---|
| *Sefer Bereishis* | **בראשית** | | 402 |
| *Sefer Shemos* | **ואלה** | | 11 |
| *Sefer Vayikra* | **ויקרא** | | 7 |
| *Sefer Bemidbar* | **וידבר** | | 206 |
| *Sefer Devarim* | **אלה** | | 6 |
| | | **Total** | **632** |

This correlation is but another example of how this teaching structure — that each lesson of the Torah should be reviewed a minimum of four times — is actually alluded to in the Torah itself.

The letter **דלת** represents the poor man (דל) who stands by the door (דלת) in order to collect charity. Just as four letters containing the letter ל corresponds to the four types of students mentioned in the Mishnah, these four letters that contain the letter ד correspond to the Mishnah in *Avos* (5:16) that lists four types of charitable donors: ארבע מדות בנותני צדקה וכו' — "There are four types of charity donors...."

### ◈ Hidden Letter Fulfillments — Nistar

As explained above, the full expansion of a letter is known as the *millui*. Every expansion can be divided into two parts. The hidden part is known as the *nistar*. For example, the letter ב is written as בית; the letters י and ת comprise the hidden portion (**בית**), for they are only pronounced, but not found in the written form of the letter ב. The hidden potential that lies within each word can be uncovered by examining the hidden part of the fulfillment of its letters. Allow me to give the reader a few examples.

### The Correlation Between the Letters ב, ח, and ט

As discussed earlier, the first ב of the Torah represents the *Beis haMikdash* (see pp. 105–106). In his commentary on *Devarim* 4:25, Rashi explains that the destruction of the First *Beis haMikdash* was brought forward by two years. In other words, it stood for a total of 410 years but it had the potential to stand for 412. These figures correspond to the numerical values of both fulfillments of the word בית. The full fulfillment has a numerical value of 412, while just the hidden fulfillment has a value of 410.

The *Beis haMikdash* was situated in the portion of Eretz Yisrael that was given to the tribe of Binyamin. When Moshe blessed each of the tribes before his death, regarding Binyamin he said: לבנימן אמר ידיד ה׳ ישכן לבטח עליו חפף עליו כל היום ובין כתפיו שכן — "To Binyamin he said, May Hashem's beloved dwell securely by Him, He shields him forever, and rests between his shoulders" (*Devarim* 33:12). This blessing refers to both the First and Second *Beis haMikdash* that were to be built on his land.

The Ben Ish Chai points out that there are only three letters in the *alef-beis* that have the hidden fulfillment of ית, namely: **בית**, **ח**ית and **ט**ית. In the *pasuk* quoted above, the word **ל**בטח, "securely," contains these three letters (ב, ח and ט). Each has a hidden fulfillment of 410, corresponding to the 410 years that the first *Beis haMikdash* stood securely. (We find this number hidden within this word by using transformation methods, as well. The letter ט is interchangeable with the letter ת, as they both belong to the lingual group; with this change, the word בטח transforms into בתח, which has a numerical value of 410. Using the At–Bash transformation, the word בטח converts into the word שנס, which also equals 410.)

The Second *Beis haMikdash* stood for 420 years — a figure that is represented by the numerical value of the combination ת"כ, which fulfills as תיו כף. These letters spell out the word כתפיו, "his shoulders," which is found at the end of the above *pasuk*. Furthermore, the rebuilding of the *Beis haMikdash* was authorized by King Koresh, who was a descendant of Yafes (יפת), the son of Noach, as Rashi explains on the passage where Noach blesses Yafes: יפת א-להים ליפת וישכן באהלי שם — "May God extend Yafes, but he will dwell in the tents of Shem" (*Bereishis* 9:27).

The word כתפיו incorporates the name יפת in the reverse order and, as we have said, letters in reverse alphabetic order symbolize the attribute of justice. This is reinforced by the fact that the Name of Hashem used in the above *pasuk* is Elokim, the Name that symbolizes judgment. A further hint to the *Beis haMikdash* can be found in the second half of the above phrase, as the words וישכן באהלי שם can also be interpreted to mean that He shall dwell in the tents of His Name, by interpreting the word שם as referring to Hashem.

Furthermore, the letters כ and ו — which surround the word כתפיו — have the same combined numerical value as that of the Name of Hashem (י-ה-ו-ה). As a direct result of the blessing received by יפת, his descendant merited to be credited with the building of the Second *Beis haMikdash* — as alluded to in the phrase ובין כתפיו שכן. Moreover, if we tally the total years that both *Battei Mikdash* stood, we get 830, the numerical value of the Aramaic word תְּלַת, which means "third," an allusion to the Third *Beis haMikdash*.

A further correlation between the letters ב'ח'ט' is found in *Osios d'Rabbi Yitzchak*. The letter ב in בראשית represents the entire Torah. With a numerical value of two, the ב represents *both* the Written and Oral Torah. The fulfillment of the ב symbolizes the *Beis haMikdash*, which existed as long as the Jewish People kept the Torah commandments. When Jewish People sinned by transgressing the

Torah, the two letters ח'ט' (which form the word "sin") took over and became separated from the ב. Thus the word בטח was broken apart, removing the security, which resulted in the destruction of the *Beis haMikdash*.

**Prayer: The Latent Power Within Each Person**

The first Belzer Rebbe, Rabbi Shalom Rokeach, gave an example of how the hidden fulfillment of a word reveals the hidden power incorporated within that word. He cited the *pasuk*: וכל שיח השדה טרם יהיה בארץ וכל עשב השדה טרם יצמח כי לא המטיר ה' א-להים על הארץ ואדם אין לעבד את האדמה — "And every tree of the field was not yet on the earth and every herb of the field had not yet sprouted, for Hashem God had not sent rain to the earth and there was no man to work the soil" (*Bereishis* 2:5). Rashi comments on this:

> *For [Hashem] had not sent rain:* And what is the reason that He had not sent rain? Because there was no man to work the soil, and there was no one who would recognize the benefit of rain. When Adam realized that rain was essential for the world, he *prayed* and it came down, so that the trees and vegetation sprouted (see *Chullin* 60b).

The Belzer Rebbe points out that the fulfillment of the word אדם is אלף דלת מם. The hidden fulfillments of these letters form the word מתפלל, "pray." The latent power within every human being is his ability to pray to Hashem.

Furthermore, this *pasuk*, from which we learn that man should pray for his needs, begins by telling us that there was a lack of vegetation in the fields: וכל שיח השדה טרם יהיה בארץ. The *Arizal* explains that the word שיח represents the eighteen blessings of the *Amidah*, which forms the central part of our daily prayers. Since the letter ש is composed from three *vav*'s — each one forming another arm of the letter — these *vav*'s have a total numerical value of eighteen (3 x 6 = 18). Moreover, the remaining two letters of the word, י and ח also total eighteen. Thus the word שיח represents a duplication of the number eighteen, corresponding to the fact that the eighteen blessings of the *Amidah* are recited twice — first, silently by the individual, and then collectively by the repetition that is led by the *chazan*.

In addition, the success of the entire world depends on the power of meaningful prayer. The Ben Ish Chai points out that the letters of the *alef-beis* that follow those of the word ארץ, "world," are those that spell the word בקש, "request." Through requests made in the form of prayers to Hashem, we acknowledge our dependence on Him for all our daily requirements.

### The Blue Thread in Tzitzis

In the chapter commanding us to wear *tzitzis*, we are told to place a blue thread, פתיל תכלת, on the fringes of our garments. The Ben Ish Chai, quoting the Gemara in *Chullin* (89a) points out that the color of this blue thread is similar to that of the blue sea, matching that of the sky, which blends with the shade of Hashem's Holy Throne. The purpose of this blue thread is to provide a link between the Jew wearing the *tzitzis* and his Father in Heaven. The fulfillment of the letters of the word אב, "father" is אלף and בית. The *hidden* fulfillment of these letters spells out the word פתיל, the thread that connects us to our Father in Heaven.

### For the Sake of Yisrael

In Rashi's commentary on the first *pasuk* of the Torah, he begins by explaining the first word בראשית, and then continues to explain the first two words, בראשית ברא. On these two words, one explanation is that the world was created for the sake of the Jewish People — בשביל ישראל. There must be a reason why Rashi divides his comments between the first word and the first two words, and why he quotes this specific *midrash* under the heading of בראשית ברא, as opposed to under the first word, בראשית.

Making use of the different alphabetic structures and the different groupings of the letters, we can appreciate the reasoning behind this comment. The middle four letters of **בראשית** are the same as the first four letters of **ישראל**. The last letter **ת** in **בראשית**, can be interchanged with the letter **ל**, as they are both letters from the lingual group. In this way, the first word of the Torah, בראשית, contains the word ישראל.

Furthermore, the second word of the Torah, ברא, fulfills as **בית ריש אלף**. Included in these letters are the five that spell out the word ישראל. Since both בראשית and ברא incorporate the word ישראל, Rashi comments under the combined heading of בראשית ברא that the world was created — בשביל ישראל — for the sake of Israel.

**Getting to the Heart of the Matter**

The Torah states: ואתה תצוה את בני ישראל ויקחו אליך שמן זית זך כתית למאור להעלת נר תמיד — "And you shall command the children of Israel that they shall take for you clear olive oil, crushed for illumination, to light a lamp continually" (*Shemos* 27:20). Rashi explains that the word תמיד, "continually," can be used to portray two meanings. It can be translated as "constantly," as in the case of the *Lechem haPanim* (Shewbread) that had to remain continually on the *Shulchan* (Table), as stipulated in *Shemos* 25:30. The freshly baked loaves would be used to push off the previous week's bread from the Table, thereby ensuring that the bread was constantly on it. On the other hand, the Menorah was kindled every evening in the *Beis haMikdash*. The excellent quality of olive oil used ensured that the flame burnt continuously during the whole night. In this context, the Hebrew word תמיד is translated as "regularly." Similarly the daily תמיד sacrifice that was offered up every single morning and evening was so named because of its regularity.

In the human body, the one organ that must simultaneously function constantly and with regularity is the heart. It begins to beat in the early stages of pregnancy, and carries on doing so, *continuously*, until death. At the same time, an efficient heart has to pump *regularly*, as well. The Hebrew word for the heart is לב. The hidden fulfillment of these letters (**למד בית**) spell out the word **תמיד**, alluding to its essential function of both a constant and regular heartbeat.

Rabbi Avraham Abulafia explains that the word לב can be read as ל + ב, meaning two times the letter ל. If we place two *lamed*s next to each other, face to face, they form the cup-shaped heart, with the two blood vessels that lead to and from the brain.

The ל on the right represents the person who learns in order to teach, while the one on the left represents the person who learns in order to do. As mentioned earlier, these two letters, ב and ל, are the first and final letters of the Torah, whose regular teaching and continuous study ensures the existence of the universe.

Moreover, in the alphabetic order, the letters that precede לב spell out the word אך, "but," which is a word that comes to exclude, whereas the letters that follow לב spell out גם, "also," a word that comes to include. Together, these neighboring letters represent the pumping action of the heart, regularly and continuously expanding to "include" more blood and then contracting to "exclude" that blood — pumping it out to nourish the body.

### ◈ Hidden Fulfillments with the Same Numerical Value as the Letter

There are five letters of the *alef-beis* whose hidden fulfillment have the same numerical value as the letter itself. They are:

| ס | נ | מ | י | ו |
|---|---|---|---|---|
| **סמך** | **נן** | **מם** | **יוד** | **וו** |

The Ben Ish Chai gives an easy way to remember them, as they are used to spell out the word סימן, "sign." Thus, because the fulfillments of each of these letters also spells out סימן, this idea is referred to as סימן בתוך סימן, "a sign within a sign." This concept is applied in practical halachah. When kosher meat is left unattended in the presence of a non-Jew, it must be wrapped with two seals to ensure that it has not been exchanged with non-kosher meat. This type of sealing is also known as סימן בתוך סימן, "a sign within a sign."

When Moshe Rabbeinu and Aharon had their initial audience before Pharaoh, in order to try and redeem the Israelites, Aharon cast down his staff and it changed into a serpent. Pharaoh, too, summoned his sorcerers who did likewise. When the serpents reverted back to their original staffs, Aharon's staff swallowed them all. The Gemara in *Shabbos* (97a) refers to this as being a נס בתוך נס, "a miracle within a miracle." The Maharsha explains that the first miracle was that Aharon's staff swallowed up the other sticks. The second miracle was that despite this great intake of sticks, Aharon's staff remained as thin as it was originally.

The fulfillment of the letters of נס as נן סמך produces hidden fulfillments that have the same numerical value as their original letter, and therefore also equal the word נס. Thus the word נס naturally incorporates within itself another word נס, providing a literal meaning to the term נס בתוך נס — "a miracle within a miracle."

◈ ◈ ◈

One of the words that is composed exclusively from the above letters is the word סיום (*siyum*), which literally means "a completion." It is customary to make a festive meal upon completing a tractate of Gemara or an order of the Mishnah. To this festivity one invites the people who have joined in with the learning program, as well as family and friends who did not participate in the learning. The Vilna Gaon explains that a person who attends a *siyum* is elevated by the learning of the one making the *siyum*, and therefore he is able to join in equally in the celebration, even though he did not contribute to the learning itself. The numerical value of each of letters of the word סיום is the same as its respective hidden fulfillment, indicating an equal participation of both parties at the סיום.

## Notrikon

In a *beraisa* taught by Rabbi Eliezer, the son of Rabbi Yossi Haglili, there is a list of thirty-two different methods that are used to interpret the Torah. The thirtieth method is known by the name of *notrikon*, a word of Greek derivative, meaning "a notation of abbreviation." When interpreting a word using the *notrikon* concept, each letter of that word is treated as the first letter of another word. For example, a word containing three letters will be explained by three complete words, whose acronym spell out the original word. Rabbeinu Chananel explains (see *Shabbos* 104b) that when medieval kings would dictate some urgent message to their scribes, they would initially jot down this message using *notrikon*, by just writing the acronym of each word. This was used either as a secret code or as a shorthand method of notation. This codified notation is one of the Divine methods of expounding the Torah, where each letter represents a complete word.

The Gemara (*Shabbos* 104b) lists a few examples of *notrikon* for words which either appear to be superfluous or contain extra letters in them. These examples are discussed in the Gemara with regard to the relevant subject of the Torah prohibition of writing two letters on Shabbos. The Gemara introduces the concept of *notrikon* in order to discuss the case when a person writes one letter of a *notrikon* word, which is self-understood to mean an entire word. Does writing one such letter constitute a transgression of Shabbos or not?

One of the examples quoted by the Gemara is a word used to explain the phrase where the angel rebuked Bilaam for having hit his mule on three occasions, while he himself was the impediment. The *pasuk* states: כי ירט הדרך לנגדי — "…for he hastened on the road against me" (*Bemidbar* 22:32). The word ירט is explained using the *notrikon* as the acronym for the words **יראה ראתה נטתה**, "she feared, she saw, she turned away." The Maharal explains that the mule was instinctively *afraid* as she sensed something was unusual. Later on, she actually *saw* the angel and consequently *turned away* from the road in order to avoid him.

Any explanation offered by the *notrikon* method needs to be approached with caution, and can only be relied upon when explained by proficient Torah scholars. Otherwise any three words beginning with the letters 'י'ר'ט' could provide an erroneous *notrikon* explanation to the original word.

The concept of *notrikon* can be used for any word in the Torah, thereby providing extra meaning to the original word that is being expanded. Just as each letter of the *alef-beis* expands into its fulfilled form, similarly each word of the Torah can be expanded using the concept of *notrikon*. The Ginas Egos points out that words can be explained using the *notrikon*, even though they do not expand in the original letter order, and they can be interpreted using both the beginning and end letters of words. A typical example is the way that Hashem's Name is represented in different acronyms or end letters in the twelve expansions that correspond to the twelve months of the year (see p. 237ff).

Another example of the *notrikon* expansion is used to explain the benefits that result from performing the mitzvah of *bris milah*. The word מילה is the *notrikon* of the phrase מי יעלה לנו השמימה — "Who can ascend to the heavens?" (*Devarim* 30:12). These same four words have final letters that spell out Hashem's Name, as it is only after a boy has been circumcised that he is able to begin to progress spiritually and draw closer to Hashem.

A further example of the use of *notrikon* is given by the Rokeach on the *gemara* (*Shabbos* 88a) which explains that the universe was created for the sole purpose of the Jewish People accepting the Torah, and if they were to refuse it, the world would automatically cease to exist. The Rokeach explains that the first word of the Torah, בראשית is a *notrikon* for this stipulation, for its letters are the acronym for the phrase: רק אם שמוע תשמע בקול י-ה-ו-ה — "Only if you will listen to the voice of Hashem" (*Devarim* 15:5).

The method of *notrikon* can be used not only to explain words in the Torah itself, but also to explain phrases used by the Gemara. One such example is brought in *Sefer Chareidim* to illustrate how each statement made by our Sages is alluded to in the actual words of the Torah. Yosef was commanded by his father to go and look for his brothers, a trip that ended with him being cast into a pit, as the *pasuk* states: **וישלכו אתו הברה והבור רק אין בו מים** — "And they cast him into the pit, which was empty; no water was in it" (*Bereishis* 37:24).

Rashi quotes a Gemara (*Shabbos* 22a) that explains the double expression used to describe the emptiness of the pit — "no water was in it." The Gemara explains: **מים אין בו אבל נחשים ועקרבים יש בו** — "There was no water in it, but there were snakes and scorpions in it." The Gemara's explanation is contained within the words of the Torah, as the letters of the words **אין בו** are the acronym of the words **אבל נחשים ועקרבים יש בו**. (Moreover, a further support of this idea is that numerical value of the hidden fulfillment of the word **בור** [pit], 726, is the same as that of the words **נחש ועקרב**.)

## Roshei Teivos and Sofei Teivos

One of the seventy-three methods for interpreting the Torah mentioned by the Rokeach is the concept of *roshei teivos* (first letters) and *sofei teivos* (final letters). This concept is based in the generative and degenerative properties of a word (which was explained in Chapter 4). In the generative process, the first letter is present during all the stages. Similarly, in the degenerative process, it is the last letter that is always present. The fact that these letters form the source of the word indicates that this positioning has special significance.

The *Arizal* explains that acronyms are always formed from letters that appear on the right-hand side of a word, thereby representing the attribute of mercy, whereas the final letters, which always appear on the left-hand side of a word, represent that of strict justice.

The Ba'al HaTurim, in his commentary to the Torah, makes frequent use of acronyms and final letters to explain many passages.

Sometimes the combined use of the *roshei teivos* and *sofei teivos* accurately portray the teachings of the Gemara. One example is from the statement made by the Gemara: כל שיש לו חולה בתוך ביתו ילך לחכם ויבקש עליו רחמים — "Anybody who has an ill person at home should go to a wise man and request that he should seek Divine mercy on his behalf" (*Bava Basra* 116a).

This statement is alluded to in the *pasuk*: והסיר ה׳ ממך כל חולי — "Hashem will remove from you every illness" (*Devarim* 7:15). The final letters of the words ממ**ך** כ**ל** חול**י** spell out the word ילך, "[he] should go." The *roshei teivos* of these same three words **מ**מך **כ**ל **ח**ולי spell out the word חכם, "a wise man." Using the acronym and the end letters together we are pointed to the advice given by the Gemara: ילך לחכם, "[he] should go to a wise man."

A second example is cited in the *gemara* (*Berachos* 30a) which details the manner in which one should direct his prayers. When praying, a person should face the direction of Eretz Yisrael. If he prays in Eretz Yisrael itself, he should face toward Jerusalem. When praying there, he should turn towards the location of the *Beis ha-Mikdash*, and ultimately direct his prayers towards the Holy of Holies. In this way, all Jewish People will be unified in prayer towards the central location of the Holy of Holies. This is the interpretation of the *pasuk*: כמגדל דויד צואריך בנוי **לתלפיות** — "Your neck is like the Tower of David, built as a model..." (*Shir HaShirim* 4:4).

The Gemara (*Berachos* 30a) states that this *pasuk* refers to the *Beis haMikdash* and explains the word תלפיות to mean תל שכל פיות פונים בו, the central place to which all mouths face in prayer. The word תלפיות is composed from the final letters of the fulfillment of the first six letters of the *alef-beis* (אל**ף** בי**ת** גימ**ל** דל**ת** ה**י** ו**ו**), thereby representing the *Beis haMikdash* as the final receptive point for all prayers. (Moreover, these first six letters represent the composition of Hashem's Name of י-ה-ו-ה, as the letters א׳ב׳ג׳ד׳ה׳ו׳ are contained within the letters י'ה'ו', those used to compose His Name. The first four letters are equal to the י, as their numerical equivalents total ten [1 + 2 + 3 + 4 = 10]. These are followed in the alphabetic order by the letters ה and ו. Thus, the first six letters of the *alef-beis* represent Hashem, to Whom all prayers are directed.)

A further example shows how the use of acronyms together with their final letters can be used to portray the teachings of the *gemara* (*Shabbos* 62b) that states that there are three things that cause a person to become poor, one of which is not being careful with the laws pertaining to washing one's hands (מזלזל בנטילת ידים). To this the Gemara concludes:

> But this is incorrect, as Rav Chisda said, "I washed my hands with handfuls of water and I was given hands full of prosperity."

After washing one's hands before a meal, one recites the *berachah* that ends with the words **על נטילת ידים**, whose acronym spells out the word עני, a poor person. This indicates that improper washing of one's hands, will cause a person to become poor. Rav Chisda is quantifying this statement. Although treating this commandment lightly will result in poverty, it also has the potential merit to make a person wealthy — if it is performed correctly. This is represented by the final two letters of each of the words **על נטילת ידים**, which have a total numerical value of 580, the same as that of the word עשיר, a rich man. The entire teaching of this *gemara* is alluded to in the combined use of the acronym and final letters of the words of the *berachah* על נטילת ידים.

Another example: In Hebrew, the sun is known by three different names, the most common one being the word שמש. The remaining two are used in the *pesukim*: האמר **לחרס** ולא יזרח — "He Who spoke to the sun and it did not shine" (*Iyov* 9:7); and: וחפרה הלבנה ובושה **החמה** — "And the moon shall be ashamed and the sun abashed" (*Yeshayahu* 24:23).

The total numerical value of the final letters of the three words used to describe the sun (שמש חרס חמה), is 365, the same as the number of days in a solar year.

◇ ◇ ◇

*Roshei teivos* and *notrikon* are, in fact, interrelated.

The Megalleh Amukos lists ten places where the *roshei teivos* of consecutive words spells out איבה, a word which appears in the *pasuk*: ואיבה אשית בינך ובין האישה — "I will put enmity between you and the woman" (*Bereishis* 3:15). This *pasuk* enumerates one of the punishments given to the Serpent for having caused the initial sin. The Serpent convinced Chavah to partake of the forbidden fruit, thereby becoming the prime source of all incorrect speech (לשון הרע). He expounds on the connection between the other phrases in the Torah that have that acronym and the effect that the initial enmity of the Serpent continues to have on future generations causing further destruction, punishment and impurity.

The *notrikon* of the word איבה appears in *pasuk*: ויאמר אליהם יוסף ביום השלישי — "Yosef said to them on the third day" (*Bereishis* 42:18). The enmity that the Serpent was instrumental in introducing into the world was apparent in the jealousy that the brothers bore against Yosef. This enmity developed, at least in part, because the brothers felt that Yosef had slandered them to their father. As a result, they sold Yosef into slavery. He was taken to Egypt, and eventually he rose to power and became viceroy, controlling the sale of Egyptian grain during the years of famine. Now, the brothers came to him to request that he sell them grain. The fact that the above *pasuk* incorporates the *notrikon* of איבה hints at Yosef's slander against them and their subsequent enmity of him. They had both been subjected to the curse of the Serpent, and it was their joint task to try to rectify this failing. For Yosef's part, he never took revenge against his brothers for the anguish that they had caused him. He sold them the grain that they had requested.

However, when Yosef accused his brothers of having come to

Egypt to spy out the land, not just to buy grain, he was hinting to them that his efforts were not enough to eradicate the transgression of slanderous speech, and there would come a time when the Jewish People would spy out the Land of Israel and speak badly about it. They would subsequently be punished and would die in the wilderness, without entering Eretz Yisrael. Consequently, the same acronym appears in Hashem's response to the report of the spies: ופגריכם אתם יפלו במדבר הזה — "But your carcasses shall drop in the wilderness" (*Bemidbar* 14:32).

The *Bnei Yisrael*'s descent to Egypt came about, then, as a result of the selling of Yosef, which transpired because of the brother's jealousy. The rectification for this sin should have been the four hundred years of the Egyptian exile. However, since this period was cut short — they left after only 210 years — "jealousy" still remained in the world. This is hinted at in the acronym איבה that is found in the *pasuk* that refers to their departure from Egypt: היום אתם יוצאים בחודש האביב — "Today you are leaving in the month of spring" (*Shemos* 13:4).

Chavah also played a role in bringing this enmity into the world. The *Arizal* points out that this is hinted at in *Bemidbar* 5:17, as it contains a passage whose acronym spells out the words חוה איבה, "the enmity [caused by] Chavah": ולקח הכהן מים קדשים בכלי חרש ומן העפר אשר יהיה בקרקע המשכן יקח הכהן ונתן אל המים — "And the *Kohen* shall take sacred water in an earthenware vessel, and the *Kohen* shall take from the earth that is on the floor of the Tabernacle and put it in the water." This *pasuk* refers to a woman whose husband becomes jealous and suspects her of being unfaithful. A further allusion to the initial sin is the use of the word עפר, "earth" or "dust," which became the staple diet of the Serpent, for its involvement. This is the only *pasuk* in all of Scripture that contains these two words in their acronym.

Another consequence of the sin of Adam haRishon is that death was introduced into the world. The laws of impurity and defilement when coming in contact with a dead body necessitated a purification process that required the use of the ashes of a red heifer. The acronym of the word איבה appears in the passage which discusses this issue: וכל אשר יגע בו הטמא — "Anyone whom the impure one will touch" (*Bemidbar* 19:22).

After the Jewish People spoke slanderously against Hashem, He punished them by sending poisonous snakes. This was to remind them that they were behaving in a manner similar to that of the Serpent who spoke slanderously, enticing Chavah to sin. That *pasuk* states: וישלח י-ה-ו-ה בעם את הנחשים — "Hashem sent the snakes, the burning ones against the people" (*Bemidbar* 21:6). When rearranged the highlighted letters also spell out איבה.

At the end of Moshe Rabbeinu's life, he wanted to finally eradicate the evil influence that resulted from the cunning speech of the Serpent. He therefore used his power of speech in positive manner, in sincere prayer, thereby trying to counteract this influence. We find this alluded to in his prayer: ואתחנן אל י-ה-ו-ה בעת ההיא — "I implored Hashem at that time..." (*Devarim* 3:23).

Hashem indicated to Moshe that the time was not yet ripe for the evil to be eliminated from the world. In the form of baseless hatred, this evil would eventually lead to the destruction of the Second *Beis haMikdash*, as explained in the Gemara (*Yoma* 10a). The first *pasuk* of the book of Lamentations, which describes the subsequent devastation, therefore contains this acronym as well: איכה ישבה בדד העיר — "How has the city that was once so populous remained lonely!" (*Eichah* 1:1).

The three other times that this acronym appears in Scripture are in connection with the rebuilding of the *Beis haMikdash* and with reference to the dynasty of David haMelech:

> ויבן את בית יער הלבנון — "And he built the house of the forest of Levanon." (*Melachim* I 7:2)
>
> אשלחך אל ישי בית הלחמי — "I will send you to Yishai the Bethlemite." (*Shmuel* I 16:1)

אז יאמרו בגוים הגדיל — "Then they will say amongst the nations, Great things...." (*Tehillim* 126:2)

This enmity will only be fully eradicated from the world with the arrival of Mashiach — may this happen speedily, in the very near future.

## Letter Permutations

There are some interesting lessons that can be learned by studying the different permutations that can be made from the letters of a word. For example:

Noach was told to build a window in the Ark, as the *pasuk* states: צהר תעשה לתבה — "A window shall you make for the Ark" (*Bereishis* 6:16). In his commentary on *Parashas Noach*, the Shach asks the question: Since there was nothing but water at the time of the Flood, what purpose could a window serve? He gives the following explanation incorporating different permutations of the word צהר, "window":

We are taught in the fifth chapter of *Pirkei Avos* that there were ten generations from Adam until Noach, to teach us the patience that Hashem displayed — for all these ten generations angered Him increasingly, until He brought upon them the waters of the flood. Over the next ten generations, from Noach until Avraham, each generation continued to be even more wicked, and based on that they deserved to be annihilated. The fact that they were not, again teaches us the extent of His patience. All these generations angered Him increasingly, and were it not for Avraham's merit, they would have been destroyed.

The question is asked as to why Avraham merited to save his generation, when his predecessor, Noach, who was also a righteous person and unique in his generation did not succeed in doing so?

As a direct result of the wickedness of Noach's generation, he and his sons were commanded to build the Ark. This large nine-hundred room structure would take 120 years to build. During this period, many people would stop and inquire as to the purpose of the enterprise. Noach would inform them that Hashem was about to annihilate the world because of their wickedness. However, they responded with insults and contempt.

During the entire 120 years Noach remained strong, despite the daily ridicule he received from the people who came to inquire about his unique project. Although *Chazal* praise Noach for his righteousness, they also point out one shortcoming that he possessed. He failed to utter a prayer on behalf of these wicked people — that they should repent and thereby avert this impending catastrophe and annihilation. Noach, being a very righteous man surely prayed regularly, but his prayers did not include his fellowmen.

In comparison, when Avraham heard about the impending danger that Lot and the inhabitants of Sodom and Amora were in, he spared no effort in praying for their salvation, despite the fact that they were "extremely wicked and evil" (*Bereishis* 18:20–33). Through the power of his prayers, Lot and his immediate family were saved. This resulted in the birth of their descendants — David haMelech and the forthcoming Mashiach. Avraham's prayer ensured the accomplishment of the purpose of Creation. He therefore merited to receive a commensurate reward that included "the reward of all of them" (see *Pirkei Avos* 5:3).

Noach is made aware of his shortcoming when he was instructed to build a window in the Ark. Although Noach, as a righteous person, needed to protect himself from outside influences, nevertheless he should have left a "window" for the unfortunate wicked people, by praying for their speedy repentance. An integral regulation of every synagogue building is that it must incorporate windows. This will remind the congregants to incorporate in their prayers those people on the outside who do not yet belong to the congregation gathered inside. The window in Noach's Ark was a lesson that prayer is not just between man and his Creator; it must also incorporate an element of בין אדם לחבירו ("between man and his fellow"), as well.

The structure of our *Shemoneh Esrei* is such that every request is made in the plural form, to combine our personal requirements together with those of the general public. Even when a personal prayer is made on behalf of an ill acquaintance, who is mentioned explicitly by name, we end this prayer by including all other ill people among the Jewish nation: "That You quickly send a complete recovery from Heaven, spiritual healing and physical healing to the patient...among the other patients of Israel." In other words, we pray for our friend's speedy recovery and, at the same time, incorporate a prayer for the remainder of the Jewish People who are suffering from illness.

The generation of Noach was doomed for total destruction in an unprecedented way. This was a time of impending צרה— the greatest calamity was about to befall mankind. Noach might have changed the situation by offering up an appropriate prayer to Hashem for their repentance. This צרה could have been averted if he would have understood the lesson signified by the "window" (צהר) which he was commanded to incorporate into the Ark. This lesson is alluded to in the conclusion of the main section of every *Shemoneh Esrei* in the words רצה ה' — "May our prayers be favorable with Hashem."

Only inclusive prayers find favor in the eyes of Hashem. The words רצה and צרה (calamity) are permutations of the word צהר (window). Our inclusive prayers (as represented by the צהר) can transform an impending calamity (a צרה) to produce a favorable conclusion — רצה, when Hashem finds favor in our prayers and saves the situation.

◈ ◈ ◈

The Chida brings an example of the use of letter permutations in explaining the importance of speaking words of Torah during a meal.

The Mishnah (*Pirkei Avos* 3:4) writes: רבי שמעון אומר שלשה שאכלו על **שלחן** אחד ולא אמרו עליו דברי תורה כאלו אכלו מזבחי **מתים** — "Rabbi Shimon states: If three people have eaten at the same table and have not spoken words of Torah together, it is as if they have eaten from the offerings of dead idols."

As mentioned earlier, the נחש, the Serpent, was the cause of the first transgression committed by Adam and Chavah — as a result of which, the concept of death was introduced into the world. The Chidah points out that the same letters that spell out the word שלחן, "table" — upon which one partakes of a meal — also spell out the word לנחש, "to a snake." The absence of Torah spoken at the שלחן provides food for the נחש.

◆ ◆ ◆

Another example is found with regard to the laws of *tefillin*. The *Shulchan Aruch* (*Orach Chayim* 44) discusses the prohibition of sleeping while wearing *tefillin*: "As long as one is wearing *tefillin* on one's head or arm, one is prohibited from sleeping — irrespective of whether it is a proper sleep or just a short nap."

The *tefillin* that are worn on the head have a large letter ש protruding from both sides. The letters of the word שין spell the word ישן, "sleep"; thus the two *shin*s indicate that *both* types of sleep — normal sleep or just a short nap — are prohibited while wearing *tefillin*.

◆ ◆ ◆

A further example is found in the *pasuk*: ויקח חמאה וחלב ובן הבקר אשר עשה ויתן לפניהם והוא עמד עליהם תחת העץ **ויאכלו** — "He took cream and milk and the calf which he had made and placed these before them; he stood over them beneath the tree and they ate" (*Bereishis* 18:8).

This *pasuk* discusses the visit made to Avraham by the three angels. The Gemara (*Bava Metzia* 86b) remarks that it only appeared as if they were eating and drinking, but they did not actually partake of any food. Although the *pasuk* explicitly states ויאכלו, that they ate, the Gemara teaches us that the word should be read as כאילו, "as if" they had eaten — a different permutation of that word.

◈ ◈ ◈

Any word, containing three letters, will form six different permutations, while a four-letter word will form twenty four permutations. Rabbi Aryeh Kaplan explained (transcribed from one of his lectures):

> From the complete twenty-two-letter alphabet $(10)^{21}$ possible permutations can be made. This equals the number of stars in the observable universe. This universe contains around $(10)^{11}$ galaxies, each one with approximately $(10)^{10}$ stars. Thus, from the permutations of the alphabet, an individual name can be formed for every star in the universe. This is in accordance with the verse that states that every star has an individual name: המוציא במספר צבאם לכלם בשם יקרא — "He Who takes out their host by number, He calls them all by name" (*Yeshayahu* 40:26).

## CHAPTER 6

# The Letters of the Alef-Beis

EACH INDIVIDUAL LETTER OF the *alef-beis* contains an infinite amount of wisdom that Hashem has placed and hidden within it. By using different techniques to analyze their properties, we can uncover some of that wisdom. Each letter has three representations: the letter itself, its fulfillment, and the term that correlates to its numerical value. In this chapter, we discuss the properties of each of the letters, as well as provide some insights into the interconnection between the letters' representations.

## THE LETTER א

The commentators write, in the name of the *Arizal*, that the letter א represents Hashem and His Glory. Since Hebrew is written from right to left, all the other letters of the *alef-beis* face away from it, so as not to gaze, so to speak, at the Divine Glory that it represents, corresponding to the concept: וראית את אחרי ופני לא יראו — "You may see My back, but My face may not be seen" (*Shemos* 33:23).

The letter א has a numerical value of one, representing the Unity of Hashem.

The fulfillment of the letter (אלף) can be translated as "prince," "teaching" or "a thousand"—depending upon how it is vowelized—and has a numerical value of 111, which is actually three number ones, symbolizing the Unity of Hashem at all levels of the number system—the hundreds, tens and units.

The Chasam Sofer points out that in *Nirtzah* (the song portion) at the end of the Haggadah, we ask: אחד מי ידע? אחד אני ידע—"Who knows One ? I know One." This question is repeated for all the numbers up to thirteen. Each question is prefaced with the word מי and the answer is given in the first person אני. The combined numerical value of these words is also 111, displaying the Unity of Hashem.

◈ ◈ ◈

The Rokeach states that אלף also represents the absolute Divine Truth that emanates from Hashem Himself. The word אמת (truth) is composed from the first, middle and final letters of the *alef-beis*. The fulfillment as אלף is similarly composed with regard to the phonetic set—the first letter being from the first group (Gutturals), the second from the middle (Linguals), and the last letter from the final (Labials) group.

Moreover, the connection between the א and אמת can be seen by transforming the letters of the *alef*'s hidden fulfillment (אלף) according to their phonetic groupings: the ל converts to a ת, as they both belong to the Linguals set, and the ף converts to a מ, as they are both of the Labials set. With these substitutions אלף becomes אמת.

## ◈ The Composition of the א

The א is formed by attaching two *yuds*, each with a numerical value of ten, to a diagonal *vav*, which has a numerical value of six. The total—the composite value—is twenty-six, the numerical value of

י-ה-ו-ה — the Name of Hashem. The letter א, with its intrinsic numerical value of one and its composite value of twenty-six, fully represents the uniqueness of Hashem by its very shape and composition. (The significance of the א being composed from two *yud*s and a diagonal *vav*, will be explained in further detail in the section dealing with the letter י.)

As mentioned, the letter א represents Hashem's Glory. After Adam haRishon ate from the forbidden fruit, Hashem had to hide some of His Glory from human perception. This is the reason that Adam was unable to remain in *Gan Eden*, for while there, he was able to appreciate Hashem's full Glory.

At the time of Creation, the letter ו in the original shape of the א was written in a vertical position — straight up and down. Another consequence of Hashem hiding His Glory was that from that point on, the ו in the letter א would be written in a diagonal position and the י that forms the foot of the א would be written in an elongated form — similar to the shape of an inverted ד (as is seen in the *Arizal*'s script). The elongation of the י represents the distancing from Hashem that resulted from Adam haRishon's sin.

### ◈ The א as an Ellipse

The Magen David views the shape of the letter א as symbolic of the elliptical orbits of the planets. Each letter י corresponds to a focal point, while the letter ו represents the axis of the ellipse.

Initially, before the sin of Adam haRishon, all the planets revolved around the sun in circular orbits — corresponding to the fact that the ו at the axis of the א was in a vertical position — creating a rotation that forms a circle, which has one focus (i.e. the center point of the circle). After the sin, the ו was tilted diagonally and elongated, and subsequently all the orbits became ellipical, with two foci. (An ellipse is, in fact, an elongated circle.) As mentioned, a result of Adam haRishon's sin was that the letter י that forms the bottom leg of the letter א was elongated to create the shape of a ד.

Yet the letter ד has a triangular value of ten (1 + 2 + 3 + 4 = 10), which is also the numerical value of י, and therefore the ד maintains a numerical connection to its previous shape as י.

The above numerical equivalency between the י and ד corresponds to the equality that is stipulated in Kepler's Second Law of Planetary Motion. Each planet's orbit creates an ellipse with the sun at one of the foci. Kepler's Law states that a planet in its orbit moves faster when it is closer to the sun and decelerates again as it moves further away. We infer from this that if an imaginary line were drawn from the sun to a planet, that line would sweep out equal areas during equal intervals of time. When the planet is far from the sun and moving slowly those sections will be long and narrow, and when it is close to the sun and moving quickly they will be short and wide. Each of these pie-shaped sections will be equal in area.

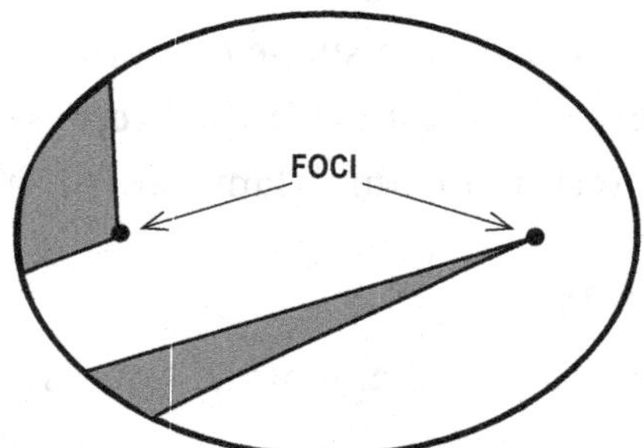


*Illustration of Kepler's Second Law of Planetary Motion*

As we said above, the two *yuds* of the א correspond to the two foci. Since the lower י has been changed to a ד, it is these letters which create the equal areas, and thus these equal sections are represented by the *alef*'s composite letters of ד and י.

It is important to point out that the Magen David, who explains how the format of the letter א alludes to the laws of planetary motion, died two years after the birth of Kepler (1571–1630). His explanation is of a Torah origin and obviously precedes that of Kepler.

The Magen David elaborates on this astronomical theme further. He points out that the letter י that forms the upper arm of the letter א is situated in a northeasterly position, and is thus symbolic of the rising of the sun at dawn which corresponds to the attribute of חסד, kindness. The lower letter י, in a southwesterly position, symbolizes the evening setting of the sun, and the attribute of דין, judgment. The numerical value of the letter א is written out as אחד, which is also an acronym for אלף חסד דין — the letter א represents both the attributes of kindness and justice. The combination of sunrise and sunset, making a complete day, is also represented by the format of the א.

## ◈ Our Connection to Hashem

The letter א, with a numerical value of one, is the first number of the units, while the letter י has a numerical value of ten, which is the first number of the tens. Each transgression against Hashem results in our distancing ourselves from Him. From the position of "one," we are moved to "ten" and then from "ten" to a "hundred." This is represented by the shape of a circle. Hashem is placed at the center and we are on the circumference. The size of the radius is a measure as to how close we are to Hashem at the center. For each transgression, the radius becomes larger, and the distance from Hashem becomes greater.

In *Devarim* 6:4 the letter ד of the word אחד is written as a large letter. This to emphasize that by serving idolatry in the form of the Golden Calf, in essence the Jewish People replaced the letter ד of the word אחד — One (God) — with the letter ר, thereby choosing a foreign god, as we find in *Shemos* 34:14 in the word אחר, "another one." These letters are written as large letters as a reminder that this mistake should not be repeated. Moreover, the numerical value of ר is two hundred, and thus represents the hundreds' place, a further distance from Hashem.

The fulfillment of the letter ד is דלת. After replacing the ד with a ר, the *millui d'millui* produces an expansion of ריש למד תיו. These nine letters have a total numerical value of one thousand, and represent a further distance from Hashem caused by the Jewish People serving the Golden Calf.

As a result of this terrible transgression, Moshe broke the two Tablets that contained the Ten Commandments, and had to ascend again to Heaven to obtain a new set. In his prayers for forgiveness, he said: נצר חסד לאלפים — "...He Who preserves His kindness for two *thousand* generations" (*Shemos* 34:7). This expression can also be explained as a prayer that Hashem should correct the distortion that was caused in the letter א by returning it to its original shape and form.

The Me'or Uketziah explains that even the combination of the letters י'ו'ר' displays the full glory of Hashem. These three letters have a total numerical value of 216, the number of letters that make up the full *Shem haMeforash*. Thus, even though a transgression increases the distance that we remove ourselves from Hashem, it does not in any way affect Hashem or His Glory.

### ◈ The Sedras That Begin with א

The Rokeach points out that there are six *alef*s in the first *pasuk* of *Bereishis*. These correspond to the six *Sedra*s which begin with the letter א. As mentioned in a previous chapter, the fulfillment of the letter א represents the word אֶלֶף, one thousand. Thus, these six *Sedra*s correspond to the six thousand years of the world's existence which is perpetuated through Torah learning. They are the first *pesukim* of the *Sedra*s of *Noach* (*Bereishis* 6:9, אלה תולדת נח), *Pekudei* (*Shemos* 38:21, אלה פקודי המשכן), *Bechukosai* (*Vayikra* 26:3, אם בחקתי תלכו), *Masei* (*Bemidbar* 33:1, אלה מסעי בני ישראל), *Devarim* (*Devarim* 1:1, אלה הדברים), and *Netzavim* (*Devarim* 29:9, אתם נצבים היום).

Similarly, the Pane'ach Raza points out there are a total of five tractates of the Oral Torah that begin with the letter א. They are: *Pe'ah* (אלו דברים), *Pesachim* (אור לארבעה עשר), *Rosh Hashanah* (ארבעה ראשי שנים הם), *Bava Kama* (ארבעה אבות נזיקי), and *Keilim* (אבות הטמאות).

Normally the number five represents the Five Books of the Written Torah and six represents the Six Orders of the Oral Torah. In order to stress their inter-relationship — and the importance of learning both of them together — the number six here is applied to the Written Torah, while the number five is used for the Oral one. True Torah wisdom can only be gleamed by combining together the teachings of the Written and Oral Torahs.

### ◇ Expanding the א: A Pathway to Wisdom

The Megalleh Amukos explains that the shape of the letter א represents the thirty-two avenues of wisdom. The shape of the letter א is composed of two *yud*s with a *vav* in the middle. One of the fulfillments of the letter ו is וו. Thus we can say that the letter א is actually composed of two *yud*s and two *vav*s, which have a combined numerical value of thirty-two, representing these avenues of wisdom. As we said earlier, these thirty-two avenues of wisdom are encapsulated in the Torah, as it begins with the letter ב and ends with the letter ל, which also have a combined numerical value of thirty-two.

Every newly-gained insight provides a stepping-stone to achieve a deeper understanding of the Torah. This is symbolized by the expansion of the middle ו into another of its fulfillments — ואו. The א in the middle can be expanded further, ad infinitum, alluding to the fact the learning process continues eternally and is never-ending. This is the meaning of the *pasuk*: ואאלפך חכמה — "And I will teach you wisdom" (*Iyov* 33:33), the wisdom that is incorporated and represented by the letter א.

◇ ◇ ◇

The symmetrical form of the letter א represents the formation of the teeth. By grouping the two *yud*s together, yielding a numerical value of twenty, and the two *vav*s together, producing a numerical value of twelve, we obtain a pattern which corresponds exactly to the symmetrical formation of the human teeth.

There are a total of twenty milk teeth on the lower and upper jaws, and an additional twelve teeth in the adult set. The Vilna Gaon points out that because teeth are formed in two stages and also work effectively as a combined set on both the upper and lower jaws, they are known as שניים. The root of this word is derived from שני, "second." Teeth are made from enamel, a material similar to ivory—which is known in Scripture as שין. The thirty-two teeth symbolize the thirty-two avenues of wisdom, hence the last set of four teeth are referred to as the wisdom teeth.

### ◈ א Represents Hashem

The fulfillment of the letter א spells out as the word אלף, which means "lord"—one who stands above and apart from the population, and controls all that transpires in his province. The Gemara in *Sanhedrin* (99a) differentiates between the meaning of the words אלף and מלך—"lord" and "king," respectively. The word אלף is used for an uncrowned ruler (מלכותא בלא תאגא), while the term מלך is used for a king that has been crowned by the populace. When Mashiach arrives Hashem (represented by the אלף) will be accepted as מלך over the entire universe.

◈ ◈ ◈

The א also displays our complete dependence on Hashem for all our daily requirements, as Scripture states: כי אתה א-להי ישעי אותך קויתי כל היום—"For You are the God of my salvation, for You I have hoped all day" (*Tehillim* 25:5). The numerical value of the words כל היום (all day) is 111, which is equal to that of אלף, the letter that displays the Omnipresence of Hashem and His ultimate power.

*Degel Machaneh Efrayim* explains that a sinner is known as a חוטא. When he transgresses, he places Hashem — as represented by the א — at the back of his mind. Thus the letter א appears at the end of the spelling of the word חוטא, as a silent, unpronounced letter. In contrast, when asking for forgiveness, our prayers begin with the words אבינו מלכנו and אשמנו, both starting with the letter א. Repentance is our realization that all that we possess emanates from Hashem. The juxtaposition of the letter א at the beginning of these words stresses our full dependence on Him.

◈ ◈ ◈

When the letter א is placed at the beginning of a verb, it provides the subject. For example, an א at the beginning of the verbs שב (to return), שמר (to guard), חלק (to divide) transforms these words into אשוב (*I* will return), אשמור (*I* will guard), אחלק (*I* will divide). As the letter א represents Hashem's unique power, its placement at the beginning of a verb, provides the subject responsible for carrying out this specific action. The letter א was chosen to represent the "I," to stress that the subject performing this action obtains his power only from Hashem. Without the express wish of Hashem, no one can even lift a finger or perform any action whatsoever. If our actions conform to Hashem's wishes, then they will prevail, as the Shlah explains on the *pasuk*: רבות מחשבות בלב איש ועצת ה' היא תקום — "Many thoughts are in man's heart, but the counsel of Hashem — only it will prevail" (*Mishlei* 19:21). The word היא in this *pasuk* can be interpreted as the acronym for אם ירצה השם, "if Hashem wants," then mans thoughts will prevail.

Similarly, the Magen David explains the *pasuk*: דעו כי ה' הוא א-להים הוא עשנו ולא (ולו) אנחנו עמו וצאן מרעיתו — "Know that Hashem, He is God, it is He Who made us and we are His, His people and the sheep of His pasture" (*Tehillim* 100:3). The written word ולא is spelled with a letter א but it should be read as ולו, with the letter ו. If a person recognizes that all that happens in the world emanates from Hashem Himself, which is represented by the letter א of the word ולא, then we are indeed His people — as the word ולו, "to Him" implies.

The letters that compose the fulfillment of the letter אלף, also spell out the word פלא, "wonder." This symbolizes the wonders and miracles that Hashem performs continually. These letters also spell out the word אפל, "darkness," because notwithstanding our perception of Hashem's wonders, His essence remains hidden from human comprehension.

◈ ◈ ◈

The letter א is symmetrical and thus when viewed from different angles its appearance remains the same. This alludes to the fact that a person, regardless of his spiritual level, has the ability to see Hashem's wonders if he so chooses.

## ◈ Correlations Between the Representations of the Letter א

### א-אלף

The letter א (אלף) can represent the number one (אלף) or the number one thousand (אלף), depending on how these letters are punctuated. The letters א'ל'ף' overlap forming a full numeric circle; "one" is at the beginning of the circle and "one thousand" is at the end, returning to the same position in the circle as the "one."

The Megalleh Amukos points out that this dual value of both the number one and one thousand corresponds to the entire history of the world. When אלף is equated to one, it refers the beginning of time, when Hashem was alone before anything else existed. When the אלף represents one thousand, it symbolizes the arrival of both Mashiach ben Yosef and Mashiach ben David at the end of time. The combined numerical values of the words משיח בן יוסף and משיח בן דויד total one thousand — for with their arrival Hashem will be acknowledged as the single ruler of the universe. This double meaning of the word אלף will then be unified into one.

Before the Great Dispersal, the entire world had one unified language. The population used this unified language to plot and rebel against Hashem in building the Tower of Babel. As a punishment, Hashem "confused their language so that they could no longer understand each other." However, the previous unity that prevailed through the use of a common language has remained in the universal use of the decimal system, which the majority of world currencies use. This gives us an indication as to how useful and unifying a universal language was in the past, and will be in the future.

◆ ◆ ◆

One of the features of the Hebrew language is that verbs and nouns are derived from either two-letter (biliteral) or three-letter (triliteral) roots. The number of biliteral roots can be calculated by taking any of the twenty-two letters and matching it with the remaining twenty-one letters and dividing the result by the number of permutations available for those same two letters. Using this formula, we arrive at the following:

$$\frac{22 \times 21}{2} = 231$$

A similar formula is used to calculate the number of possible triliteral roots:

$$\frac{22 \times 21 \times 20}{2 \times 3} = 1{,}540$$

The Ginas Egos points out that the word ישראל can be read as יש + ראל, "there are רא"ל," and that the numerical value of רא"ל is 231, the number of biliteral roots in the *alef-beis*. Moreover, when the letter א represents one thousand (אלף), the numerical value of the word ישראל is 1,540, corresponding to the number of triliteral roots.

The way that the letter א portrays the Uniqueness of Hashem was discussed in the previous section dealing with the shape of the letters. In the chapter dealing with *gematria*, we explained how the generative and degenerative development of the word אחד signifies the unique power of Hashem.

As we have said, the א is composed from two *yud*s and a *vav*, which together have a total numerical value of twenty-six, representing the full Name of Hashem. The *mispar katan* of twenty-six is eight, and there are a total of eight letters in both of the four-letter Names י-ה-ו-ה and א-ד-נ-י — the written and articulated forms of Hashem's Name. The triangular value of the number four is ten, the numerical value of י. Appropriately, both of these four-letter Names are represented by the two *yud*s which form the א. Moreover, the first of these two four-letter Names of Hashem begins with a י, the second Name ends with a י, and in between them there are six letters — six being the numerical value of the letter ו.

The unification of these names is hinted at in the three letters of the word אחד. The ח and ד — with numerical values of eight and four, respectively — refer to the *eight* letters of the two *four*-letter Names. Thus the ח and ד in the word אחד come to explain the composition of the letter א.

It is interesting to note that in Aramaic the number one is spelled simply as חד, for these two letters represent the true unity of these two Names of Hashem — the articulated form together with the written form.

The power that is housed within the combination of these two four-letter names can only be properly understood by the use of Kabbalah. These Names are hinted at in the Gemara in *Chagigah* (13a) which quotes from *Sefer Ben Sira*: במופלא ממך אל תדרוש ובמכוסה ממך אל תחקור — "That which is far removed from your understanding (מופלא), you shall not inquire about; and that which is hidden (מכוסה) from you, you shall not study."

The phrase מופלא ממך אל תדרוש, "that which is far removed from your understanding, you shall not inquire about" is a reference to those who are not on the appropriate level to study these hidden secrets. The highlighted letters, פ'ל'א', spell out אלף, which represents this hidden wisdom.

An additional hint to the Divine Names in the above quote is found in the word ובמכוסה. The numerical value of the Name of Hashem of י-ה-ו-ה (twenty-six, כו) and that of אדנ-י (sixty-five, סה), together form the word כוסה, a further reference to the hidden secrets that are contained with Hashem's Names.

The combined numerical value of these two Names is ninety-one (26 + 65 = 91), the same as the numerical value of the word אמן, "*Amen*." For this reason, after hearing the recitation of a blessing mentioning Hashem's Name, the appropriate response is to answer אמן. This unification of both the written and pronounced Names is exhibited by the correlation of the numbers: Ninety-one is the triangular value of the number thirteen, which is the numerical value of אחד, One.

Furthermore, the word אחד is composed from three letters, which will produce six permutations. We have already explained in the section entitled "Pyramidial Values," how the number six converts to ninety-one, alluding to the fact that Hashem's unifying power expands in all the six directions (see p. 156).

◈ ◈ ◈

The word אחד has both a numerical value and a *mispar katan* of thirteen (1 + 8 + 4 = 13), alluding to both the unity and uniqueness of Hashem that is represented by the letter א.

The *mispar katan* of the fulfillment as אלף is twelve (1 + 3 + 8 = 12), corresponding to the twelve tribes, who unified the Jewish People in their service of Hashem. The word אחד also represents the family unit of Yaakov and his twelve sons. Yaakov (1), together with the *eight* (8) sons born to Leah and her maidservant, and the *four*

(4) sons born to Rachel and her maidservant, correspond to the numerical values of the letters 1 + 8 + 4. Therefore, Yaakov with his twelve sons, were the first who were able to collectively declare the Unity of Hashem, with the proclamation: **שמע ישראל ה' א-להינו ה' אחד** — "Hear O Israel, Hashem is our G-d, Hashem is *One*!"

The three letters of the word **אחד** have six permutations, which produces a total numerical value of seventy-eight (6 x 13 = 78). The sum of all the integers from one to twelve also equals seventy-eight (1 + 2 + 3 + 4 + 5 + 6 + 7 + 8 + 9 + 10 + 11 + 12 = 78). Moreover, the total numerical value of Hashem's Name as it appears three times in the proclamation of **י-ה-ו-ה מלך י-ה-ו-ה מלך י-ה-ו-ה ימלך** is also seventy-eight (26 + 26 + 26 = 78). The declaration of Hashem's Unity (**ה' אחד**) could only be made when there was unity among the twelve tribes. This was accomplished at the end of Yaakov's life, when the twelve brothers lived in harmony, and all previous feelings of jealousy had been dispeled.

These letters — **א'ח'ד'** (1+ 8 + 4) — represent a uniqueness and singularity. The product of these three numbers is thirty-two (1 x 8 x 4 = 32), the numerical value of the word **יחיד**, "singular." These same integers form the equation (1 + 8) x 4 = 36, which is the numerical value of the word **לבד**, "alone."

The *millui d'millui* of the letter **א** is **אלף למד פא**, which contains a total of eight letters. In the section dealing with the letter **ח**, we shall explain how the *mispar katan* of each multiple of eight decreases as the multiples increase, until the *mispar katan* reaches the number one, after which it repeats the same pattern — beginning at eight and decreasing to one — in a perpetual manner. (It is interesting to note that the number twenty-six is the only other number which follows this pattern in its *mispar katan*.) The *mispar katan* of the last letters of this second fulfillment (**אלף למד פא**) total thirteen (1 + 4 + 8 = 13), equating to the *mispar katan* of the word **אחד**. This reinforces the Unity of Hashem that is displayed by the letter **א**.

*Osios d'Rabbi Yitzchak* explains that there is a correlation between the masculine and feminine form of the word אחד. It makes no difference if this word is in the masculine (אחד) or feminine (אחת) form since the two letters ד and ת can be interchanged, as they both belong to the Linguals group.

## The Letter ב

The numerical value of the letter ב is two. The Torah begins with the letter ב, and thus it represents the entire Torah—both the written and the oral. The fulfillment of the ב is בית, meaning a house. The second fulfillment is בית יוד תיו, which has a *mispar katan* of twenty-nine, and a final *mispar katan* of two. (The final *mispar katan* is formed by continually adding the digits of the *mispar katan* until a one-digit result is achieved [2 + 9 = 11; then 1 + 1 = 2].) Thus the numerical value of the letter ב is equal to the final *mispar katan* of its fulfillment. The *mispar katan* of each of the letters of the hidden portion of the *beis*'s second fulfillment—יוד and תיו—also equals two.

The numerical value of the first fulfillment בית is 412. By adding to it the value of the *mispar katan* of the second fulfillment, twenty-nine, we arrive at the total of 441, the numerical value of the word אמת, "truth." The connection between the ב (Torah) and אמת is reinforced in the *pasuk*: ראש דברך אמת—"Your very first utterance is truth" (*Tehillim* 119:160).

The letter ב can be composed from the combination of the letters ד and ו, the latter forming the base. Since the numerical value of the letter ב is two, it represents the beginning of diversification, separation, difference and disparity. Alternatively, these two letters can combine to form the letter ה. The ב and ה possess similar shapes and are also interchangeable using the At–Bach alphabetic structure.

The letter ב can also be composed from three *vavs* (ו), which have total numerical value of eighteen (3 x 6 = 18). The Mishnah (*Pirkei Avos* 5:25) states that eighteen is the recommended age for marriage and the setting up of a new home. This is hinted at in the meaning of the fulfillment of the letter ב — which represents a house (בית).

### ◈ Correlations Between the Representations of the Letter ב

**ב-בית-שני-שתי-תרי**

As just mentioned, the fulfillment of the letter ב is בית, meaning a house. With its numerical value of two, the ב represents the second of the Ten *Sefiros*, that of חכמה, wisdom. We find a connection between these two ideas in the *pasuk*: בחכמה יבנה בית — "With wisdom a house is built" (*Mishlei* 24:3).

As explained elsewhere, the fulfillment of בית represents the *Beis haMikdash*. This can be seen from the first word of the Torah, בראשית; by expanding the large letter ב, we can read it as **בית** ראשית, the large house of utmost importance, referring to the *Beis haMikdash*, the Holy Temple, which served as the Jewish House of primary importance.

In the first *Beis haMikdash*, the Holy Ark housed the two tablets containing the Ten Commandments. The Gemara in *Yoma* (21b) states that the Holy Ark was not present in the Second *Beis haMikdash*; in its place, a black rock, known as the אבן שתיה, protruded from the ground. Furthermore, the word **שתי**ה incorporates the representation of שתי. Thus the representations of ב-בית-שני-שתי are all interrelated.

We received the Torah after Moshe Rabbeinu had spent forty days in Heaven to obtain it. These forty days are symbolized by the numerical value of the letter מ, which when added to the words שני and שתי form the words שנים and שתים, respectively.

In the At–Bash transformation, the letter ב is interchangeable with the letter ש. Thus, בית becomes שתי. Moreover, the fulfillment of the letter ש is שין, the same letters that form the word שני.

Similarly, in the Ayik–Bekar alphabetic structure the letter ב transforms to ר, and thus the word בית can become תרי, which means "second" in Aramaic.

The ב represents the two inclinations — the *yetzer ha-ra* (the evil inclination) and the *yetzer ha-tov* (the good inclination) that are "housed" within every person. In order to overcome the *yetzer ha-ra* and refrain from following the wrong path, it is necessary to have יראת שמים, fear of Hashem. The letters of the word יראת incorporate the letters that spell תרי with the addition of the letter א, which represents the requisite fear of Hashem that enables a person to subdue his *yetzer ha-ra*, so that he can serve Hashem correctly with *both* of his inclinations.

◈ ◈ ◈

The correlation of ב–בית–שני is reflected in the physical construction of *tefillin*. The *tefillin shel rosh* display two (ש) *shins* — one on either side of the בית, the special housing which contains the parchments. In the At–Bash alphabetic structure the ב transforms into the letter ש. The letter ש fulfills as שין, which also spells out the word שני.

The ב is known as both שני, "second," and שתי, "two." Thus if we substitute these words for the ב in the term אלף–בית, the result is the combination of אלף–שני–שתי. The final two letters of these words (אלף–שני–שתי) spell out the word תפילין, *tefillin.*

◈ ◈ ◈

Alternatively the letter ב corresponds to the two redeemers who are destined to come to deliver the Jewish nation, Mashiach ben Yosef and Mashiach ben David. The numerical value of ב' משיח, the two Mashiachs, equates to that of the word שני.

◈ ◈ ◈

As mentioned earlier, the letter ב represents both the Oral Torah and the Written Torah. Without the complete Torah one would not know how to properly serve Hashem. In Chapter 101 of *Tehillim*, David haMelech praises the importance of purity and truth in serving Hashem: **הלך בדרך תמים הוא ישרתני לא ישב בקרב ביתי** עשה רמיה — "He who walks the path of perfect innocence, he shall serve Me. There shall not dwell in the midst of My House one who practices deceit" (*Tehillim* 101:6–7). This *pasuk* combines all of the above-mentioned interpretations for the meaning of the letter *beis* (ב–בית–שני–שתי–תרי). The word ביתי, "My House," incorporates the meanings of ב–בית, while the word ישרתני, "he shall serve Me," comprises the letters used in שני–שתי–תרי.

Every Jewish home (בית) is required to have a *mezuzah* affixed to its doorposts. The *mezuzah* guards and protects the Jewish home and its contents, as implied in the *pasuk*: הנה לא ינום ולא יישן שומר ישראל — "Behold, neither does He slumber or sleep, the Guardian of Israel" (*Tehillim* 121:4). The letters of the word ישן, spell out the word שני, thereby connecting the words בית, "house," and שני together.

Hashem's Name of שד-י is written on the outer surface of the *mezuzah*. This Name is an acronym for שומר דלתות ישראל, "Guardian of the gates of Yisrael," and represents Hashem in His capacity as our Protector. By using the letters of the Linguals set, ד'ט'ל'נ'ת', we can transform this Name into both the words שני and שתי.

A *mezuzah* contains the first two chapters of the *Shema*, which are written on twenty-two lines corresponding to the number of letters of the *alef-beis*. The final *pasuk* of each of these two chapters, instruct us to "write them on the doorpost of your house and upon your gates." In the first chapter of the *Shema*, the word *mezuzos* is spelled מזזות, whereas in the second chapter it is spelled מזוזות, incorporating an extra letter ו. The complete *pasuk* in the first chapter therefore contains twenty-four letters, whereas the corresponding one in the second chapter contains twenty-five letters. These correspond to the twenty-five letters contained in the first *pasuk* of the *Shema* — שמע ישראל י-ה-ו-ה א-להינו י-ה-ו-ה אחד — and the twenty-four letters contained in our response: ברוך שם כבוד מלכותו לעולם ועד.

## THE LETTER ג

As we have said, the letter א represents unity, while the letter ב represents duality. The letter ג, with a numerical value of three, represents a degree of separation and dilution. For example, the word *get* (a bill of divorce) begins with a letter ג because it represents separation.

The correlation between the number three and the concept of separation is alluded to in the passage: **והשטן** עמד על ימינו **לשטנו** ויאמר ה' אל **השטן** יגער ה' בך **השטן** ויגער ה' בך הבחר בירושלם הלא זה **אוד** מצל מאש — "And the *Satan* was standing on his right, to accuse him. And [the angel of] Hashem said to the *Satan*, 'May Hashem rebuke you, O *Satan*; may Hashem Who chose Jerusalem rebuke you. Did he not merit this as he was plucked from the fire?'" (*Zechariah* 3:1–2). This phrase contains the word *Satan* four times, each instance separated by three words. This spacing dilutes and thus weakens the power of the *Satan*.

The *shofar* blasts on Rosh Hashanah are meant to confuse the *Satan* in order to weaken his power. The Rokeach points out that it is for this reason that all the *shofar* blasts are performed in sets of three.

The Maharil states that the word אוד, mentioned above, alludes to Rosh Hashanah, as its first day can never fall on a Sunday, Friday or Wednesday — the first, fifth and fourth day of the week — which coincide with the numerical values of the letters א'ו'ד'.

◇ ◇ ◇

The letter ג fulfills as גימל, which can be translated as either "to nourish," "benevolent," "a camel" or "a bridge."

The eight letters that make up the hidden fulfillment of the word גימל (גימל יוד מם למד) have a final *mispar katan* of three, the same as the numerical value of the original letter ג. The complete fulfillment contains a total of twelve letters, a number whose *mispar katan* is also three.

The *mispar katan* of גימל is eleven, which equates to the *mispar katan* of Hashem's Name of אדנ-י. The word גימל also equals twenty-six, when adding the *mispar katan* of each of the levels of its generative sequence:

| | | | | |
|---|---|---|---|---|
| ג | = | 3 | = | 3 |
| גי | = | 3 + 10 | = | 4 |
| גימ | = | 3 + 10 + 40 | = | 8 |
| גימל | = | 3 + 10 + 40 + 30 | = | 11 |
| | | **Total** | = | **26** |

Thus the ג also connects to both of Hashem's Names of י-ה-ו-ה and אדנ-י.

The letter ג is unique in that it is the only letter of the *alef-beis* whose standard fulfillment (גימל) is comprised of four letters. It is symbolic of both of the four-letter Names of Hashem of י-ה-ו-ה and אדנ-י. Appropriately, the letter ג is the first letter in the alphabetic sequence that is adorned with three crowns, known as תגין (this will be elaborated on in Chapter 7). The second fulfillment of the letter ג spells out גימל יוד מם למד, which has a total numerical value of 257, alluding to the נזר ("tiara") that adorns the letter ג, as the word נזר also has a numerical value of 257.

◆ ◆ ◆

The ג is composed from a combination of the letters ז, ו and the letter י as its foot to the left. Together, they form the word זיו — the shine and luster of Hashem's Countenance. Any two of these three composite letters can join together to represent Hashem, each in a different way. The two letters ו and י are both used in spelling Hashem's

Name. The *mispar katan* of the letters ו and ז total thirteen, the same as of the word אחד, thereby displaying the Unity of Hashem. Also, the fulfillments of the letters י and ז (יוד and זין) have a total numerical value of eighty-seven. As mentioned earlier, eighty-seven is the numerical value of the words of אני י-ה-ו-ה, "I am Hashem."

Moreover, there is a unique connection between the number three, the number eighty-seven and the shining Countenance of Hashem. When adding the numerical values of the letters of Hashem's Name of י-ה-ו-ה, as well as the numerical values of both the four letters that precede them and the four letters that follow them in the alphabetic order, we obtain the following:

| | | | |
|---|---|---|---|
| Hashem's Name | ה + ו + ה + י | = | 26 |
| Letters Before | ד + ה + ד + ט | = | 22 |
| Letters Before | ו + ז + ו + כ | = | 39 |
| **Total Numerical Value** | | **=** | **87** |

The total numerical value of these three transformations of Hashem's Name equate to the fulfillment of the composite letters of the letter ג.

The numerical value of three has significance with regard to the natural divisions within the *alef-beis*. Each letter of the *alef-beis* possesses a unique numerical value that naturally divides them into three distinct groups. The first group consists of the letters ranging from א until ט, which possess corresponding numerical values of the units, ranging from one until nine. These total forty-five (1 + 2 + 3 + 4 + 5 + 6 + 7 + 8 + 9 + = 45), a number that has a *mispar katan* of nine (4 + 5 = 9), representing eternal truth.

The second group is comprised by the letters from י until צ, which have numerical values ranging from ten to ninety, incorporating the tens. These total 450 (10 + 20 + 30 + 50 + 60 + 70 + 80 + 90 = 450), which again has a *mispar katan* of nine (4 + 5 + 0 = 9).

The third group is represented by the letters from ק to ץ, which have numerical values ranging from one hundred until nine hundred, incorporating all the hundreds. These total forty-five hundred (100 + 200 + 300 + 400 + 500 + 600 + 700 + 800 + 900 = 4500), which also has a *mispar katan* of nine. These three individual groups each display the eternal truth that is incorporated into each of the letters of the *alef-beis*. The three letters that make up the composition of the word אמת, "truth," have respective numerical values of one, forty and four hundred, representing the units, tens and hundreds of our number system. This same division of the letters is formed by the Ayik–Bekar alphabetic structure.

*Midrash Talpios* explains that we also find that the entire *alef-beis* is divided into three sections with regards to the number of crowns that each letter contains. The letters of שעטנז גץ are each adorned by three crown. The letters בדה חקי have one crown each, while the letters of מלאכת סופר have no crowns at all. These three groupings of the letters are alluded to in the word אותיות, "letters," which is mentioned three times in *Yeshayahu* (41:23, 44:7, 45:11). Moreover, the ג is the first letter of the *alef-beis* to possess three crowns.

## ◈ Correlations Between the Representations of the Letter ג

### ג-שלש

In the Ayik–Bekar transformation method, the letters ג, ל and ש belong to the same alphabetic set (אי"ק בכ"ר גל"ש), and therefore can be interchanged. Thus each of the letters of the word שלש can be transformed into the letter ג.

### ג-גימל-שלש

The Gemara in *Shabbos* 88a (see p. 161) explains the correlation between the number three and how the Torah was given. Scripture is divided into three sections known as Torah, *Nevi'im* and *Ke-*

*suvim*. Likewise, it was given to a nation which is divided into three groups: *Kohen*, *Levi* and *Yisrael*. The Torah was given to us by Moshe Rabbeinu, who was the third oldest in his family, after three days of abstention and purification, in the third month of the year. These groups of triplicates are incorporated in the combination of the meanings of ג-גימל-שלש and are hinted at in the hidden fulfillment of the letter ג (**גימל**), which is an acronym for **יום משה לחדש**.

The three sections of the Written Torah are the *Five* Books of Moses, the *eight* Books of the Prophets and the *eleven* Books of Writings. The "base" of this arithmetic progression of 5, 8, 11 is three, providing the "base" for the entire Torah that was given in a triplicate form.

The Magen David explains that the letter ג represents the three Patriarchs in whose merit we received the Torah. Since they were the first to "coronate" Hashem as the Master of the universe, it is appropriate that this letter should be the first one to be adorned with three crowns.

The Patriarchs are symbolized by the three-armed letter ש, each corresponding to one of the arms. Thus they are represented in the first letter ש of the word **שלש**. The second letter (ל) of this representation fulfills as the word למד, and represents the learning and teaching of the entire Torah, which we received in triplicate form. The last ש in this representation (**שלש**) alludes to the three groups — *Kohen*, *Levi* and *Yisrael* (כהן לוי ישראל) — who received the Torah and are obliged to learn it.

Moreover, the Gemara in *Kiddushin* (30a) teaches us that a person should divide his learning hours into three parts. He should allocate a third of his time to Chumash, a third to Mishnah, and a third to learning Gemara. This explains the different permutations of the ג-גימל-שלש and the lessons they come to portray.

### ג-תְלַת

The Torah states: למען ירבו ימיכם וימי בניכם על האדמה אשר נשבע ה׳ לאבתיכם לתת להם כימי השמים על הארץ — "In order to prolong your days and the days of your children on the land that Hashem has promised to your forefather to give them, like the days of the Heaven on the earth" (*Devarim* 11:21).

Hashem promised the *three* Patriarchs the Land of Israel, for the sake of building the *Beis haMikdash* so that there would be a place for His *Shechinah* to dwell. The first *Beis haMikdash* stood for 410 years and the second one for 420 years, totaling 830 years. Eight hundred and thirty is the numerical value of the word **לתת**, "to give." The Aramaic word for three is **תלת**, the same letters as the word **לתת**.

## THE LETTER ד

ד

The letter ד has a numerical value of four. It fulfills as **דלת**, which translates as "door," and represents the poor man standing at the doorway when collecting charity. The second fulfillment is **דלת למד תיו**, which is comprised of nine letters — nine symbolizing absolute truth. The *mispar katan* of the word **דלת** is eleven, the same as the *mispar katan* of the Name of **אדני**. This Name acts like a doorway that leads to His other Names. Eleven is also the *mispar katan* of the fulfillment of the previous letter ג, which explains their juxtaposition in the *alef-beis*.

It is interesting to note that from the entire *alef-beis*, this letter ד has the highest numerical value for its hidden fulfillment, alluding to the extent of the poor man's deficiency.

The numerical value of the Name of **אדני** is sixty-five, which equates to that of **מזוזה**, *mezuzah*, which is placed on the doorway (**דלת**) of our homes. This corresponds to the *pasuk*: **אשרי אדם שמע לי לשקד על דלתתי יום יום לשמר מזוזת פתחי** — "Fortunate is the man who listens to me to watch by my doors day by day, to guard the doorposts to my entrances" (*Mishlei* 8:34).

Spelling out the word **דלת** in a progressive generative sequence

(ד-דל-דלת), results in a *mispar katan* of twenty-two (when adding up the *mispar katan* of each of these letters) and a final *mispar katan* of four (2 + 2 = 4). This is the same as the numerical value of the original letter ד.

Although this letter belongs to the seven simple shaped letters, its format resembles two *vavs*, one vertical and one horizontal. Each letter ו fulfills as ואו, with a numerical value of thirteen, the same as the word אחד. The fulfillment of these two *vavs* have a combined numerical value of twenty-six, the same as Hashem's Name.

The opening *pasuk* of the שמע reads: שמע ישראל ה' א-להינו ה' אחד — "Hear O Israel, Hashem is our G-d, Hashem is One." The Unity of Hashem is proclaimed by the word אחד, which ends with a large ד. As explained elsewhere, a large letter can be interpreted as if it were doubled. When using the fulfillment of the composite letter ו (ואו) this large ד equates to fifty-two, since it is equivalent to four *vavs* (4 x 13 = 52). Appropriately, this large letter ד is used in the *pasuk* that contains the Name of Hashem twice, for together that also equals fifty-two (26 + 26 = 52).

We know that Eliyahu haNavi is destined to announce the arrival of Mashiach. His name (אליהו) also has the numerical value of fifty-two. With his arrival, the complete universe will acknowledge the Unity of Hashem as portrayed by ה' אחד.

## ◈ Correlations Between the Representations of the Letter ד

### ד-דלת

The letter ד has a very similar shape to that of the final letter ך, signifying a connection between them. The letter ד is articulated as דלת representing the poor man (דַל) who collects charity by going from door to door (דֶלֶת). The final letter ך is known as the כף פשוטה, which denotes "an outstretched and open hand." The similarity between these two letters stresses the importance of giving charity to the poor person, generously and with an open hand.

*Tehillim* 74:21 states: אל ישב דך נכלם עני ואביון יהללו שמך — "Let them not turn back the oppressed in shame, let the poor and destitute praise Your Name." If one does not give generously to the poor, he will become oppressed. This is appropriately expressed by the use of the combination of the letters ך + ד to spell the word דך, "oppressed," in this *pasuk*.

We mentioned in the previous section that the juxtaposition of the letters ג and ד represents the giving of charity to the needy, as it is the acronym of גומל דלים. The fulfillment of the letter ג is גימל and that of the letter ד is דלת. The *mispar katan* of each of these fulfillments is eleven. We have previously shown how all the digits from one to ten form five groups, each totaling eleven. The number eleven symbolizes the pairing together of two diverse numbers — in the same fashion that a donor (גומל) is paired together with the recipient (דלים). If we add together the *mispar katan* of both of these two letters, we get twenty-two, a number that represents the entire *alef-beis*.

The second fulfillments of גימל and דלת are גימל יוד מם למד and דלת למד תיו. Six of these seven words (excluding the word מם) have a *mispar katan* of eleven. If we combine the six sets to make three groups of two's, then each group has a combined *mispar katan* of twenty-two. These letters are followed in the alphabetic order by the letters ה and ו, respectively, which have a combined numerical value of eleven. They fulfill as הה and וו, which also have a combined numerical value of twenty-two.

The letter ד is similar in shape to the letter ר, apart from the upper right hand corner. Just as the letter דלת represents the poor person, similarly, the letter ריש represents the pauper who is known as רש, an impoverished person. The combination of these two letters forms the word רד, which signifies a person who has lost his wealth and has fallen from his previous financial status.

The letter ד, with its numerical value of four, has a triangular value of ten (1 + 2 + 3 + 4 = 10) — the numerical value of the first letter of Hashem's Name of י-ה-ו-ה. Thus, this י incorporates the numerical values of the first four letters of the *alef-beis*.

During the festival of Sukkos, we sit in *sukkos* (booths). The numerical value of the word סוכה (*sukkah*) is ninety-one, the same as that of the written and articulated Names of Hashem.

The Gemara (*Sukkah* 8b) mentions that there are eight types of *sukkos*. These are grouped into two sets of four and represented by the acronyms סוכת גנב"ך and סוכת רקב"ש (a detailed explanation of these can be found in the Gemara itself). These groups correspond to the combination of Hashem's two four-letter Names, which, as we have said, equates to the numerical value of the word סוכה.

The Festival of Sukkos is also the time when we include a special prayer for rain, known as *Tefillas Geshem*. Rain is the most important requirement that enables vegetation to grow and produce our essential foods. By praying for rainfall, we are acknowledging our total dependence on Hashem for our daily essentials. Without His continuous kindness, we would all starve. We have already explained how the letter א represents the unifying power of Hashem. On Sukkos we are commanded to take the ארבע מינים, the Four Species. The letters of the word ארבע spells out רעב-א our appreciation that without the provisions supplied by Hashem (א) we would remain hungry and starve (רעב).

## The Letter ה

ה

The numerical value of the letter ה is five, and is composed from the letters ד + י; and the sum of these letters' *mispar katan* is also five. Alternatively, it can be composed from the letters ד + ו, which have a combined final *mispar katan* of one, thereby displaying the Unity of Hashem.

This letter fulfills in one of four different ways: הא, הה, הי or היא, which translate as "behold," "to take seed" or "to be broken."

The Magen David begins his explanation of the letter ה by quoting a *pasuk* that refers to propagation: הא לכם זרע וזרעתם את האדמה — "Here is seed for you, sow the land" (*Bereishis* 47:23). He points out that since the first word in this phrase is an expansion of the letter ה, the ה must be connected to reproduction, as well.

When a woman gives birth to a child, she creates the next generation. Women are referred to by the general term נקבה, female. In the Hebrew language, most words ending with a ה are feminine. Here, too, the ה of נקבה indicates the feminine gender, and it can be read as **ה** + נֶקֶב. The word נֶקֶב means an opening, in this case the opening through which childbirth transpires. Thus, the word נקבה symbolizes the female in a very literal way.

The last of the Ten *Sefiros*, מלכות — through which Hashem's blessings emerge directly into our physical world — is referred to as the feminine *Sefirah*. As stated above, the first ה in Hashem's four-letter Name represents the *Sefirah* of בינה, the *Sefirah* that is responsible for conception. Counting upwards from the last *Sefirah* towards the first one, the *Sefirah* of בינה is the seventh *Sefirah*. This connection between the number seven and the letter ה is hinted at in the *pasuk*: עקרה ילדה **שבעה** — "The barren woman has given birth to seven" (*Shmuel* I 2:5). These three words — עקר**ה**, ילד**ה** and שבע**ה** — each end with the letter ה. Rashi explains that the phrase עקרה ילדה שבעה refers to Chanah, the wife of Elkanah. Yet Chanah had only five children, not seven. Rashi points out that the numerical value of the word שבעה is 377, which equates to the value of שמואל, the son whom Chanah bore. Thus, the *pasuk* can be read as עקרה ילדה שמואל. However, *Osios d'Rabbi Yitzchak* explains that the word שבעה here is a reference to the seventh *Sefirah*, בינה, which, as we said, is the source of fertility.

In speaking of an unborn child the Gemara uses the expression:

עובר ירך אמו — "the fetus inside the mother['s womb]" (*Gittin* 23b), explaining that although the unborn child is within its mother, they are two separate entities. The letter ה is one of only two letters which are made up of two disjointed parts. This is likened to a fetus in its mother's womb — two separate entities yet very much connected.

The ה is composed from the letter ד and the inverted letter י, which forms its foot. The letter ד fulfills as the word דלת which represents the opening, the "doorway," of the mother's womb, as we find in the *pasuk*: כי לא סגר **דלתי** בטני — "For He did not shut the doors of my womb" (*Iyov* 3:9). The inverted small letter י represents the developing fetus that is usually in a head-down position prior to birth. Their combination forms the letter ה, representing the expression עובר ירך אמו, the fetus that is fully enclosed within the womb.

The Gemara in *Menachos* (29b) explains the shape of the letter ה with the following words:

> Why was this physical world created through the use of the letter ה? Because this world is comparable to an entrance hall [that leads to the banquet suite of the next world], and anybody is at liberty to leave if he so wishes. (This is denoted by the wide opening at the bottom of the letter.) And why is the foot of the letter hanging [on the left hand side]? To allow those who repent to return and rejoin [through the upper aperture]. Why does the person not return through the bottom hole [through which he originally departed]? This supports Reish Lakish who said: "What is the meaning of [the *pasuk*]: 'With the cynics he will act cynically, but to the humble He will grant favor' (*Mishlei* 3:34)? It means that if one wants to purify himself, they will help him to achieve this; and if one wants to defile himself, they provide an opening for him to do so." And why is there a crown on the letter ה? Hashem says, that if he repents, then I will bind him with a crown.

This passage is almost identical to the passage that discusses the significance of the letter ק. These two letters, ה and ק, are the only ones that are composed from two distinct disjointed parts, as they both represent very similar ideas. I will combine their teachings together in this section, but they apply equally to both letters.

Both of these letters represent a sinner who wants to repent and return to the correct path.

Rambam (*Hilchos Teshuvah*. ch. 2) explains that proper repentance requires a firm and sincere commitment not to repeat that sin in the future. His repentance is complete when he is faced with the opportunity to repeat that transgression, yet withstands the temptation and does not sin.

The Rambam also lists the virtues of repentance (ibid., ch. 7). A sincere repentant becomes even closer to Hashem than a righteous person who never sinned at all. The sinner who repents has the added advantage of having overcome his evil inclination. For this effort, he rises to a higher level than a righteous person who never had to withstand a similar temptation.

The Rambam expounds on the Gemara's explanation as to why the "return" cannot be effected through the bottom opening of these letters. He explains that since the former sinner is sincere in his desire to repent and withstands the temptation to repeat his sin, Hashem gives him a different route back — a separate gate is created towards the top of these two letters through which he can now enter and become close to Hashem Himself.

The Ben Ish Chai states that the closeness to Hashem that the repentant person achieves is alluded to in the passage: רחצתי את רגלי איככה אטנפס דודי שלח ידו מן החור ומעי המו עליו — "I have washed my feet, how can I soil them? My Beloved One stretched out His hand through the hole, and my insides are stirred because of Him" (*Shir HaShirim* 5:3–4).

This *pasuk* refers to the sinner who has made a complete commitment to repent and return to Hashem, which is alluded to in the first part of this passage: רחצתי את רגלי איככה אטנפס — "I have washed my feet, how can I soil them?" The letters of the words את רגלי ("my feet") spell out אל תרי"ג, "to 613," as the washing the soiled feet represents a return to the observance of the 613 commandments of the Torah. As a direct result of this sincere repentance, Hashem stretches out His Hand, as it were, through the hole at the side of the ה order to accept his repentance. This is the meaning of the second half of the passage: דודי שלח ידו מן החור — "My Beloved One stretches out His hand through the hole."

The Rokeach points out that a universal repentance is destined to take place before the arrival of Mashiach, when the entire Jewish People will return to the correct Torah path. This is alluded to in the phrase: שלח ידו מן החור — "[Hashem] stretches out His hand through the hole." The words שלח ידו have a numerical value of 358, the same as for the word Mashiach (משיח).

There is a difference of opinion in Halachah as to the construction of the final letter ה in Hashem's four-letter Name. The Beis Yosef holds that both *hei*s have the same format, namely that of a ד and a י. The Arizal, however, maintains that the final letter takes the form of a ד and a ו. The Shlah writes that these two opinions give rise to a true argument that can be classified as לשם שמים, an argument to determine the true wish of Hashem. Since these arguments are for the sake of understanding the ultimate truth, Hashem combines them both to form the expression דודי (דו + די), one of true affection and love.

However, both opinions are incorporated in the phrase דודי שלח ידו — "My Beloved One stretches out His hand," as the same letters are used to form the word ידו. Hashem will always stretch out His Hand to assist the repentant.

Of these two opinions, which format makes it easier for him to return? It is the ה when it is composed from a ד and a י, for it leaves a larger aperture, and therefore assists him to climb back into the fold.

The Chasam Sofer points out that this idea is reinforced in our *davening*, when we say: הפותח יד בתשובה לקבל פושעים וחטאים — "[You] Who opens a hand to the repentant, to welcome rebels and sinners." The phrase "opens a hand" (יד) is used here to indicate that Hashem helps a person to repent, since, as we said, the combination of י and ד to form the letter ה creates a larger aperture in the ה, facilitating repentance.

The Magen David gives an interesting insight into how the shape of the letter ה indicates repentance. In the spelling of Hashem's Name of י-ה-ו-ה, the letters י and ו precede the letter ה in both the first and second part of the Name. These two letters represent the wicked person who has turned his back away from Hashem and His commandments, in that they appear behind the *hei*s in the spelling of His Name. Yet when these same two letters are used to form the lower part of the letter ה, they complete the composition of the ה, which represents subjugation. When a sinner wishes to repent, he subjugates himself to Hashem's commandments, Thus, the shape and composition of the letter ה, and its position within the spelling of Hashem's Name, represent the journey of the repentant sinner.

Hashem wants the wicked to repent, waiting patiently for them to do so. This theme is stressed in the final part of the *Ne'ilah* prayer of Yom Kippur, quoting from the prophet Yeshayahu: יעזב רשע דרכו ואיש און מחשבתיו וישב אל ה׳ וירחמהו ואל א-להינו כי ירבה לסלוח — "The wicked should abandon their ways, and the men of iniquity their thoughts, and return to Hashem, Who shall have mercy on them, and [return] to our God, for He will freely pardon him" (*Yeshayahu* 55:7).

This *pasuk* contains a total of fifteen words, which corresponds to the number of words contained in the fifth *berachah* of the *Amidah* prayer, which specifically refers to repentance:

> השיבנו אבינו לתורתך וקרבנו מלכנו לעבודתך והחזירנו בתשובה שלמה לפניך ברוך אתה ה׳ הרוצה בתשובה — Bring us back, our Father, to your Torah, and bring us near, our King, to Your service, and influence us to return in perfect repentance before You. Blessed are You, Hashem, Who desires repentance.

This *berachah* also begins and ends with the letter ה, as it represents repentance.

The Eitz Yosef points out that in all of the *Amidah,* we refer to Hashem as "our Father" only in this *berachah* of repentance and in the following one where we pray for forgiveness. This teaches us that even when a son has rebelled against his Father, if he repents and seeks forgiveness from his Father in Heaven, he is welcomed back with compassion. The Rokeach points out that in all of Scripture Hashem is referred to as the "Father" of the Jewish People a total of fifteen times.

The Chasam Sofer comments that the numerical value of the word רשע, meaning a wicked person, is 570, and that of the word דרך, the path that one pursues, is 224. If we subtract the numerical value of the word דרך from that of the word רשע — symbolizing the wicked person's departure from his previous evil ways — we get 346, which is the numerical value of the word רצון, "[Hashem's] will." Hashem's explicit desire that the wicked person abandon his evil ways is substantiated in this mathematical equation, providing a literal interpretation to the *pasuk* in *Yeshayahu* cited above: **יעזב רשע דרכו** ואיש און מחשבתיו — "The wicked should abandon their ways, and the men of iniquity their thoughts."

The Baruch sheAmar has a different interpretation of how the shape of the letter ה represents repentance. He explains that when the letter ה is composed from the letters ד and י, the top of the letter ד symbolizes the spiritual heavens above us and the World to Come. The vertical side of the letter ד represents this physical world, through which one can reach the spiritual heights of the next world. The small foot of the letter ה is an inverted י, with the foot of the letter pointing upwards, representing the Jewish soul that naturally aspires to return to its original source. This Jewish soul has a constant choice to make while living on this physical planet. He can either fall down through the deep hole, formed by the floor of the letter ה or, alternatively, he can aspire to gain spiritual heights, climbing upwards in order to gain his allotted place in the World to Come.

There are two different types of repentance. The lower form is known as תשובה מיראה — a repentance instigated by the fear of receiving Divine retribution. This lower form is represented by the letter ה, which has a numerical value of five. The higher form is referred to as תשובה מאהבה, a repentance instigated by a pure love of Hashem and a desire to obey His wishes; this form is represented by the letter ק, which has a numerical value of one hundred. In order to go from תשובה מיראה to תשובה מאהבה, one needs to multiply the numerical value of ה by twenty to get to that of ק (5 x 20 = 100). The numerical value of the word עשרים, "twenty," is 620, which equates to the value of the word כתר — the crown that Hashem binds onto every repentant person. The Chasam Sofer points out that even if this wicked person had been previously guilty of the punishment of כרת, of being cut off from the rest of the Jewish People, his sincere repentance has the power to switch the order of these letters from כרת to produce a כתר, a crown. This is not just a play on the order of the letters; it has a deeper meaning, as well.

The Gemara teaches us that sincere repentance has the inherent power to change all previously committed transgressions into positive merits. Repentance is one of the positive commandments of the Torah. Yet, without a transgression, there can be no repentance. Thus, a person's repentance is instigated by his previous sin. It is therefore understandable why even the sentence of כרת can be changed through repentance, to produce a כתר, a suitable and appropriate crown, as repentance provides many new merits.

These two types of repentance are represented by the two formats of the letter ה itself. The loftier תשובה מאהבה, a repentance that is instigated by pure love of Hashem, is represented by the format of ד + י, since the letter י was used to create the higher spiritual sphere of the World to Come. The second type, תשובה מיראה, a repentance that is instigated by the fear of receiving Divine retribution, is represented by the format of ו + ד, as the letter ו represents the stick that is used to punish the wicked.

The letter ה represents repentance and a return to the teachings of the Torah. The prophet admonishes us: דרשו ה' בהמצאו — "Seek Hashem when He is to be found" (*Yeshayahu* 55:6). Where is He to be found? The answer is in the wording of the *pasuk*. The word בהמצאו can be understood to mean בה + מצאו, "[Hashem] is to be found within the letter ה," the letter that represents repentance.

There appears to be another connection between the letters ה and ק which is mentioned in the *pasuk*: ורדפו מכם חמשה מאה ומאה מכם רבבה ירדפו — "Five of you will pursue one hundred, and one hundred from among you will pursue ten thousand" (*Vayikra* 26:8). The first part of the *pasuk* connects the number five with that of one hundred, corresponding to the numerical values of the letters ה and ק, respectively. As stated above, the number twenty is the multiple needed to get from ה to ק. In the second part, the *pasuk* connects the number one hundred with the number ten thousand, which has a five times higher multiple (100), than the first part of the *pasuk*.

The Gemara in *Sanhedrin* (60b) brings down that initially the two luminaries, the sun and the moon, were created of equal size. However, the moon complained that it was impossible for two kings to share the same crown. As a result, Hashem reduced it in size.

However, we are told that with the advent of Mashiach the diminished light of the moon will return to its original strength, as the prophet tells us: והיה אור הלבנה כאור החמה וכו' — "And the light of the moon shall be like the light of the sun..." (*Yeshayahu* 30:26).

The final letter ה of Hashem's Name represents the final *Sefirah* of מלכות, Kingship, and, as we have said, can be written as combination of ו + ד or י + ד. The Magen David explains that the final letter ה of Hashem's Name corresponds to the moon, which shared the same royal crown with the sun at the time of Creation. The letter ה when written as a combination of ו + ד represents the moon in its original state, before it was diminished in size. When written as

י + ד, it represents the moon in its diminished form, as the letter י is smaller and is actually a contracted form of the letter ו. The fact that the moon will regain its formal strength is alluded to in the hidden fulfillment of the letter י (יוד), as the combination of the letters ד and ו represent its original illumination.

### ◈ Correlations Between the Representations of the Letter ה

**ה–הא–הה–הי**

Possessing a numerical value of five, the letter ה represents the Five Books of the Written Torah. Each of the above fulfillments signifies a different aspect of the Written Torah. The Ten Commandments were written on two tablets of stone, each containing five commandments. This is symbolized by the expansions of הי and הה respectively. The unifying power of the Torah is represented by the expansion of הא, which has a numerical value of six, thereby representing the six orders of the Oral Torah. The combined expansions of הה and היא have a numerical value of twenty-six, a number that equates to the numerical value of י-ה-ו-ה, the Name Hashem used when He gave us the Torah.

We have already discussed how the Al–Bam alphabetic structure symbolizes Torah learning and teaching. We have also discussed why the letters א and ל are chosen to begin the Al–Bam alphabetic structure (see p. 62ff). The total numerical value of the three common expansions, הא–הה–הי, is thirty-one, the same as the numerical value of the opening set (א"ל) of Al–Bam.

The Unity of Hashem is further displayed by the above three fulfillments in the following manner: The expansion הה has a *mispar katan* of one, which intrinsically represents the Unity of Hashem. The other two expansions, הא and הי, each have a *mispar katan* of six, which correspond to the letter ו. This fulfills as ואו, with a numerical value of thirteen, which equates to the word אחד, One, thereby representing the Unity of Hashem, as well. Furthermore, the letters of the expansion as הא have numerical values of five and one respectively. By summing the squares of these numbers we arrive at twenty-six ($5^2 + 1^2 = 26$), the same numerical value as Hashem's Name.

◆ ◆ ◆

The *Zohar* states that there are four levels of Creation: (1) *Atzilus*, (2) *Beriyah*, (3) *Yetzirah*, and (4) *Assiyah*. The *Arizal* explains that each of these levels corresponds to the standard fulfillments of Hashem's Name. These fulfillments are referred to according to the fulfillment of the letter ה that appears in each one (either הא, הה or הי). The standard fulfillments are:

יוד + הי + ויו + הי = 72
יוד + הי + ואו + הי = 63
יוד + הא + ואו + הא = 45
יוד + הה + וו + הה = 52

The Shlah points out that the total numerical value of these fulfillments is 232, the same as the word ממקומו, "from His place." It is therefore appropriate that we use this expression in the praises of *Kedushah* when the entire congregation proclaim together: מלא כל הארץ כבודו — "The whole world is filled with His Glory," which is immediately followed by the *pasuk*: ברוך כבוד ה' **ממקומו** — "Blessed is the Glory of Hashem from *His place*" (*Yechezkel* 3:12). Moreover, the word מקום also equates to Hashem's Name of י-ה-ו-ה using the multiplication method of squared numbers, as we explained elsewhere (see p. 153).

The Ben Ish Chai explains, in the name of the *Arizal*, that the five human senses are displayed by different alternative expansions of Hashem's Name. The fulfillment of יוד הא ואו הא represents the sense of touch. Sight is through the eye, עין, with a numerical value of 130, which is five times the numerical value of the Divine Name (5 x 26 = 130). Hearing is represented by expanding His Name into יוד הי ואו הה, which has a total numerical value of fifty-eight, the same as that of the word אזן, ear. The sense of smell is represented by the expansion יוד הי ואו הי, with a total numerical value of sixty-three, which equals that of the word חוטם, the nose. Taste is also represented by the expansion יוד הי ואו הי. If we add twenty-two — the number of letters in the *alef-beis* — to sixty-three, the sum is eighty-five (63 + 22 = 85), the numerical value of the word פה, mouth, through which the letters are articulated.

## ה-הא-הה-הי-חמשה

The letter ה is also known as חמשה, the representation of the numerical value of the letter. The letters ח'מ'ש'ה' also spell out the word שמחה, "joy" or "happiness," which can only be truly achieved through the medium of learning Torah — the חמשה חומשי תורה, the Five Books of the Torah.

There is also another, deeper meaning to the connection between the three expansions of הא-הה-הי and the words שמחה/חמשה.

The Torah tells us that it was through the evil power of Amalek that His full four-letter Name of י-ה-ו-ה was divided into two. His Throne was also affected by Amalek's evil actions. The Torah writes: ויאמר כי יד על כס י-ה מלחמה לי-ה-ו-ה בעמלק מדר דר — "And He said: 'There is a hand on the Throne of Hashem; Hashem maintains a war against Amalek, from generation to generation'" (*Shemos* 17:16).

Rashi points out that Hashem's Name is spelled using only the first two letters (י'ה'). This abridged Name of י-ה has the power to regenerate into the full Name with the arrival of Mashiach. The expansion of these two letters יוד הא has a total numerical value of twenty-six, the same as His complete four-letter Name. The evil power of Amalek accomplished to further obscure the full radiance of Hashem's power from the world. This is indicated by the fact that the full numerical value of His Name is hidden in a concentrated form inside the Name of י-ה.

The Shlah points out the sum total of the numerical values of the three common fulfillments of Hashem's Name of י-ה is ninety-one (26 [יוד הא] + 30 [יוד הה] + 35 [יוד הי] = 91), the same as that of the word אמן and the combined numerical values of His two Names of י-ה-ו-ה and אדנ-י. In the responsive prayer that is said in *Kaddish*, אמן יהא שמה רבא — "Amen, may His Name be made great," we are asking for the restoration of Hashem's former glory in this world.

The three expansions of the letter ה are formed by the use the letters of 'י'ה'א. They have a total numerical value of ninety-one, the same as אמן, as the expansion of Hashem's Name will ultimately be accomplished by the annihilation and destruction of the evil forces of Amalek. This period will reveal His true greatness, as represented by the full original spelling of His Name, and bring with it the ultimate שמחה into the world.

◈ ◈ ◈

As part of the inauguration of the *Mishkan*, each of the twelve princes brought offerings on the Altar. The Torah lists their exact contributions: ולזבח השלמים בקר שנים אילם חמשה עתדים חמשה כבשים בני שנה חמשה — "And for the peace-offering sacrifice, two cattle, five rams, five he-goats, five sheep in their first year..." (*Bemidbar* 7:23). Rashi, under the same heading of אילם עתדים כבשים, explains two parts of the above-quoted phrase. He writes:

> These three varieties correspond to the *Kohen*, *Levi* and *Yisrael*, and to the three parts of Scripture. There are three sets of five, corresponding to the five Books of the Torah, the five Commandments that were written on the first Tablet, and the five that were written on the second Tablet.

These three sets of five also correspond to the three different fulfillments of the letter ה. As stated above in the name of the Shlah, the sum total of the numerical values of the three common fulfillments of Hashem's Name of י-ה is ninety-one. It is interesting to note that the numerical value of the acronym of the words אילם עתדים כבשים, used in the above *pasuk*, totals ninety-one, as well.

The Megalleh Amukos points out that by using a multiplication factor on all these three expansions of Hashem's Name, we obtain the following:

| | | | | |
|---|---|---|---|---|
| יוד x הא | = | 20 x 6 | = | 120 |
| יוד x הה | = | 20 x 10 | = | 200 |
| יוד x הי | = | 20 x 15 | = | 300 |
| | | **Total** | = | **620** |

Six hundred and twenty is the numerical value of the word כתר — the royal Crown of Hashem that will be restored with the eradication of Amalek and the arrival of Mashiach.

## The Letter ו

ו

The letter ו has a numerical value of six, and fulfills in one of three different ways: וו, which has a numerical value of twelve and translates literally as a "hook"; ואו, which has a numerical value of thirteen — the same value as the unifying word of אחד, One; or ויו, which has a numerical value of twenty-two — the same as the number of letters in the *alef-beis*.

A unique property inherent in the letter ו is that the three integers which sum up to its numerical value of six — one, two and three (1 + 2 + 3 = 6) — also produce a product of six when they are multiplied together (1 x 2 x 3 = 6). These three integers represent the three physical measurements of length, breadth and depth. The dimension of length produces a left- and right-hand side; that of breadth, a concept of forward and backward; while that of depth, the directions of up and down. They form the six dimensions of the physical creation, represented by the three factors of six. Every cubic shape is comprised of six sides, and the circumference of a circle is six times larger than its radius.

Since the letter ו represents the six dimensions of the physical world, it must also represent the Name of Hashem, because all achievements in this world are only possible through His help and consent. The full Name of Hashem, the *Shem haMeforash*, consists of seventy-two sets of three letters each. The Magen David points out that this Name is also represented in the letter ו, as the fulfillment וו equates to seventy-two by means of the multiplication method ([6 x 6] + [6 x 6] = 72). In addition, the triangular value of the number six is twenty-one, which corresponds to the numerical value of another of Hashem's Names, that of אהי-ה.

### ◈ The Vav's Usage: Conjunctive and Convertive

The letter ו can be used either as a conjunction (*vav hachibur*), joining two subjects together, or as a conversion (*vav hahipuch*), changing the tense of a verb from the future tense to the past tense or vice versa. This duality is alluded to in the fact that when a *vav* is used as a composite letter, it appears as a straight line, because it is actually two *vav*s interlocked — the upright ו representing the conjuctive and the upside-down one representing the conversive.

An example of the conjunctive ו is found in the *pasuk*: אשר בחרת באברם והוצאתו מאור כשדים **ו**שמת שמו אברהם — "Who chose Avram, brought him out of Uhr Kasdim, and made his name Avraham" (*Nechemiah* 9:7). The word שמת translates in the past tense as "placed" or "made," and in the above context the letter ו is used to connect the two phrases together.

An example of the conversive ו is found in the *pasuk*: **ו**שמת בטנא — "And You shall place it in a basket" (*Devarim* 26:2). In this case the letter ו changes the word שמת from the past to the future tense.

It is interesting to note that the alternative spellings of this letter's fulfillments — either as וו, ואו or ויו — are all palindromes. They read equally from left to right and from right to left, alluding to the conversing and the joining properties of this letter.

The first time the Torah uses the letter ו as a connecting letter is in the very first *pasuk* of the Torah: בראשית ברא א-להים את השמים ואת הארץ — "In the beginning of Hashem's creating the heavens and the earth" (*Bereishis* 1:1). It is the twenty-second letter and it appears in the sixth word. The first time that the Torah uses the letter ו to change the tense of a verb is in the twenty-second word, in the *pasuk*: ויאמר א-להים יהי אור ויהי אור — "And Hashem said, 'Let there be light and there was light'" (ibid. 1:3).

Mathematically, the fulfillments וו (numerical value = 12) and ואו (numerical value = 13) represent the connective and conversive properties of this letter in the following way:

| | |
|---|---|
| 12 x 12 = 144 | 13 x 13 = 169 |
| 21 x 21 = 441 | 31 x 31 = 961 |

The two *vavs* are connected by multiplying them together. When reversing the integers as above, the products are similarly reversed. This is a unique attribute of the numbers twelve and thirteen.

For all other numbers a similar formula applies in that the final *mispar katan* of the respective products will be the same. In most cases, the *mispar katan* itself will also be the same. For example:

| NUMBER | | PRODUCT | MISPAR KATAN | FINAL MISPAR KATAN |
|---|---|---|---|---|
| 15 x 15 | = | 225 | 9 | 9 |
| 51 x 51 | = | 2,601 | 9 | 9 |
| 146 x 146 | = | 21,316 | 13 | 4 |
| 641 x 641 | = | 410,881 | 22 | 4 |
| 1,024 x 1,024 | = | 1,048,576 | 31 | 4 |
| 4,201 x 4,201 | = | 17,648,401 | 31 | 4 |

## ◈ The Vav's Juxtaposition in the Alef-Beis

The Magen David explains the juxtaposition of the letters of 'ה'ו'ז in the alphabetic sequence.

We have already explained how the letter ה represents repentance. The ו represents woe and grief, through its fulfillment as ויו. This fulfillment spells out the word ווי, an expression of woe and grief, as we find in the Gemara where a sinner exclaims: **ווי אבדה נפש** — "Woe to the loss of my soul" (*Beitzah* 17a). Moreover, the shape of the letter ו represents the מטה א-להים, Hashem's Staff, with which He punishes the wicked for their wrongdoing. The numerical value of the word מטה is fifty-four, equal to that of the word דן, "justice." The next letter in the alphabetic sequence, ז, with a numerical value of seven, can symbolize either the שבעה מדורי גיהנם, "the seven depths of *Gehinnom*," into which a sinner can descend or, conversely, the spiritual enjoyment of Shabbos, the seventh day of the week.

The juxtaposition of these three letters serves as a warning to the sinner who does not utilize the gateway to repentance — represented by the letter ה — that Hashem leaves open for him. This will be followed by Hashem's retribution, using His Staff — symbolized by the letter ו. If these warning are insufficient to cause the sinner to repent, then he will receive his ultimate punishment in *Gehinnom* — represented by the letter ז.

Alternatively, if repentance is performed (ה), then the following letter ו is conjunctive, connecting him to the spiritual world of Shabbos and divine bliss, represented by the letter ז. (This idea is further elaborate in the section on the letter ז.)

◈ ◈ ◈

Every commandment in the Torah is introduced either with the word ויאמר or with וידבר, both of which begin with the letter ו. The fact that the ה precedes the ו in the alphabetic order teaches us that only after one has properly repented for previous wrongdoings can he hope to keep the commandments. Moreover, the shape of the letter ו is similar to that of a *shofar*, which is used to arouse the Jewish People to repent and return to their adherence of all its commandments.

### ◈ The Vav as a Hook

Each Hebrew word has a root. The letter ו is unique in the Hebrew language in that there is only one word whose root begins with this letter. The word is וו, as we find: **ווי העמודים**, "the hooks of the pillars" (*Shemos* 38:10) in reference to the *Mishkan*. The Radak, in *Sefer HaShorashim*, explains: "These were pegs that protruded from the pillars, in the shape of a letter ו; they were used to hang the carcasses of the sacrifices when they were being skinned."

The phrase **ווי העמודים** is mentioned a total of *six* times during the account of the *Mishkan*. Moreover, in the above *pasuk* from *Shemos*, the word **ווי** appears as the *sixth* word of the *pasuk* — a further connection to the letter ו, via its numerical value.

Another of the instances where the **ווי העמודים** is mentioned is in the *pasuk*: **ואת האלף ושבע המאות וחמשה ושבעים עשה ווים לעמודים** — "And from the 1,775 [*shekalim*] he made hooks for the pillars" (*Shemos* 38:28). The Megalleh Amukos points out that the total of the numerical values for the twenty-two letters of the *alef-beis* is 1,495. When the total of the lower numerical values of the five final letters (280) is added to that figure, it produces a total of 1,775, which corresponds to the 1,775 *shekalim* of silver that were used to make the hooks for the pillars in the *Mishkan*.

### ◈ The Correlation Between the Representations of the Letter ו

**ו–וו**

There are five occasions when the name Yaakov (**יעקב**) is spelled with an extra letter ו (**יעקוב**). Rashi, in his commentary to *Vayikra*

26:42, explains that these correspond to five places where the name of Eliyahu haNavi is written without a letter ו. Yaakov "took" this letter as a security to ensure that Eliyahu will come and herald the redemption of his children with the advent of Mashiach. appropriately the letter ו appears in the first *pasuk* of *Shemos* (Exodus) five times.

(The five places that the name יעקוב appears with the letter ו are: *Vayikra* 26:42; and *Yirmeyahu* 30:18, 33:26, 46:27, and 51:19. The five places that the name Eliyahu is spelled without the letter ו are: *Melachim* II 1:3, 1:4, 1:8, 1:12; and *Malachi* 3:23.)

The Maharal explains that this guarantee was sealed by a handshake. As the letter ו resembles a finger, five of them together represent the hand. As the numerical value of the letter ו is six, this handshake represents the number thirty. The Mishnah at the beginning of *Ohalos* states that each hand is composed of thirty segments. We have previously explained how the Mishnah in *Avos* (6:6) teaches us that Kingship is attainable through thirty attributes. These thirty attributes will eventually be recognized at the time of Mashiach, when mankind will proclaim Hashem as King of the universe.

The ו also fulfills as a double letter וו, representing both Redeemers — Mashiach ben Yosef and Mashiach ben David. The dual properties of the letter ו, that can both convert and unify, is ideally suited to represent the arrival of Mashiach, who will return mankind in their unified service of Hashem.

The Shlah provides another meaning as to the significance of the handshake mentioned above:

The creation of the human being is referred to as the יציר כפיו, the handiwork of Hashem's hands, as it were. Every human hand contains a total of four fingers and one thumb. Each finger has three separate bones and the thumb has two — a total of fourteen bones, which is also the numerical equivalent of the Hebrew word for "hand" (יד). If we study more closely the first and second fulfillment of Hashem's Name, we will find that these letters parallel the fingers of the human hand.

The first fulfillment:

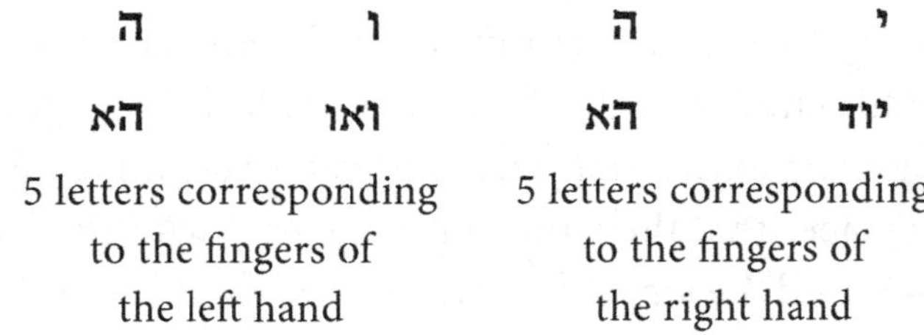

| ה | ו | ה | י |
|---|---|---|---|
| הא | ואו | הא | יוד |
| 5 letters corresponding to the fingers of the left hand | | 5 letters corresponding to the fingers of the right hand | |

The total numerical value of the letters corresponding to the right hand is twenty-six, while those of the left total nineteen. The right hand is therefore the stronger of the two.

The next fulfillment produces the corresponding number of letters for each bone on the fingers and thumb.

The second fulfillment:

| הא | ואו | הא | יוד |
|---|---|---|---|
| הא אלף | ואו אלף ואו | הא אלף | יוד ואו דלת |
| 14 letters corresponding to the bones in the fingers of the left hand | | 14 letters corresponding to the bones in the fingers of the right hand | |

As mentioned earlier, the evil power of Esav through his descendant Amalek succeeded in dividing the goodness that is revealed to us through Hashem's full Name. Thus, He is now referred to by only the first two letters, י-ה. The fulfillment of these two letters corresponds to the fingers and bones contained in one hand. Thus the handshake that Eliyahu gave to Yaakov was given as a security until the evil power of Amalek would eventually be eradicated, and His full Glory fully appreciated.

When a Jew wakes up in the morning, he ritually washes his hands. This is performed by alternatively washing the right hand followed by the left one, three times each. Since each hand corresponds to half of Hashem's Name, washing the right hand followed by the left one, represents His full Name. Performing this three times in an alternate fashion, corresponds to a triple revelation of His Name. This begins our preparation for a new day in our service of Hashem, which will bring us nearer to that ultimate proclamation that contains His Name three times — **ה' מלך ה' מלך ה' ימלך לעולם ועד**.

## ו–ואו

The *vav*'s fulfillment of ואו has a numerical value of thirteen. The Radak writes, in his *sefer* entitled *Michlal*, that there are thirteen different translations and/or uses of the letter ו in the Hebrew language. These are listed below, together with an example of each.

1. As an introduction to a new topic or idea:
   ויהי בימי אחשורוש — "*And* it was in the days of Achashverosh" (*Megillas Esther* 1:1).
2. To indicate that something is missing from the text (which is incorporated in the extra letter ו):
   ואלה בני צבעון ואיה וענה — "And these are the sons of Ziv'on: *and* Aiah and Anah..." (*Bereishis* 36:24). There were additional descendants, too, but they are not specifically mentioned, as they all died childless. They are, however, incorporated by the addition of the extra letter ו at the beginning of the name of Aiah.
3. To indicate an alternative, such as either or etc.:
   ומכה אביו ואמו מות יומת — "He who smites *either* his father *or* his mother shall be put to death" (*Shemos* 21:15).
4. The omission of the letter ו in a list of articles or names:
   ראובן שמעון לוי — "Reuven, Shimon, Levi..." (*Shemos* 1:2).
   Listing the omission of the letter as one of its uses is substantiated by the Ibn Ezra's remarks on *Shemos* 1:4, where he lists six different ways that the letter ו is used as a conjunction to join a list of nouns together. They are:

(a) Between people's names:

**בני שם עילם ואשור וארפכשד ולוד וארם וכו'** — "The sons of Shem; Elam *and* Ashur *and* Arpachshad *and* Lud *and* Aram" (*Bereishis* 10:22).

(b) Connecting each article:

**בנפך ארגמן ורקמה ובוץ וראמת וכדכד** — "Precious stone, purple wool *and* embroidered work *and* fine linen *and* corals *and* rubies" (*Yechezkel* 27:16).

(c) Connecting articles, *except* the first two:

**טור אדם פטדה וברקת** — "a row of odem, pitdah *and* barekes" (*Shemos* 28:17).

(d) Grouping articles in a sequence:

**דן ונפתלי גד ואשר** — "Dan *and* Naftali, Gad *and* Asher" (*Shemos* 1:4).

(e) Connecting articles, only after the first in the list:

**מר ואהלות קציעות** — "Myrrh *and* aloes, cassia" (*Tehillim* 45:9).

(f) Connecting articles by its omission:

**אדם שת אנוש** — "Adam, Sheth, Enosh" (*Divrei HaYamim* I 1:1).

5. To indicate a priority in time; translated as "after":
**וירם תולעים ויבאש** — "It became infested with worms *after* it stank" (*Shemos* 16:20). Rashi explains that this is an inverted *pasuk*; it should be understood as, it first stank and later became infested with worms, for such is the nature of all things that become wormy.

6. Translated as "as":
**אם לא ישבעו וילינו** — "...without being satisfied *as* they sleep" (*Tehillim* 59:16).

7. To equate two subjects; translated as "just as...so":
**הדלת תסוב על צירה ועצל על מטתו** — "*Just as* a door turns on its hinge, *so* does a lazy man on his bed" (*Mishlei* 26:14). (Extensive use is made of this in *Mishlei*.)

8. To answer a conditional statement; translated as "then":
   **אם בחקתי תלכו וכו' ונתתי גשמיכם בעתם** — "If you will go in My statutes...*then* I will provide you with rain" (*Vayikra* 26:4).

9. Used in place of the letter **ב**; translated as "with":
   **וכלי זעמו לחבל כל הארץ** — ...*with* the weapons of His fury, to destroy all the land" (*Yeshayahu* 13:5).

10. Used in conjunction with the word **לא** to make a question; translated as "will you not?":
    **ולא יתן נא לעבדך** — "*Will you not*, please give it to your servant?" (*Melachim* II 5:17).

11. Translated as "with" or "including":
    **ויהי כל נפש יצאי ירך יעקב שבעים נפש ויסף היה במצרים** — "And all the people that descended from Yaakov were seventy souls, *including* Yosef who was in Egypt" (*Shemos* 1:5).

12. Translated as "but":
    **ויאמרו אליו לא אדני ועבדיך באו לשבר אכל** — "They said to him, 'No, my lord! *But* your servants have come to buy food'" (*Bereishis* 42:10).

13. Translated as "when":
    **ביום השלישי וישא אברהם את עיניו** — "On the third day, *when* Avraham raised his eyes..." (*Bereishis* 22:4).

◈ ◈ ◈

The letter **ו** belongs to one of the seven simple letters, which are used to compose the remaining ones. The letters of the hidden fulfillment of the expansion of **ואו**, have numerical values of six and one, respectively. There are a total of seven letters in the *alef-beis* that use the letter **ו** in their composition (א'ב'ה'ח'ל'מ'ס'), six of which always use it, while one, the letter **ה**, may be formed with or without it (**ד + י** or **ד + ו**), as explained previously. The quantitative use of the letter **ו** as a component part of the compound letters of the *alef-beis* is accurately represented by the hidden fulfillment of the ואו expansion.

◈ ◈ ◈

At birth יעקב was so called as this name represents the עקב, the heel, always being treated as inferior by his brother Esav. After Yaakov had successfully defeated the Angel of Evil (see *Bereishis* 32:29), he was given the more prestigious name of ישראל, which spells out לי ראש, "I have a head." He had now proven himself and was not to be considered as a lowly person any longer, but as one who was capable of achieving great spiritual heights and even defeating angelic powers.

Normally the shape of the letter ו is a straight vertical line, with a letter י, superimposed as its head. However, when this letter is incorporated as a component part to form other letters, it has only the lower part, the straight line without the *yud*-shaped head. The Magen David explains that when used as a component part, the letter ו represents the inferior name יעקב. Therefore only the lower part of the letter is used. However, when it appears as a separate letter in a word, representing the higher status of ישראל, the complete form of the ו is used, with the י as its head.

◈ ◈ ◈

We have previously explained how the number nine represents eternal truth. The word שקר, "falsehood" has a numerical value of six hundred, and a *mispar katan* of six. One might expect, therefore, that the number six would represent falsehood. Yet, the *Zohar* refers to the straight letter ו as the "letter of truth." Mathematically, this can be explained by the fact that there is a numerical connection between the letter ו and the word אמת. The triangular value of ו is twenty-one, and the numerical value of אמת, "truth," is 441, which is $21^2$. Appropriately, the letter ו is referred to as the "letter of truth."

◈ ◈ ◈

As we have said, the numerical value of the letter ו is six, and that of its fulfillment of ואו is thirteen. These two numbers are connected in that the pyramidial value of six equals the triangular value of thirteen ($1^2 + 2^2 + 3^2 + 4^2 + 5^2 + 6^2 = 91$ and $1 + 2 + 3 + 4 + 5 + 6 + 7 + 8 + 9 + 10 + 11 + 12 + 13 = 91$).

### ו–וו–ואו

Hashem's four-letter Name will produce twenty-four different permutations. However, since the letter ה is repeated in its spelling, it will produce only twelve distinct permutations, corresponding to the twelve months of the yearly cycle.

In some *siddurim* before the *Musaf* prayer said on *Rosh Chodesh*, there is a list of the twelve months with the *pasuk* that represents that month. Each of these *pesukim* contains an acronym which spells out one of the permutations of Hashem's Name.

The twelve permutations and their corresponding months are as follows:

| | | |
|---|---|---|
| Nisan | ישמחו השמים ותגל הארץ | (*Tehillim* 96:11) |
| Iyar | יתהלל המתהלל השכל וידוע | (*Yirmeyahu* 9:23) |
| Sivan | ידתיו ולצלע המשכן השנית | (*Shemos* 26:19–20) |
| Tammuz | זה איננו שוה לי | (*Esther* 5:13) |
| Av | הסכת ושמע ישראל היום | (*Devarim* 27:9) |
| Elul | וצדקה תהיה לנו כי | (*Devarim* 6:25) |
| Tishrei | ויראו אותה שרי פרעה | (*Bereishis* 12:15) |
| Cheshvan | ודבש היום הזה יהוה | (*Devarim* 26:15–16) |
| Kislev | וירא יושב הארץ הכנעני | (*Bereishis* 50:11) |
| Teves | ליהוה אתי ונרוממה שמו | (*Tehillim* 34:4) |
| Shevat | המר ימירנו והיה הוא | (*Vayikra* 27:33) |
| Adar | עירה ולשרקה בני אתנו | (*Bereishis* 49:11) |

The Me'or V'Shemesh makes some interesting observations regarding these permutations and their correlation to the months that they represent.

The phrases that contain the permutations of the letters of Hashem's Name allude to the major events that occur within the respective month. To give one example: the phrase for the month of Nisan (**י**שמחו **ה**שמים **ו**תגל **ה**ארץ) translates as "the heavens will be glad and the earth will rejoice." On the fifteenth of Nisan the Jewish People were redeemed from their Egyptian exile, and it is in Nisan that they are destined to be redeemed again in the future with the coming of Mashiach, as taught by the Gemara (*Rosh Hashanah* 11a). Nisan, therefore incorporates a period of exile during the first part of the month and a period of redemption in the second half. The Rokeach points out that in the above phrase the letters of the word ותגל also spell out the word גלות, "exile," and those of the word ישמחו also spell out the word ומשיח, Mashiach — both alluding to the major events that occurred and will occur within that month.

The month of Tishrei is the month in which we affirm Hashem as the supreme and universal King. The permutation of His Name for this month is: **ו**יראו אות**ה** שר**י** פרע**ה**. This acronym is appropriately used in the *pasuk*: **והיה** ה' למלך על כל הארץ ביום ההוא יהיה ה' אחד ושמו אחד — "Hashem will be King over the entire world; on that day, Hashem will be One and His Name will be One" (*Zechariah* 14:9).

When looking at the twelve combinations of His Name, the Me'or V'Shemesh finds a similar and unique relationship between any two months that are six months apart. These "twin" months interlock with each other. Take, for example, the month of Elul, and its corresponding counterpart six months later, the month of Adar:

Elul: **ו**צדק**ה** ת**ה**יה לנו כ**י**
Adar: עיר**ה** ולשוק**ה** בנ**י** אתונ**ו**

We can immediately notice a similarity in these patterns. For each pair, the *hei*s will be in the same position. In this example, both the first and second letters are the letter ה.

Moreover, the fourth and second letters in the *pasuk* for Elul spell out יה, while the fourth and second letters of its corresponding month, Adar, provide the וה that completes the spelling of Hashem's Name. This interesting phenomena works in reverse as well. If we begin with Adar, it is the third and second letters that make up the יה; thus the third and second letters of the phrase for Elul should provide the וה — and, in fact, they do! These unique combinations work for any two months that are six months apart.

The Me'or V'Shemesh also discusses the relationship between the fifteenth day of the month of Av and the corresponding day six months later, the fifteenth of Shevat. From his explanation it becomes apparent that not only is there a very close relationship between a month and its counterpart six months later, there is a connection between any given day in a month and its corresponding day in its twin month. The Gemara compares the festival of Pesach, on the fifteenth day of Nisan, to that of Sukkos, on the fifteenth day of Tishrei.

Each pair of twin months are twenty-six weeks apart from each other, corresponding to the numerical value of Hashem's Name (26). Moreover, these pairs are symbolized by the conjunctive power of the letter ו as they are alluded to in its numerical value, six, being that the twin months are six months apart. When the letter ו is spelled out as וו, it represents the double periods of six months that make up a yearly cycle. The fulfillment of ואו represents this same feature, but with the additional thirteenth month of the lunar leap year.

◈ ◈ ◈

The phrase whose acronym represents the month of Nisan is the only one which is mentioned twice in Scripture. The first time is in *Tehillim* (96:11): **ישמחו השמים ותגל הארץ ירעם הים ומלאו** — "The heavens will be glad and the earth will rejoice; the sea and its fullness will roar." In this *pasuk* the remaining words also begin with letters of Hashem's Name. The second time this phrase appears is in *Divrei HaYamim* (I 16:31): ישמחו השמים ותגל הארץ ויאמרו בגוים ה' מלך — "The heavens will be glad and the earth will rejoice; let them say among the nations, 'Hashem rules!'"

The question is: Which *pasuk* represents the month of Nisan? The answer is the *pasuk* in *Tehillim*. As explained, the "twin" months are interrelated. Nisan's twin month is Tishrei. The permutation of Hashem's Name for Tishrei is ו-ה-י-ה, which is the same combination that appears in the *pasuk* in *Tehillim* when starting from the end of the *pasuk* moving backwards. The interconnectivity of these two months is thus an integral part of this *pasuk*; therefore, it is the appropriate one to represent the month of Nisan.

◈ ◈ ◈

Rabbi Yonasan Eibeshutz explains that the twelve calendar months correspond to the twelve tribes of Israel and to the twelve stellar constellations in the following manner:

| MONTH | TRIBE | MAZAL | ZODIAC SIGN |
|---|---|---|---|
| Tishrei | Reuven | מאזנים | The Scales (Libra) |
| Cheshvan | Shimon | עקרב | The Scorpion (Scorpio) |
| Kislev | Levi | קשת | The Archer (Sagittarius) |
| Teves | Yehudah | גדי | The Goat (Capricorn) |
| Shevat | Yissachar | דלי | The Water Bearer (Aquarius) |
| Adar | Zevulun | דגים | The Fish (Pisces) |
| Nisan | Yosef | טלה | The Ram (Aries) |
| Iyar | Binyamin | שור | The Bull (Taurus) |
| Sivan | Dan | תאומים | The Twins (Gemini) |
| Tammuz | Naftali | סרטן | The Crab (Cancer) |
| Av | Gad | אריה | The Lion (Leo) |
| Elul | Asher | בתולה | The Virgin (Virgo) |

Just as there is a close tie between any two *pesukim* that represent twin months, there is also a connection between any two tribes that correspond to these months and to their respective signs of the zodiac.

For example, Reuven and Yosef correspond to each other in the above chart and they were the firstborns of Leah and Rachel, respectively — Yaakov's two original wives. It was Reuven who tried to save Yosef from being sold to the Egyptian merchants, as related in *Bereishis* 37:29. Similarly, Shimon corresponds to Binyamin and it was therefore appropriate that Yosef keep Shimon imprisoned in Egypt as a guarantor that Binyamin would be brought down to Egypt, as mentioned in *Bereishis* 42:24.

The Megalleh Amukos explains a connection between the months of Nisan and Tishrei, the Name of Hashem and their corresponding zodiac signs. These two months both contain a *yom tov* of seven days' duration. Pesach requires a thorough physical removal of all *chametz* (leavened bread), while Tishrei is the time for a spiritual removal of all traces of sin. The square of the numerical value of the first two letters of Hashem's Name is 225 (יה x יה = 15 x 15 = 225). This is the same as the numerical value of the words מזל מאזנים, the zodiac sign of the Scales, which corresponds to the month of Tishrei. Similarly, the square of the numerical value of the last two letters of His Name is 121 (וה x וה - 11 x 11 = 121), the same as that of מזל טלה, the zodiac sign of the Ram, corresponding to the month of Nisan. These two months are further interconnected by the custom on the first night of Rosh Hashanah to partake of the head of a ram, an animal that represents the zodiac sign for the month of Nisan.

## ו–ויו

The Torah states: והיה עקב תשמעון את המשפטים האלה — "And it shall be because of your obedience to the mitzvos…" (*Devarim* 7:12). The word עקב literally means "heel," the bottom of the foot, symbolizing the epoch at the *end* of time, and has a numerical value of 172. The third fulfillment of the letter *vav*, as ויו, also connects to 172 as it has a multiplication value of 172. This is achieved by totaling the products of the squares for each letter (36 + 100 + 36 = 172).

We have previously explained, in the section dealing with the At–Bash alphabetic structure, the observance of Shabbos by the entire Jewish nation will precipitate the early arrival of Mashiach. This same message is alluded to in the above *pasuk*: **והיה עקב תשמעון את המשפטים האלה** — the highlighted letters spell out the word **שבת**.

This fulfillment (ויו) has a numerical value of twenty-two, the same as the number of letters in the *alef-beis*. We have previously explained how the alphabetic structure is a natural proclamation of ה' ימלך, the crowning of Hashem as the King of the universe. This will coincide with the fulfillment of the phrase of והיה עקב **תשמעון** את המשפטים האלה and the arrival of Mashiach.

### ו–וו–ואו–שש

The numerical value of letter ו is six — **שש**, which is composed of six *vavs*, each forming another arm of the letter **ש**.

Previously we explained the concept of the Ten *Sefiros*. With regard to the way they interrelate with the physical world, the Ten *Sefiros* are divided into two parts. The higher three form one group and the lower seven, the second group. Each of the *Sefiros* corresponds to a different part of the human body. The sixth (ו) *Sefirah* of the lower group is known as יסוד and corresponds to the area connected to the mitzvah of מילה (circumcision), which is what David haMelech was referring to when he said: **שש** אנכי על אמרתך — "I rejoice over your word" (*Tehillim* 119:162). The mitzvah of *milah* is connected to the letter ו and its numerical value of six. The word **שָׂש** in the *pasuk* can also be read as **שֵׁש**, and **שש** has a *mispar katan* of six.

The *Sefirah* of יסוד is said to correspond to יוסף, whose name has a numerical value of 156, which is six times the numerical value of Hashem's Name (6 x 26 = 156).

◈ ◈ ◈

The life history of Yosef duplicated that of his father Yaakov. Rashi quotes a Midrash that explains the phrase: אלה תלדות יעקב יוסף — "These are the chronicles of Yaakov; Yosef…" (*Bereishis* 37:2). Rashi explains: "Everything that happened to Yaakov, happened to Yosef as well. Both were hated by their respective brothers, who wanted to kill them." The Magen David explains that the fulfillment of the letter ו as וו represents this duality in their life histories. These similarities are alluded to in the introductory word of the above passage, אלה, "these." The numerical value of אלה is thirty-six, which is six squared. This is represented by the fulfillment of וו, which is the letter ו squared.

The closeness that Yaakov enjoyed with his beloved son Yosef is reflected in the fact that the numerical value of יעקב is 182, a number that is seven times the numerical value of Hashem's Name, while the numerical value of יוסף is six times that of His Name. Their combination — thirteen times the value of Hashem's Name — is indicative of their special bond, the **אחדות** (unity) between father and son. This unity and common goal in their lives is represented by the fulfillment of this letter as **ואו**, which has the same numerical value as the word אחד, unity. Furthermore, the first two letters (**וא**ו), having a numerical value of seven, represent Yaakov, and final letter (וא**ו**), with a numerical value of six, represents Yosef.

## ו-וו-שש

The Midrash writes: "The six things that were taken away from Adam haRishon after he sinned will be returned with the arrival of Mashiach" (*Bereishis Rabbah* 12:6). *Tehillim* 72:17 refers to Mashiach as ינין שמו — which is written as ינין but is pronounced as יִנּוֹן, replacing the second י with a ו. The hidden fulfillment of the word שש

is שין שין, which combine together to produce the name ינין. These six (ו) items will again be returned to the human race with the arrival of ינין, Mashiach, thereby connecting the letter ו to the word שש and to Mashiach, who is destined to come in the *sixth* millennium of the world's existence.

This is reinforced by the *Mesorah*, which comments that only twice in Scripture does the word תולדות appear in its full written form (with two *vavs*). The first time is in *Bereishis* 2:4: אלה תולדות השמים והארץ — "These are the products of the heavens and the earth...." This refers to the world before the sin of Adam haRishon. The second time is at the end of *Megillas Rus* (4:18), in listing the lineage of David haMelech as the ancestor of Mashiach: ואלה תולדות פרץ — "These are the generations of Peretz...." Thus these two *vavs* allude to the time before the sin — before the six things were taken away — and to the time after Mashiach's arrival — when they will be returned to Adam's descendents.

The last three *pesukim* of *Megillas Rus* list the ten generations from Peretz to David haMelech. *Megillas Rus* has a total of eighty-five *pesukim*, the same as the numerical value of בועז (Boaz), Ruth's husband. All but eight of these *pesukim* begin with the letter ו. David haMelech compensates for these *vavs* in *Tehillim* 119; there, the word עדתיך, "Your testimonies," is spelled with an extra ו (עדותיך) on eight occasions. (That chapter of *Tehillim* is structured in groups of eight: the first eight *pesukim* all begin with the letter א, the second eight all begin with the letter ב, and so on.) The Chasam Sofer points out that first letters of the eight *pesukim* in which the word עדותיך appears with and extra ו, spell out מדה בן פרץ — "the characteristic of the son of Peretz," which is an allusion to Mashiach.

### ו-ואו-שש-ששה

The recitation of the *Shema* is the acceptance of Hashem's absolute sovereignty by our declaration that He is One, Unique and Indivisible. With this declaration we are subordinating all aspects of our lives to His will: שמע ישראל ה׳ א-להינו ה׳ אחד; after which we say: ברוך שם כבוד מלכותו לעולם ועד.

Each of these declarations contains six words, which correspond to the two *vavs* in the fulfillment ואו. These declarations proclaim the Unity of Hashem, which is represented by the א in that fulfillment.

The *Shema* is repeated twice daily—once in the morning and once in the evening. The word שש can be an acronym for the doubled recitation of *Shema*: שמע שמע, interconnecting the representations of ואו and שש.

◈ ◈ ◈

The letter ו represents the six orders of the Mishnah (ששה סדרי משנה). The six arms of its representation as שש allude to the Oral Torah. The ה of ששה symbolizes the *five* books of the Written Torah, which are can only be properly understood with the explanations of the *six* orders of the Oral Torah. Thus, the letter ו and its representations of שש and ששה allude to the interconnectivity of both Torahs.

### ו-שש

There is another connection between the letter ו, with a numerical value of six, and its representation as שש. In Hebrew, the word linen can be translated either as בד or שש. The word בד has a numerical value of six and is derived from the word לבד, alone—single. Linen is the only natural fiber that grows as long singular, vertical strands, and thus requires no combing or carding before weaving. The fact that linen grows as *singular* strands corresponds to the word בד. The word שש—which, as we have said, also means six—is also alluded to in the natural shape of linen. A cross-section of one strand, when viewed under a higher-powered microscope, has a perfect hexagonal (six-sided) shape.

## THE LETTER ז

The letter ז has a numerical value of seven and fulfills as זין. This expansion has a final *mispar katan* of thirteen, the same as for the word אחד, signifying the Unity of Hashem. The generative expansion of the word זין (ז–זי–זין), has an initial *mispar katan* of twenty-eight (when adding the *mispar katan* of each of the levels of the generative sequence) and a final *mispar katan* of one (2 + 8 = 10 and 1 + 0 = 1), which again reinforces the Unity of Hashem.

Seven represents the basic time unit of a week, the triangular value of seven is twenty-eight, corresponding to the seven words and twenty-eight letters contained in the first *pasuk* of the Torah.

This fulfillment of זין translates as "weapon" or "sword." The first time that a weapon was used to kill a person was in the seventh generation from Creation, when Lemech killed both Cain and TuvalCain. (The seven generations are: Adam, Kayin, Enoch, Irad, Mechuyael, Methushael and Lemech.)

### ◈ The Seven Sefiros

As mentioned earlier, the universe was created through the medium of the Ten *Sefiros*. Counting from the top downwards they are:

כתר
חכמה
בינה
חסד
גבורה
תפארת
נצח
הוד
יסוד
מלכות

These Ten *Sefiros* were the tools used to created the world. Of these ten, the first three are completely hidden from human intellect. The remaining seven *Sefiros* correspond to the seven days of the week. This internal division, between the three upper the seven lower *Sefiros*, are portrayed by the shape the letter ז as it is written in the Torah script, with three תגין, three crowns, vertically above the letter. The actual letter ז represents the seven lower *Sefiros*. The three perpendicular crowns represent the three higher *Sefiros* that funnel spirituality into the lower seven *Sefiros*. Of these three crowns, the middle one is slightly taller and represents the first *Sefirah* of כתר, the other two upper *Sefiros*, חכמה and בינה, flank it on either side.

### ◈ ז Represents Sustenance

The second fulfillment of ז (זין יוד נון) contains nine letters, representing the absolute truth that is contained within it. This second fulfillment is special in that all these nine letters belong to the group of seven simple letters, being a unique feature of the fulfillments of the letters ז and נ.

Elongating the letter ז produces a final letter ן, representing an extension of these channels of the *Sefiros*. These two letters combine to form the word זן — the food and sustenance that is so vitally important and essential to guarantee continued life for all living matter. The word זן has a numerical value of fifty-seven, equating to that of the word אוכל, "food," and also to that of the word דגן, "grain." The Rokeach points out that the first blessing of the Grace After Meals appropriately contains a total of fifty-seven words. In this same blessing, the word זן is first mentioned as the seventh word: ברוך אתה ה' אלהינו מלך העולם **הזן** את העולם כלו — "Blessed are You, Hashem, our God, King of the Universe, Who nourishes the entire world."

The two letters ז and ן belong to the same set in the Ayik–Bekar alphabetic structure (ז'ע'ן'), indicating that they are interconnected. The three letters ז'ע'ן' have numerical values of seven, seventy and seven hundred, respectively, and thus share the same *mispar katan* of seven. On Shabbos, which is represented by the number seven, the Jewish People enjoyed a double portion of Manna, the heavenly bread that sustained them for forty years in the desert. This double portion is indicated by the double *mispar katan* of seven in the letters of the word זן.

In the weekly cycle, the Jewish People are commanded to enjoy the seventh day of Shabbos as a day of rest. Similarly in the yearly cycle, the farmer is commanded to let his field remain fallow, during the entire seventh year of *shemittah*. After every seven *shemittah* cycles, the fiftieth year is the *Yovel* (Jubilee) year. This *Yovel* year was proclaimed as "…a year of freedom throughout the land for all its inhabitants" (*Vayikra* 25:10). These two similar periods of freedom are symbolized by the letters ז and ן, with numerical values of seven and fifty, respectfully.

We have previously discussed how the *pasuk* in *Tehillim* (72:17) refers to Mashiach by the name of ינין שמו, and that the word is written as ינין, but pronounced as יִנּוֹן. The hidden fulfillment of the three letters of the above-mentioned Ayik–Bekar set become זין עין נון, which combine together to produce both the names ינין and ינון. Complete freedom will be accomplished when the entire Jewish nation observes the mitzvah of Shabbos, *shemittah* and *Yovel*, because it will precipitate the arrival of Mashiach.

## ◈ Correlations Between the Representations of the Letter ז

**ז–זיין–שבעת**

With its numerical value of seven, the letter ז represents the seventh day of the week, Shabbos, which is sanctified by the recitation of *Kiddush* on Friday night. This is derived from the *pasuk* that states:

זכור את יום השבת לקדשו — "Remember the Shabbos day in order to sanctify it" (*Shemos* 20:8).

This remembrance is performed by making *Kiddush* over a goblet of wine, as the Gemara (*Pesachim* 105a) interprets the words "Remember the Shabbos" to mean: זכרהו על היין — "Remember it on wine." The word יין, "wine," has a numerical value of seventy, the same as that of the letter ע. Moreover, the Friday night *Kiddush* contains seventy words. Thus the letter ז, with its representation of שבעה, can also be articulated as שבעת (when the letters ה and ת appear at the end of a word which is in the feminine form, they can be interchanged for each other — thus שבעה can also be read as שבעת), whose letters spell out ע + שבת, representing the sanctification of Shabbos through wine.

Sometimes, the fulfillment of the letter ז is spelled זיין, with a double letter *yud*. The fulfillment of זיין can be read as יין + ז, alluding to the sanctification of Shabbos through the recitation of *Kiddush* over wine (יין).

The Gemara states: מתנה טובה יש לי בבית גנזי ושבת שמה — "I have a valuable gift in My Storehouse, named Shabbos" (*Shabbos* 10a). The word גנזי, "My Storehouse," has a numerical value of seventy. By interchanging the letters of the Palatals group (ג'י'כ'ק'), it is appropriate that the word גנזי transforms into the word זיין, as both represent Shabbos.

In our Friday night song of לכה דודי we say: שמור וזכור בדבור אחד השמיענו א-ל המיחד — "'Safeguard and Remember,' in a single utterance the One and Only Hashem made us hear."

The Ben Ish Chai points out that the word שבת itself incorporates a duality of the זכור and שמור. These were both articulated simultaneously in one utterance by Hashem when He gave us the Ten Commandments. The fulfillment of the letters of שבת expand into שין בית תו. These letters spell out the words שני תיבות, "two words," alluding to the two words שמור וזכור that were uttered as a single word.

The Vilna Gaon observes that all the items that characterize the day of Shabbos have a *mispar katan* of seven. These are listed below.

| | NUMERICAL VALUE | MISPAR KATAN |
|---|---|---|
| נר (candle) | 50 + 200 = 250 | 2 + 5 + 0 = 7 |
| יין (wine) | 10 + 10 + 50 = 70 | 7 + 0 = 7 |
| חלה (*challah*) | 8 + 30 + 5 = 43 | 4 + 3 = 7 |
| דג (fish) | 4 + 3 = 7 | = 7 |
| בשר (meat) | 200 + 300 + 2 = 502 | 5 + 2 = 7 |

As we have said, the final *Sefirah* of מלכות acts like a junction through which the effects of all the other *Sefiros* pass, before they can be useful in this physical world. The *Sefirah* of מלכות is the seventh *Sefirah* of the lower group, and thus it represents Shabbos, which is appropriately named שבת מלכתה, the Shabbos Queen.

The sixth *Sefirah* of the entire group is תפארת, Splendor. This *Sefirah* therefore represents the timely preparation on Friday for the Shabbos Queen. This is the meaning of the words of the Shabbos prayer: תפארת עטה ליום המנוחה ענג קרא ליום השבת — "With splendor He engulfed the day of rest, He declared Shabbos a delightful day...."

## THE LETTER ח

The letter ח has a numerical value of eight and fulfills as the word חית, which has a *mispar katan* of thirteen, the same as that of the word אחד, thereby signifying, once again, the Unity of Hashem. Sometimes the fulfillment is spelled חת; both fulfillments translate as "gracefulness" or "fear." An example of its use is found in the *pasuk*: ויהי **חתת** א-להים על הערים — "And there was a Divine fear on the cities" (*Bereishis* 35:5).

The letter ח is very similar in shape to the letter ה. Both belong to the Gutturals group of א'ח'ה'ע', and are therefore interchangeable with each other. The letter ח represents the mitzvah of *milah*, which is performed on the eighth day. Avraham, who was the first person to be commanded to perform this mitzvah, had the letter ה added to his name prior to him being able to have children.

The ח is composed by combining the letters ו + ד, which have a total numerical value of ten, and a *mispar katan* of one, returning again to the Unity of Hashem.

Every seventh year is known as a *shemittah* year, when all fields lie fallow. The year following seven such *shemittah* cycles is known as a year of *Yovel*. In the Torah script, the letter ח is composed from two *zayins*, joined by two thin lines that form its roof. These double letter ז, represent the seven *shemittah* cycles, each one encompassing seven years, that are immediately followed by the *Yovel* year. They are symbolized by the juxtaposition of the letters ז and ח, which is itself composed from two *zayins*.

Regarding the fiftieth year of *Yovel*, the Torah writes: וקדשתם את שנת החמשים שנה וקראתם דרור בארץ לכל ישביה יובל היא תהיה לכם — "You shall sanctify the fiftieth year and you shall proclaim freedom throughout the land for all its inhabitants, it is a Yovel year for you" (*Vayikra* 25:10). The numerical value of the word דרור, "freedom," is 410, the same as the hidden fulfillment of the letter **חית**, Moreover, the letter ח represents the *Sefirah* of בינה, which is the eighth *Sefirah* when counting upwards from the bottom, and it is through the power of this *Sefirah* that freedom and redemption are effected.

We have already explained how the composition of the letter א — being made up from two *yud*s and a diagonal *vav* — has a total numerical value of twenty-six, the same as that of Hashem's Name of י-ה-ו-ה. The *mispar katan* of each of these three letters 'י'ו'י totals eight (1 + 6 + 1 = 8), demonstrating a correlation between these two numbers. Moreover, being that the written Name of Hashem, י-ה-ו-ה, is articulated as א-דנ-י, together they contain eight letters.

### ◈ Unique Properties of the Number Eight

There are some very unique mathematical properties of the number eight that have a direct connection with Hashem's Name of י-ה-ו-ה and its numerical value of twenty-six.

The Shlah explains that the numerical values created in the generative process of Hashem's Name produces a mathematical series that begins with the number one and ends with the number eight, in the following manner:

| | | | | |
|---|---|---|---|---|
| י | = | 10 | = | 1 + 2 + 3 + 4 |
| י-ה | = | 15 | = | 1 + 2 + 3 + 4 + 5 |
| י-ה-ו | = | 21 | = | 1 + 2 + 3 + 4 + 5 + 6 |
| י-ה-ו-ה | = | 26 | = | 5 + 6 + 7 + **8** |

Moreover, the *mispar katan* of the numerical value of Hashem's Name (26) is eight (2 + 6 = 8). If we repeat this calculation for multiples of twenty-six, as shown below, a unique pattern is formed.

| A | | | | | | | | B |
|---|---|---|---|---|---|---|---|---|
| **1** | x 26 | = | 26 | 2 + 6 | | | = | **8** |
| **2** | x 26 | = | 52 | 5 + 2 | | | = | **7** |
| **3** | x 26 | = | 78 | 7 + 8 | = 15 | 1 + 5 | = | **6** |
| **4** | x 26 | = | 104 | 1 + 0 + 4 | | | = | **5** |
| **5** | x 26 | = | 130 | 1 + 3 + 0 | | | = | **4** |
| **6** | x 26 | = | 156 | 1 + 5 + 6 | = 12 | 1 + 2 | = | **3** |
| **7** | x 26 | = | 182 | 1 + 8 + 2 | = 11 | 1 + 1 | = | **2** |
| **8** | x 26 | = | 208 | 2 + 0 + 8 | = 10 | 1 + 0 | = | **1** |
| **9** | x 26 | = | 234 | 2 + 3 + 4 | | | = | **9** |
| **10** | x 26 | = | 260 | 2 + 6 + 0 | | | = | **8** |

The higher the multiple in the left hand column (A), the smaller the final figure becomes on the right hand column (B). An increase in the multiple of Hashem's Name produces a decrease in its *mispar katan*.

The Shlah explains that this represents Hashem's humility, and he points out that this idea is reinforced by the *gemara* which says: "Rabbi Yochanan says: Wherever you find the greatness of Hashem there you find His humility" (*Megillah* 31a).

This pattern also applies to multiples of the number eight, as well as to numbers that have a *mispar katan* of eight. For example:

| | | | | |
|---|---|---|---|---|
| **1** x 8 = 8 | | | = | **8** |
| **2** x 8 = 16 | 1 + 6 | | = | **7** |
| **3** x 8 = 24 | 2 + 4 | | = | **6** |
| **4** x 8 = 32 | 3 + 2 | | = | **5** |
| **5** x 8 = 40 | 4 + 0 | | = | **4** |
| **6** x 8 = 48 | 4 + 8 | = 12 | 1 + 2 = | **3** |
| **7** x 8 = 56 | 5 + 6 | = 11 | 1 + 1 = | **2** |
| **8** x 8 = 64 | 6 + 4 | = 10 | 1 + 0 = | **1** |
| **9** x 8 = 72 | 7 + 2 | | = | **9** |
| **10** x 8 = 80 | 8 + 0 | | = | **8** |

The *mispar katan* that results from the multiples of the number eight moves progressively towards the number one, symbolizing a special unifying power latent within the number eight. For example, circumcision, performed on the eighth day, brings the newborn into the covenant of Avraham, thereby unifying him with the Jewish People.

This unique feature of the numbers eight and twenty-six is alluded to in the *pasuk*: אתה הוא י-ה-ו-ה לבדך וכו' — "It is You alone, Hashem..." (*Nechemiah* 9:6). The numerical value of the words אתה הוא equals 418, the same as that of the fulfillment of the letter ח as חית. The next word in the *pasuk* is Hashem's Name, which, as we know, has a numerical value of twenty-six. The last word in this phrase לבדך, “alone,” alludes to the fact that only these two numbers — eight and twenty-six — possess the unique feature of the *mispar katan* decreasing as the corresponding multiples increase.

As stated earlier, the ח can be formed by joining two *zayins* together. Normally each individual letter ז is adorned by three crowns, known as תגין. However, when they are joined together to form the letter ח, they do not have these crowns. This is because when two adorned letters join to compose one of a higher value, they lose their crowns, thereby displaying humility. This humility is reinforced by the fact that as the progression of the multiples of the number eight increases, the resultant *mispar katan* decreases, as enumerated above.

### ◈ Correlations Between the Representations of the Letter ח

**ח-שמונה**

The only other number that forms a similar pattern in the final *mispar katan* of the multiples is the number fifty-five. This number also represents the unique bond between Hashem and the Jewish People. The Maharal of Prague gives the following explanation.

The number sequence begins with units, progresses to tens and then to hundreds. When the numbers belonging to the units progress into the higher section of tens, or the numbers in the tens progress to the hundreds, they can be paired off together as follows:

| | | | | | |
|---|---|---|---|---|---|
| 1 + 9 | = | 10 | 10 + 90 | = | 100 |
| 2 + 8 | = | 10 | 20 + 80 | = | 100 |
| 3 + 7 | = | 10 | 30 + 70 | = | 100 |
| 4 + 6 | = | 10 | 40 + 60 | = | 100 |
| 5 is left singly without a partner | | | 50 is left singly without a partner | | |

The numbers five and fifty represent the uniqueness of the Jewish nation and their unity with Hashem, as reinforced by the *pasuk* which describes the Jewish People as: הן עם לבדד ישכן ובגוים לא יתחשב — "They are a people who dwell alone and amongst the nations they are not reckoned" (*Bemidbar* 23:9). The Jewish People are described by the use of the word הן, being composed from these two unique letters that stand alone, without a suitable partner. The Gemara in *Sanhedrin* 76b explains that הן is the Greek equivalent for "one."

The word הן has a numerical value of fifty-five and a final *mispar katan* of one (5 + 5 = 10; 1 + 0 = 1). Thus, the two letters of הן are used to express the unique unity that exists between Hashem and His People via an inherent property of the number fifty-five.

The progression of the final *mispar katan* of the multiples of the number fifty-five is in reverse order to that obtained by the multiples of the number eight and twenty-six:

| | | | | | | | |
|---|---|---|---|---|---|---|---|
| **1** | x 55 = | 55 | 5 + 5 | = 10 | 1 + 0 | = | **1** |
| **2** | x 55 = | 110 | 1 + 1 + 0 | | | = | **2** |
| **3** | x 55 = | 165 | 1 + 6 + 5 | = 12 | 1 + 2 | = | **3** |
| **4** | x 55 = | 220 | 2 + 2 + 0 | | | = | **4** |
| **5** | x 55 = | 275 | 2 + 7 + 5 | = 14 | 1 + 4 | = | **5** |
| **6** | x 55 = | 330 | 3 + 3 + 0 | | | = | **6** |
| **7** | x 55 = | 385 | 3 + 8 + 5 | = 16 | 1 + 6 | = | **7** |
| **8** | x 55 = | 440 | 4 + 4 + 0 | | | = | **8** |
| **9** | x 55 = | 495 | 4 + 9 + 5 | = 18 | 1 + 8 | = | **9** |
| **10** | x 55 = | 550 | 5 + 5 + 0 | = 10 | 1 + 0 | = | **1** |

This similarity between the series formed by the multiples of eight, twenty-six and fifty-five is hinted at in the word שמונה, as it spells out שמו + נה, which can be understood as "[the multiples of]

His Name (שמו) [form a similar pattern to that of the multiples of] נה (55)."

◈ ◈ ◈

The letter ח is the acronym for חיים, "life." The human body is only brought to life when the נשמה, the spiritual soul, enters the body. A physical body without a soul remains as dead as a stone. The letters of the word שמונה spell out the word נשמה, "the soul," as it is the spiritual soul that provides life to a person.

Alternatively, the word שמונה can also be translated as "to count." On Yom Kippur, the *Kohen Gadol* entered the Holy of Holies to sprinkle the blood, and counted up to the number eight, as the Mishnah enumerates: וכך היה מונה : אחת - אחת ואחת - אחת ושתים - אחת ושלש - אחת וארבע - אחת וחמש אחת ושש - אחת ושבע — "And this is how he counted: one, one and one, one and two, one and three, one and four, one and five, one and six, one and seven" (*Yoma* 5:3).

## The Letter ט

The letter ט has a numerical value of nine, which represents the virtue of eternal truth and fulfills as either טת or טית, which translates as "goodness." When fulfilled as טת, it has a *mispar katan* of thirteen, the same as the word אחד, signifying the Unity of Hashem. The second fulfillment of the alternative spelling טית (טית יוד תיו) has a final *mispar katan* of nine, the same as the numerical value of the original letter ט.

Thus, the letter ט is connected to the numbers nine and thirteen, and the letter itself portrays the absolute and indestructible nature of the truth. Appropriately, the fulfillment of Hashem's Name has a total of nine letters (יוד הא וו הא), and that of Elokim, thirteen (אלף למד הא יוד מם).

The truth that was incorporated into Creation is displayed by the first three words of the Torah (בראשית ברא אלהים), in that their final letters spell out the word אמת, the truth that is sealed within the Torah. The first two words בראשית ברא contain a total of nine letters, while the third word, the Name of Elokim, as we have said, fulfills into thirteen letters.

### ◈ The Shape and Composition of the Letter ט

The creation of the human embryo is aptly represented by the number nine in various ways. From all the letters of the Hebrew *alef-beis*, the only one that is shaped in a way that forms a receptacle with a small aperture on the top is the letter ט, which is composed from a ז and either a כ or נ, where the כ or נ is bent slightly inwards. This shape closely resembles the female womb that houses a human embryo during its nine months of gestation. The triangular value of the number nine is forty-five, the same as the numerical value of the word אדם, "man," representing the development of the human fetus during the nine months of pregnancy.

The *Zohar* explains that a person's souls originates from one of the three spiritual worlds. These worlds are represented in the decimal system in the groupings of the integers in the tens, hundreds and thousands, while the physical world is represented by the units. In the composition of the letter ט, both options (ז + כ or ז + נ) incorporate values from the units (7 = ז) and from the tens (20 = כ and 50 = נ). Thus the birth of a physical body combined with a higher spiritual soul at the end of the nine months of pregnancy is represented by the shape and composition of the letter ט.

Moreover, the nine-month gestation period is alluded to in the molecular structure of DNA — which is the basis of each human cell — in that the DNA structure is displayed in the pattern of the multiples of the number nine (see p. 147).

During these nine months of pregnancy, the developing fetus is taught the entire Torah, which he then forgets again at birth. Every birth mentioned in Scripture is introduced with the phrase ותהר ותלד — "...and she conceived and bore a child." The letters of the word ותהר, "she conceived," can also spell out the word תורה alluding to the Torah that is taught during the nine months of pregnancy. Both the Torah and the human soul are timeless and indestructible, and are, therefore, aptly represented by their close association to the number nine.

◈ ◈ ◈

As mentioned, the ט, with a numerical value of nine, is the only letter that forms a receptacle-shaped container. All the higher *Sefiros* are filtered into the ninth *Sefirah*, יסוד, before being funneled into the final *Sefirah*, מלכות, which is the gateway to the physical world. Correspondingly, the number nine is the final one of the units, before the tens begin.

When the ט is formed from ז + כ it has a composite numerical value of twenty-seven, which produces a *mispar katan* of nine — the same as the numerical value of the complete letter. This represents the complete truth that is encapsulated in each of the twenty-seven letters of the entire *alef-beis*. Alternatively, when the ט is composed from ז + נ, it forms the word זן, the maternal nourishment that a baby receives during the nine months of gestation. Once a baby is born, this nourishment is supplied through his פה, his mouth; the shape of the letter פ is in fact similar to that of a ט when the latter is rotated ninety degrees counter-clockwise.

## ◈ Correlations Between the Representations of the Letter ט

### ט-תשעה

In the section dealing with *mispar katan,* we explained the significance of the number nine and its connection to the concept of אמת, truth. With the arrival of Mashiach, the complete and absolute truth will manifest itself to the entire world. This revelation will occur at the time of the תְּשָׁעָה, our final Salvation. Thus, the letter ט connects to the word תשעה, as they both relate to the revelation of the absolute truth.

## THE LETTER י

י The letter י has a numerical value of ten, and the fulfillment translates as "hand" or "possessions." It is the smallest of all the letters, representing the self-nullification that every Jew must strive for, to become a true servant of Hashem. In Hebrew, the written shape of the letters are suspended from the top of a line with the base resting on the line below. The י however is the only letter of the *alef-beis*, which is suspended in mid-air. This is representative of the Jew who is suspended as well, because he has nothing to stand upon on his own and must rely on Hashem's Providence.

The letters of the fulfillment of י (יוד) all belong to the group of simple letters. The total numerical value of the hidden fulfillment of this expansion (**יוד**) is ten, the same as that of the letter itself. The double fulfillment can be written as **יוד ואו דלת**, which has a final *mispar katan* of eight. We have already explained how the multiples of eight progress towards the number one, thereby displaying the humility and the unity of Hashem. Furthermore, its generative sequence (י–יו–יוד), also has a final *mispar katan* of one (when adding the *mispar katan* of each of the levels). This again displays the Unity of Hashem that is inherent in this letter.

### ◈ Correlations Between the Representations of the Letter י

**י–יוד**

We have previously explained how the Ten *Sefiros* are represented by the four letters of Hashem's Name of י-ה-ו-ה. The letter י

represents the first two *Sefiros* — כתר and חכמה. Divine wisdom was given to Shlomo haMelech, as the *pasuk* states: וי-ה-ו-ה נתן חכמה לשלמה — "And Hashem imbued Shlomo with wisdom..." (*Melachim* I 5:26).

The letter י in Hashem's Name represents the Divine wisdom that is incorporated in the *Sefirah* of חכמה. Wisdom is comparable to a flame from which another flame can be lit without diminishing its original illumination. Similarly, the hidden fulfillment (וד) has the same numerical value as the י itself, representative of the fact that although Divine wisdom was bestowed upon Shlomo haMelech, in no way was the original Divine wisdom weakened. The Divine wisdom that was given to Shlomo haMelech is symbolized by the hidden fulfillment of the letter י, which duplicates the original letter.

◆ ◆ ◆

The Kli Yakar, in his commentary on the priestly blessing (*Bemidbar* 6:25), gives a profound explanation regarding the connection between the letter י and its fulfillment as יוד. He quotes the Gemara in *Niddah* (31a) that states: "There are three partners that form the human being: Hashem, the father and the mother. The father provides the white semen from which five parts are formed. They are: the bones, sinews, the nails, the brain and the white part of the eyeball. The mother provides a further five items: the blood, the skin, the flesh, the hair and the black part of the eyeball. Hashem provides [ten distinct parts to the living body]: the living spirit; the divine spirit; the facial countenance; the senses of sight, hearing and speech; the power to walk; wisdom; insight and knowledge."

The ten discernible items jointly provided by the parents are all incorporated in the י — the revealed portion of the fulfillment (**י**וד) — while the other ten items, which are provided by Hashem, are incorporated in the hidden portion of the fulfillment (י**וד**). This partnership between Hashem and the parents is symbolized by the *complete* fulfillment of the letter. Hashem is the majority shareholder in human creation, and each parent remains in a humble minority, signified by the use of the smallest letter to represent this partnership. A person feels indebted to Hashem for all His kindness and praises Him, as expressed in the *pasuk*: **יודו לי-ה-ו-ה חסדו** — "Praise Hashem for all His kindness" (*Tehillim* 107:8). Praise is expressed as a fulfillment of the letter **י**, as highlighted above.

The universe was created through the use of four basic ingredients (Ramban explains that this is called "*hule*" in Greek): **אש** (fire), **מים** (water), **רוח** (air), and **עפר** (dust). All were used to create man, the pinnacle of Creation. The acronym of these four items has a numerical value of 311, the same as that of the word **איש**, "man."

The *Shulchan Aruch* in *Orach Chayim* 219 writes that there are four types of salvations that require a special prayer of thanksgiving to be recited: after having returned safely from traveling overseas, after having traveled across a desert, after having recovered from a major illness, and after being released from captivity. Each of these four salvations corresponds to one of the four ingredients used in Creation. Water corresponds to the sea traveler; dust, to travelers across the deserts; fire, to recovering from a major illness, which normally is accompanied by a high temperature; and air corresponds to being released from captivity. After experiencing a salvation from one of these four life-threatening dangers, one recites *Birchas haGomel*, a prayer thanking Hashem.

The *Shulchan Aruch* suggests a mnemonic to remember these four occurrences from the words of the prayer we recite during *Shacharis* in praise of Hashem: וכל החיים יודך סלה — "Every living thing will praise You, *selah*." The word **חיים** is a *notrikon* for these four occurrences:

**ח**בוש captivity
**י**סורים illness
**י**ם sea travel
**מ**דבר crossing the desert

The above expression of praise incorporates the fulfillment of יוד (וכל החיים **יודך** סלה) and thus displays a connection between the number four — which represents here the four salvations — and the letter י, since the triangular value of the number four equates to the numerical value of י.

### י-יוד-עשר

The Ba'al HaTurim, in his commentary to *Bemidbar* 11:16, enumerates seventy descriptive Names of Hashem. *Osios d'Rabbi Yitzchak* explains that these seventy Names are represented by the letters of the word עשר.

Seventy, as Ba'al HaTurim points out is the numerical value of the letter ע. The fulfillment of the Name א-להים is אלף למד הי יוד מם, with a total numerical value of three hundred, the same as that of the letter ש. The generative value of א-להים is two hundred — א (1) + אל (31) + אלה (36) + אלהי (46) + אלהים (86) — which is also the numerical value of the letter ר.

The letter י, with a numerical value of ten, appropriately symbolizes holiness, as the *pasuk* points out: העשירי יהיה קדוש לה' — "Every tenth one shall be holy to Hashem" (*Vayikra* 27:32).

The correlation between the letter י and the word עשר vis-à-vis Hashem's seventy Names is alluded to in the words of the *pasuk*: י-ה-ו-ה יסעדנו על ערש דוי — "Hashem will fortify him, on the bed of misery..." (*Tehillim* 41:4). The first word of this phrase is itself the Name of Hashem. The numerical value of the second word (יסעדנו) is two hundred and thus corresponds to the generative value of the Name א-להים. The second and third words (יסעדנו על) have a combined numerical value of three hundred. These, therefore, represent the numerical value of the fulfillment of the Name א-להים, as explained above. The final two words in the *pasuk* (ערש דוי) also spell out the words עשר יוד, thereby providing a correlation between these three different representations of the letter י (י-יוד-עשר).

Furthermore, the Ba'al HaTurim points out that the Torah refers to the Jewish People also with seventy names. The fact that Hashem describes the Jewish nation with seventy names, the same number as His own, displays an affection that He has for His Chosen People. This is alluded to in the name ישראל, as both the ש and ר represent the Name of א-להים. The remaining letters of the name ישראל also represent Hashem — each in their own specific way.

This intimacy between Hashem and His People is also displayed in a mathematical format. The final *mispar katan* of the word ישראל equals one, thereby connecting them to the Omnipresent. Using the At–Bash transformation, the name ישראל produces מבגתכ, which has a *mispar katan* of fifteen. This equates to the numerical value of His Name of י-ה. In the Al–Bam alphabetic structure ישראל converts to שיטלא, which has a *mispar katan* of seventeen, the same as the *mispar katan* of His Name of י-ה-ו-ה. Furthermore, the *mispar katan* of the word אורייתא, the Aramaic word for "Torah," is also seventeen, and equates to the numerical value of the word טוב, "good." This affectionate bond is only formed when the Jewish People learn His Torah, for we know from the Zohar: קודשא בריך הוא אורייתא וישראל חד הוא — "Hashem, Israel and the Torah are one unit."

We have already explained how the letter א represents Hashem, and the letter ל portrays the learning and teaching of Torah. The hidden fulfillment of the word למד is comprised of the letters מ'ד', which convert, using the At–Bash formula, into the letters י'ק'. The latter pair have a numerical value of 110, the same as the hidden fulfillment of the letter א (אלף), illustrating the intimate connection that Hashem has with His nation, who learn His Torah.

This unifying bond is also expressed in the *Amidah* of Shabbos *Minchah*, when we say: אתה אחד ושמך אחד ומי כעמך ישראל גוי אחד בארץ — "You are One and Your Name is One, and who is like Your people Israel, *one nation* on earth." The numerical value of the phrase גוי אחד is thirty-two, the same as the word לב, which are the first and final letters of the Torah. Our adherence to the Torah ensures that we remain as "the one nation on earth" who have a unique bond with Him.

◈ ◈ ◈

The combination of י–יוד–עשר is indicative of the Ayik–Bekar alphabetic structure, which represents the correct separation and giving of tithes and charity. We have previously explained how tithes are allocated by separating ten percent of our produce. By their correct separation, the donor receives Hashem's blessings, which is represented by the letter י, with a numerical value of ten. This is indicated by the doubling up of the numerical values of the letters in the second set of the Ayik–Bekar structure, which is mirrored by the fulfillment of the letter י into the word יוד, thereby doubling its numerical value in the fulfilled form. The word עשר translates as "ten" and also as "wealthy," since receiving His special blessing results in wealth. This special mitzvah of giving ten percent of one's income to charity is symbolized in the combination of י–יוד–עשר.

◈ ◈ ◈

The Shlah, in his commentary to the *siddur* on the *pasuk*: פותח את ידך ומשביע לכל חי רצון — "You open Your hand, and satisfy every living thing with its desire" (*Tehillim* 145:16), interprets the phrase פותח את ידך to mean the "opening up of the *yuds*" — a reference to the space through which Hashem's blessing filters down to us. This space is achieved by stretching out, in a sense, the written and articulated Names of Hashem י-ה-ו-ה and אדנ-י. One Name begins with the letter י and the other ends with the same letter. Furthermore, he interprets the word פותח as פתח + ו, referring to the opening or the expansion of the six letters between the two *yud*s. The fullness of Hashem's blessings filter through to mankind via the expanded space occupied by these two Names. Thus we are praising Hashem for expanding that space and allowing us to receive even greater benefit.

Moreover, in that praise we are acknowledging that Hashem provides sustenance to all mankind. Sustenance is known as זן, which has a numerical value of fifty-seven. As explained above, the bountiful amount of sustenance is represented by the word עשר, which has a numerical value of 570 — ten times the numerical value of the word זן. The word עשר, therefore, aptly represents the prosperity that a person enjoys when Hashem showers His blessings on him by "opening His Hand."

◈ ◈ ◈

These different representations of the number ten (י-יוד-עשר) correspond to the Ten *Sefiros* through which the world was created. As explained earlier, in order to interact with the physical world, each of the higher one's resources are channeled through to the next lower *Sefirah*, with the lowest one acting as a gateway through which the effect of the other *Sefiros* are routed (see *Sefer Yetzirah*, for a further understanding of this esoteric concept). Thus, each one of these ten *Sefiros* incorporates within itself all of the other *Sefiros* as well. All these concepts are indicated by the combination of י-יוד-עשר. The hidden fulfillment of י (וד) alludes to the complete array of the other *Sefiros* that is incorporated within each of the *Sefiros*. The tenth and final *Sefirah* (מלכות) is represented by the word עשר, whose letters spell out the word שער — the gateway for all the other *Sefiros*. The numerical values of the letter י (10), its fulfillment as יוד (20), and its second fulfillment as יוד וו דלת (466) total 496 — the same as that of the word מלכות.

◈ ◈ ◈

The י, being the smallest of the letters, represents the concept of אין סוף, and corresponds to infinity. It represents a small dot, from which all the other letters of Hashem's Name can be formed. Elongating the letter י, forms the letter ו and by extending it in both directions, the letter ד is formed. From these three letters, 'י'ו'ד, we can also compose the letter ה, thereby completing the letters required to spell out Hashem's Name. The three letters of the fulfillment יוד belong to the simple letters, as simple letters represent Hashem's uniqueness.

The fulfillment of the letter י also connects to Hashem's Name of י-ה-ו-ה through it numerical equivalency. When substituting the triangular value of the letter ד (1 + 2 + 3 + 4 = 10) for its numerical value in יוד (10 + 6 + 4 = 20), the fulfillment of the letter י equates to twenty-six (10 + 6 + 10 = 26), the numerical value of Hashem's Name.

The number twenty-six is written in Hebrew letters as כו, the fulfillment of which spells out כף + וו. The hidden fulfillments of these letters (כף + וו) have a total numerical value of eighty-six, the same as that of the Name of א-להים. The number twenty-six, as represented by the letters of כו, therefore incorporate both the Names of Hashem and Elokim. We see from this how this small seed-size letter י grows and develops until it represents the Name of Hashem, which further transforms into the Name of Elokim, as well.

Alternatively its fulfillment into יוד doubles the numerical value (10 + 10), which also represents the Name of אדנ-י in the following way: The triangular value of the number ten is fifty-five, the same as the combined numerical value of the first three letters of **אדנ-י**. Therefore, אדנ + י is represented by the fulfillment of the letter י.

Thus, the letter י correlates to each of Hashem's three Names — י-ה-ו-ה, א-להים and אדנ-י.

(It should be noted that Hashem's actual Name is י-ה-ו-ה — all the other Names by which He is known are descriptive ones, known collectively as שם כנוי, "a descriptive name." The word כנוי has a numerical value of eighty-six, the same as that of א-להים, which is His primary descriptive Name, and the first one used in the Torah.)

◆ ◆ ◆

The Torah states: וידעת היום והשבת אל לבבך כי י-ה-ו-ה הוא הא-להים בשמים ממעל ועל הארץ מתחת אין עוד — "You are to know this day and take to your heart that Hashem is the only God — in the Heavens above and on the earth below — there is no other" (*Devarim* 4:39).

As stated earlier, the composition of the letter א is made up from two *yuds* separated by the diagonal letter ו, and the fulfillment of the letter י represents the Names of י-ה-ו-ה and א-להים. The two *yuds* correspond to the phrase י-ה-ו-ה הוא הא-להים בשמים ממעל ועל הארץ מתחת. The upper letter י corresponds to Hashem Elokim "in the Heavens above," and the lower one to Hashem Elokim "on the earth below." The Ba'al HaTurim points out that the phrase אין עוד appears a total of six times in all of Scripture (see *Yeshayahu* 45:5, 45:6, 45:21, 45:22, 46:9; and *Yoel* 2:27), corresponding to the diagonal ו in the letter א. Thus this entire *pasuk* is explained by the composition of the א.

As we have mentioned many times, each letter displays the Unity of Hashem, and intrinsic in each letter is an infinite amount of wisdom. The Unity of Hashem is incorporated in the directive to take to heart (והשבת אל לבבך) the wisdom incorporated in all of the letters of the *alef-beis*. The word לבבך is composed from the words לב + בך. The first part לב, with a numerical value of thirty-two, represents the thirty-two avenues of wisdom; the word בך has a numerical value of twenty-two, the same as the number of letters in the *alef-beis*. Therefore, one must take to "heart" the "thirty-two" avenues of wisdom that are derived from the study of the Hebrew *alef-beis*, with which the entire Torah is written. (The first and final letters of the Torah are ב and ל, which combine to form the word לב.)

*Daniel* 7:9 refers to Hashem as עתיק יומין, "the Ancient One." By using the At–Bash formula, the letter ק can be replaced by a letter ד, transforming the word עתיק into עתיד, which contains the same letters as the word ידעת. This reference to Hashem as עתיק יומין thereby corresponds to the phrase וידעת היום, tying it in with the *pasuk* from *Devarim* quoted above. Thus, the reference to Hashem as "the Ancient One" refers to Him as being the unique power — אין עוד.

## THE LETTER כ

The numerical value of the letter כ is twenty. It fulfills as the word כף, which has a numerical value of one hundred, and a final *mispar katan* of one. The second fulfillment can be spelled out as **כף פא**, which also has a final *mispar katan* of one. This reinforces the Unity of Hashem, which is symbolized by the letter and its fulfillment.

The fulfillment of the letter כ into the word כף is used to convey five different meanings:

1) a spoon, as in כף אחת — "one spoon" (*Bemidbar* 7:14).
2) forcing, as in: **הלכף** כאגמן ראשו — "forcing his head down like a sickle" (*Yeshayahu* 58:5).
3) protective wings, as in: נשא לבבנו אל **כפים** — "Let us lift up our hearts with our hands" (*Eichah* 3:41), i.e. in a protective gesture.
4) a weighing pan, as in: **כף** מזניים — "the pan of a scale" (Mishnah *Beitzah* 3:6).
5) a dome shape, as in: **כופין** את הסל לפני האפרוחים — "Invert a basket in front of a baby chick's [nest]" (*Shabbos* 128b) — forming a dome-shaped step to facilitate the chicks entering their nest.

The letter כ belongs to the seven simple letters, and it is used in composing another seven letters: ק'פ'ס'מ'ל'כ'ט'. The actual shape of the letter כ, with its rounded edges, resembles that of a dome lying on its side.

When used at the beginning of a word to compare two objects, it is known as the כף הדמיון — the comparative כ. The letter כ has a symmetrical shape, consisting of two parallel lines, which bend round to meet each other. Thus, drawing an analogy between two similar objects and connecting them together, is represented in the actual shape of this letter.

An example is found in the *pasuk*: כי כמוך כפרעה — "...for you are like Pharaoh" (*Bereishis* 44:18). In this example, there are two comparative *chaf*s, and, as Rashi explains, a double analogy is found in comparing Yosef to Pharaoh, and also in comparing Pharaoh to Yosef. (See Rashi, there, for further explanation.)

◈ ◈ ◈

If we separate Hashem's Name into two halves (יה + וה), the numerical values of the halves — fifteen and eleven, respectively — can be achieved by summing various combinations of the numbers from one to ten.

The respective numerical equivalencies can be formed by the following sets:

| וה | | יה | |
|---|---|---|---|
| 10 + 1 | = 11 | 10 + 5 | = 15 |
| 9 + 2 | = 11 | 9 + 6 | = 15 |
| 8 + 3 | = 11 | 8 + 7 | = 15 |
| 7 + 4 | = 11 | **Total** | **= 45** |
| 6 + 5 | = 11 | | |
| **Total** | **= 55** | | |

These eight sets total one hundred (45 + 55 = 100), the numerical value of כף.

At every circumcision a special chair is reserved in honor of Eliyahu haNavi, who is attributed with the title of being the מלאך הברית, the angel of the covenant. He is personified by the expression that was declared on Mount Carmel: י-ה-ו-ה הוא הא-להים — "Hashem is God" (*Melachim* I 18:39). These Names of Hashem (י-ה-ו-ה and א-להים) have numerical values of twenty-six and eighty-six respectively, while that of the word מילה, circumcision, is eighty-five.

The Name Elokim has a special connection with the commandment of *milah*, as it was through its use that this commandment was given: וימל אברהם את יצחק בנו בן שמנת ימים כאשר צוה אתו **א-להים** — "Avraham circumcised his son Yitzchak, at the age of eight days old, as Elokim commanded him" (*Bereishis* 21:4).

There are further numerical connections here: Avraham, who lived in the twentieth (the numerical value of כ) generation from Creation, was one hundred (the numerical value of כף) years old, when he circumcised his eight-day-old son, Yitzchak (eight being the total number of sets in the above grouping).

The letter כ is known as the כ כפופה, the bent letter כ. We can find numerical connections between this term and the above explanation, as well. The first two letters of **כף** כפופה have a numerical value of one hundred. The final two letters of כף כפו**פה** have a numerical value of eighty-five, the same as that of the word מילה. The middle letters of the כף כ**פו**פה have a numerical value of eighty-six, the same as that of א-להים. The letter כ in כף **כ**פופה, with a numerical value of twenty, represents a crown (see below). The purpose of the circumcision is to remove the foreskin and reveal the עטרה, crown. The Aruch explains the word עטרה as היקף דבר מכל צד ככתר — "something similar to a crown that fully surrounds." Thus the commandment of circumcision is incorporated in the expression of כף כפופה.

### ◈ כ—The Royal Letter

The three letters that compose the word מלך, "king," appear in a reverse alphabetic order, representing the attribute of justice, as it is the monarch's responsibility to maintain law and order among his subjects. When using the word מלך with reference to the Divine King, the reverse order also indicates that His monarchy has different parameters to that of a human king. A human king requires a population to rule over, whereas the Divine King is required by the population for all their needs, as expressed in the sentiment: כל העולם צריכים לו והוא אין צריך להם — "The complete universe needs Him, but He does not require them."

It is interesting to point out that when anointing the kings of the dynasty of David haMelech, special oil was smeared on their heads, in the shape of the letter כ.

The shape of the letter כ is symmetrical along the horizontal, and has rounded edges both inside and outside. This unique symmetrical shape represents a weighing scale. The two letters that follow it in the alphabetic sequence, the ל and מ, are both composed from the letters כ + ו, with a numerical value of twenty-six. The letter כ, therefore, demonstrates how Hashem sits in judgment and carefully weighs everything in Divine Judgment.

The letter כ also represents the throne (כסא) on which the king sits. As the tallest and most regal letter of the *alef-beis*, the ל represents royalty and nobility. Thus, these letters portray a royal monarch sitting on his throne. The letter מ, as the middle one of the complete *alef-beis*, is representative of the phrase: מקרב עמך — "from among your nation," a reference to the fact that a king is usually chosen from among the people over whom he will rule.

## ◈ Correlation Between the Representations of the Letter כ

**כ–כף**

The fulfillment of the letter כ into כף, translates as a spoon or the palm of the hand, which acts as a receptacle that is capable of holding objects.

The letters 'כ'ף also spell out the word פך, a small jug. The two letters that are in juxtaposition to the כ in the *alef-beis* form the word כלי, which means "vessel." The fulfillment as כף represents a vessel containing all of His blessings, as symbolized by the *pasuk*: כף אחת עשרה זהב מלאה קטרת — "One spoon of gold, its weight ten *shekalim*, filled with incense" (*Bemidbar* 7:14).

We have previously discussed how the alphabetic structure of Ayik–Bekar displays full Divine blessings. The first set of letters (אי"ק)

has numerical values of one, ten and one hundred, respectively. Similarly, in the above *pasuk*, the numerical value of the word כף is one hundred, the word אחת translates as "one" and עשרה as "ten." The second set of letters (בכ"ר) represents the ברכה, the reward — the spoon of incense that contains the blessing.

The Mishnah (*Tamid* 5:2) explains that the incense-offering was a powerful *segulah* for material wealth. Thus, the *Kohen* who performed it could become wealthy. Consequently, the privilege of performing this service in the *Beis haMikdash* was allocated only to people who had not done so before, to give as many as possible the opportunity to benefit. This great gift is alluded to by the juxtaposition of the *pesukim*: "They shall place incense before You" (*Devarim* 33:10) and "Bless Hashem his possessions and favor the work of his hands" (ibid. 33:11).

◈ ◈ ◈

The blessings symbolized by the אי"ק continue in the next set of בכ"ר. This represents the acronym of ברכה — the blessing that is stored in the receptacle of the כף, the spoon, that has the ability to make the impoverished רש into a wealthy man. His blessings require a storage receptacle in which to hold them — namely the כף. This connection between the ברכה and the כף highlights the similarity in shape between the two letters of ב and כ.

The fulfillment of כף, with a numerical value of one hundred, symbolizes the daily requirement to recite one hundred blessings. The Baruch sheAmar views the shape of the letter כ as having the same shape as two *vavs* lying sideways facing each other, alluding to the twelve tribes (6 + 6 = 12) who are all obliged to recite these one hundred daily blessings.

### כ-עשרים

The letter כ represents a כתר, a crown. The Mishnah, in the fourth chapter of *Pirkei Avos,* writes: "There are three different types of crowns: the Crown of the Torah, the Crown of Priesthood, and the Crown of Kingship. But the crown of possessing a Good Name stands higher than the previous three."

The Crown of Priesthood (כתר כהנה) is symbolized by the letter כ itself. The Crown of Torah is represented by the letter ב. (We have previously explained how the letter ב, with a numerical value of two, represents both the Written and Oral Torah.) The letter כ and the letters that follow it in the alphabetic sequence (ל and מ), form the word מלך, representing the Crown of Kingship.

The topic of the above Mishnah is further elaborated on in the sixth chapter of *Pirkei Avos*, where it states: גדלה תורה יותר מן הכהנה ומין המלכות — "Torah is greater than either Priesthood or Kingship."

The striking similarity in the shape of the letters ב and כ, indicates a deeper connection. (Incidentally, the ב and כ have other similarities, as well: Both are part of the same set in the אי"ק בכ"ר alphabetic structure, and both possess a *mispar katan* of two.)

The fact that the ב (Torah) appears earlier in the alphabetic order than the כ (Priesthood) and the מ'ל'ך' combination (Kingship), supports the idea that Torah is greater than both Priesthood and Kingship, as mentioned in the Mishnah.

Moreover, the numerical value of the words כתר תורה, the Crown of Torah, equates to the words עשרים וששה, the written out form of the number twenty-six. Thus the true crowning glory of the Torah is the fact that it incorporates within it Hashem's Divine wisdom.

This is reinforced by a comment made by the Sifsei Kohen on the *pasuk* describing the fashioning of the Golden Ark: ונתת אל הארן את העדת אשר אתן אליך — "You shall put into the *Aron* the Testimony that I shall give you" (*Shemos* 25:16). This *pasuk* contains twenty-six letters. Moreover, it begins with the letter ו and ends with the letter ך, which have a combined numerical value of twenty-six.

◈ ◈ ◈

In Hebrew, all the integers in the units will produce a corresponding multiple number in the tens by adding ים as a suffix. For example, the number שלש, three, becomes thirty—שלשים. This holds true for all the numbers with the exception of the number twenty, **עשרים**, which is formed as the plural of the number ten (עשר), rather than the plural of the number two.

*Osios d'Rabbi Yitzchak* gives an explanation for the above anomaly. There it is explained that this plural form correlates to three of Hashem's Names: א-הי-ה, י-ה and י-ה-ו-ה. The total numerical value of these Names is sixty-two (15 + 21 + 26 = 62). Multiplying this number by ten (עשר), produces a total of 620, which is the numerical value of the word עשרים and the word כתר. We've already explained how the letter כ symbolizes the three types of crowns; therefore, it is appropriate that עשרים is the representation for the letter כ.

The basic monetary unit used in the Torah is the *shekel* (שקל) and each Jew was obligated to donate half a *shekel* yearly towards the cost of the Temple sacrifices. The *shekel* was comprised of twenty *geirah* (גרה); therefore, half a *shekel* is the equivalent of ten *geirah*. The phrase used in the commandment: מחצית השקל בשקל הקודש עשרים גרה השקל—"Half a *shekel*, by the holy *shekel*, the *shekel* is twenty *geirah*" (*Shemos* 30:13).

Using the At–Bash method, the letters of the word שקל transform into the letters ב'ד'כ', which have a total numerical value of twenty-six, the same as that of Hashem's Name. Appropriately, this coin is referred to as שקל הקודש, the "holy *shekel*." The numerical value of the word שקל is 430, which equates to the combined numerical values of Avraham (אברהם = 248) and Yaakov (יעקב = 182). The numerical value of the word *geirah* (גרה) equals that of the Yitzchak (יצחק = 208). Thus, the *shekel*, with a value of twenty *geirah*, represents all three Patriarchs. Furthermore, the fulfillment of יצחק, spelled as **יוד צדיק חית קוף**, has a total numerical value of 620, the same as the words עשרים and כתר.

## THE LETTER ל

ל

The letter ל has a numerical value of thirty, and fulfills as the word למד, which means "to learn" or "to teach." It is also found in the expression מלמד בקר, "an ox goad," which is the yoke with which one trains and controls an animal's instincts. The second fulfillment becomes למד מם דלת which has a *mispar katan* of thirty—the same as the numerical value of the letter itself—and a final *mispar katan* of three. Three and thirty are the numerical values of the letters of ג and ל, respectively, which both belong to the same set in the אי"ק בכ"ר alphabetic structure.

The ל is composed from the letter כ, as the base, and the letter ו, as its neck. Together they have a numerical value of twenty-six, the same as Hashem's Name.

### ◈ ל Represents Monarchy

As mentioned earlier, the ל is the tallest of all the letters and therefore symbolizes the nobility and majesty of a king. The fulfillment למד translates as "learning," alluding to the requirement of a Jewish monarch to study Torah daily.

The Mishnah in *Pirkei Avos* (6:6) writes: המלכות נקנית בשלשים מעלות—"Royalty is acquired with thirty prerogatives," the same as the numerical value of the letter ל. The ultimate aim of Creation will be achieved when Hashem will be universally acknowledged as the King of the entire universe, as expressed in *Zechariah* (14:9): ביום ההוא יהיה ה' אחד ושמו אחד—"On that day Hashem will be One, and His Name will be One." Appropriately, the word יהיה ("[Hashem] will be") has a numerical value of thirty. Similarly, on Rosh Hashanah, we are commanded to blow the *shofar*, through which we coronate Hashem. This blowing is divided into two parts, the first set of which are the thirty blasts that are blown before *Musaf*.

The ל is among the five letters (א'ל'מ'ס'ם') that are composed from the letters כ and ו. It is interesting to note that when these letters are written in their fulfilled states, they each contain two of these five letters:

| | |
|---|---|
| א | אלף |
| ל | למד |
| מ | מם |
| ס | סמך |
| ם | מם |

### ◈ Correlation Between the Representations of the Letter ל

#### ל-למד

A special Divine unity is expressed in the fulfillment of the letter ל (למד). In this fulfillment, both the ל and the מ have composite values of twenty-six, the numerical value of Hashem's Name. When accepting Hashem's sovereignty, we say: שמע ישראל ה' א-להינו ה' אחד — "Hear O Israel, Hashem is our G-d, Hashem is One" (*Devarim* 6:4). This *pasuk* mentions Hashem's Name twice, corresponding to the composite value of each of the first two letters in the fulfillment (למד). Furthermore, the *pasuk* contains two large letters — ע and ד — which have a combined numerical value of seventy-four, the same as that of the fulfillment למד. These two large letters spell out the word עד, "to testify," which has a numerical value equal to that of למד — Torah study. This connection is reinforced by the Gemara in *Sanhedrin* (7), which states: "In the Heavenly Tribunal, a person will be asked to testify regarding his Torah study."

#### ל-למד-שלשים

As mentioned, the numerical value of the letter ל is thirty, שלשים. However, the word שלשים can also be understood to mean a high-ranking officer or a superior, as in: ושלשים על כלו — "and officers over them all" (*Shemos* 14:7). The lesson to be learned is that in order for a student to learn from his teachers (למד), he needs to respect them and treat them as his superiors (שלשים).

## The Letter מ

מ

The letter מ has a numerical value of forty and fulfills as the word מם. Its hidden fulfillment is the same as the letter itself. Both its regular and final form (ם) are composed from the letters ו + כ — representing the Unity of Hashem, and the *mispar katan* of the fulfillment מם is eight, which, as explained earlier, also represents the Unity of Hashem. A further connection is its ordinal value; מ is the thirteenth letter in the *alef-beis* — thirteen being the numerical value of the word אחד, thereby reinforcing the Unity of Hashem that is symbolized by this letter.

Although the מ represents unity, it also symbolizes diversification, for the addition of a letter מ at the end of a word transforms it into a plural. For example, the word ילד becomes ילדים, "children," by adding the suffix ים.

The final letter ם and the letter ס have a very similar shape. The final ם is sometimes used to represent the shape of a square, and the ס, a complete circle.

Moreover, they both belong to the same set in the Ayik–Bekar alphabetic structure, each with a *mispar katan* of six. The letter מ, with a numerical value of forty, alludes to the forty days that Moshe spent in Heaven before the giving of the Torah. Thus this letter represents the Written Torah. As we know, the Written Torah can only be understood correctly through the interpretations and teachings of the Oral Torah. Appropriately, the hidden fulfillment of the the letter מ is a final ם, which, when using its higher numerical value, has a *mispar katan* of six, thereby representing the Oral Torah. The combination of both formats of the letter מ represents the unity of the Written and Oral Torah together. Moreover, it was in the fortieth generation after the giving of the Written Torah that the Oral Torah was compiled.

Rambam, in his introduction to his codification of Jewish Law, enumerates forty generations from Moshe Rabbeinu to Rav Ashi. Moshe gave us the Written Torah while Rav Ashi compiled the Babylonian Talmud. With its completion, Rav Ashi "sealed" the revelation contained in the Oral Torah. Both the Written Torah and the Oral Law are symbolized by the fulfillment of the letter מ, which is comprised of two letters (מם) each having a numerical value of forty.

The letter ס also has a *mispar katan* of six, which when combined with the ם produces the idiom for the Torah as **סם** חיים — "the spice of life" (see *Ta'anis* 7a). Moreover, there is close connection between the final letter ם and the fulfillment of the word סמך. They both have the equivalent numerical value of six hundred (when taking the higher numerical value of five hundred for the final ך).

◈ ◈ ◈

If a matter is brought for judgment to a local *beis din* and is found to be too complex a case to rule on, the Torah lays down the procedure that should be followed. The relevant passage begins: כי יפלא ממך דבר למשפט וכו' — "If a matter of judgment will be concealed from you..." (*Devarim* 17:8).

The hidden fulfillment of the letter מ is another ם and that of the letter ס is מך. Combining the hidden fulfillments of these letters produces the word ממך, "from you." Since both the Written and Oral Torah are represented by the letters מ and ס, it is appropriate that this passage, which deals with complex matters, begins with the phrase: כי יפלא **ממך** דבר למשפט.

◈ ◈ ◈

Both the normal and final letters מ, are composed from the letters ו + כ. We have already explained how the letter ו represents the מטה א-להים, Hashem's Staff. The movement of His staff controls world events. Hashem's Divine Power was displayed in the ten plagues that were brought on **מצרים**, Egypt. This retribution against **מצרים** is symbolized by the two *mems*, in that their respective shapes correspond to the angle that the Divine Staff was held. In the open מ the "staff" (ו) is leaning backwards, poised to deliver a blow, while in the final ם the "staff" is upright, indicating that the "slap" has already been given.

The Rokeach points out that in the *pasuk* that introduces the first plague, where the waters changed to blood, the letter מ appears twenty-two times—more times than in any other *pasuk* in Scripture. Twelve are regular *mems* and ten are final ones (as highlighted): **ויאמר ה' אל משה אמר אל אהרן קח מטך ונטה ידך על מימי מיצרים על נהרתם על יאריהם ועל אגמיהם ועל כל מקוה מימיהם ויהיו דם והיה דם בכל ארץ מצרים ובעצים ובאבנים**—"And Hashem said to Moshe: 'Say to Aharon, Take your staff and stretch our your hand over the waters of Egypt—over their rivers, over their canals, over their reservoirs, and over all their gatherings of water—and they shall become blood; there shall be blood throughout the land of Egypt, even in wooden and stone vessels" (*Shemos* 7:19). The use of both the regular מ and the final ם alludes to the "hitting action" mentioned above.

◆ ◆ ◆

The final letter ם is four-sided in shape and has a higher numerical value of six hundred. This symbolizes Mashiach, who will gather in all the Jewish exiles from the four corners of the globe, and who is destined to come within the sixth millennium from Creation.

The letter מ is used to represent the central figure of **מלך המשיח**, as it is the central—i.e. the middle—letter of the twenty-seven-letter *alef-beis*. The מ is followed by the letter נ; together they produce the acronym **מלך נאמן**, "the faithful king," an expression referring to Mashiach.

The significance of the juxtaposition of the letters מ and נ in the alphabetic order is further displayed by the fact that the fulfillment of the letter נ is incorporated into the word of **ינון**, a name which refers to Mashiach. Moreover, the letter נ is the fourteenth letter of the *alef-beis* — fourteen being the numerical value of David (דוד), the ancestor of the Messianic dynasty.

◈ ◈ ◈

The first separation that took place at the time of Creation was between the two dissimilarities of light and darkness. The next division was between two similar items — a separation between water and water (בין מים למים). The word מים is composed from the letters מ and י. The numerical value of each of these letters equals the numerical value of its respective hidden fulfillment. This duplication alludes to the reflective and mirror-like properties of water.

The letter מ, with a numerical value of forty, represents the minimum quantity of forty cubic *se'ah* of water (מים) that is required for *mikveh* to be kosher. We have previously explained how the At–Bash alphabetic transformation method represents repentance. In At–Bash, the letter מ converts to a י; thus the word מים becomes ממם or $מ^3$, which represents a cubic measure — the forty cubic *se'ah* of water in a *mikveh*.

### ◈ Correlation Between the Representations of the Letter מ

**מ–מם**

The fulfillment of the מם is comprised of a מ פתוח, an open מ, and a ם סתום, a closed מ. The open letter symbolizes the revealed portion of the Torah, while the closed one represents its hidden teachings. This combination of מם indicates that however much of the revealed Torah we have learned and understood, there is always at least an equivalent amount that still remains hidden. This letter's fulfillment continues to fulfill again into מם מם, *ad infinitum*. This symbolizes the eternity of the Torah as the wellspring of knowledge in both its revealed and hidden parts. The Magen David explains that the letter מ represents both the revealed and hidden teachings of the Written and Oral Torah. Any additions to the Torah would be represented by the inclusion of a conjunctive letter ו, forming the word מום, "blemish." The Torah is completely perfect and any external additions would only be detrimental.

◈ ◈ ◈

The first מ in the fulfillment of מם represents the first redeemer, Moshe Rabbeinu, while the final ם in this fulfillment represents the final redeemer — Mashiach. Thus, the fulfillment of the letter מ represents complete redemption.

When Hashem instructed Moshe to go to Egypt to redeem the Jewish People, he was very hesitant to do so. After seven days of delay, he finally said: ויאמר בי אדני שלח נא ביד תשלח — "Please, my Lord, send by the hand whomever You will send" (*Shemos* 4:13).

*Targum Yonasan* explains this dialogue. Moshe understood that he was not to be the ultimate and final redeemer. Because he knew that the Jewish People were destined to suffer further exiles, in this *pasuk* he was asking Hashem to send Eliyahu together with Mashiach immediately, to bring about the Final Redemption and save the Jewish People further persecutions. This is supported by the Rokeach, who adds that the numerical value of the words ביד תשלח ("whomever You will send") is 754, which equates to the numerical value of the words of שלח אליהו ומשיח, "Send Eliyahu and Mashiach."

## The Letter נ

The נ has a numerical value of fifty and fulfills as the word נון; this fulfillment has a final *mispar katan* of nine (50 + 6 + 700 = 756; 7 + 5 + 6 = 18; 1 + 8 = 9), the number that represents eternal truth. This number is also alluded to in the letter's second fulfillment, as it contains nine letters (נון ואו נון).

The נ represents the fifty gates of wisdom commonly known as the נ' שערי בינה. Repentance is effected through the third *Sefirah* of בינה. Appropriately we allocate fifty days of the Jewish year specifically for repentance. These begin with the first day of the month of Elul and end fifty days later on Hoshana Rabbah.

When using the lower numerical value of the final *nun* (50), the generative value of the fulfillment (נ–נו–נון) has a final *mispar katan* of five (50 + 56 + 106 = 212; 2 + 1 + 2 = 5), which is the numerical value of the letter ה. Both the letters ה and נ belong to the same group in the Ayik–Bekar alphabetic structure and have a *mispar katan* of five. Although the letter נ belongs to the simple letters, it has a shape that combines features from both the letters ו and ז, which together have a numerical value of thirteen, the same as the numerical value of אחד, One — thereby displaying the Unity of Hashem.

The three letters ו'ז'נ' represent Hashem in another way as well. They fulfill as ואו זין נון, which has a total numerical value of 186 — the same as that of the word מקום, a reference to Hashem. The fulfillment as נון has a numerical value of 106, which equates to the combined numerical values of three of His Names: י-ה-ו-ה + אדנ-י + י-ה (26 + 65 + 15 = 106).

The letters used in the first fulfillment of the letter נ (נון) and the second fulfillment (נון וו נון) are all simple letters. The only other letter with this property is the letter ז. In fact, the shape of the letter נ is similar to that of the letter ז with a bent foot.

The letter נ is one of three letters whose fulfillments begin and end with the same letters. These letters are: ו (ואו), מ (מם) and נ (נון).

Another unique property of the letter נ is that the product of its numerical value (50) multiplied by its ordinal value (14) is the higher numerical value of the final letter ן (700).

### ◈ The Inverted Letter נ

*Parashas Beha'aloscha* begins with the instructions regarding the kindling of the Menorah. This was the only vessel in the *Mishkan* that was made entirely from pure gold. It was comprised of seven branches, twenty-two goblets, eleven knobs and nine flowers which were all hewn out of a single golden block. The Menorah, therefore, contained a total of forty-nine component parts (7 + 22 + 11 + 9 = 49), corresponding to the forty-nine words in Chapter 67 of *Tehillim*, which is often written in the shape of a Menorah. This chapter is often recited after counting the forty-nine days of *Sefiras haOmer*.

Further on in *Parashas Beha'aloscha*, at the end of the tenth chapter of *Bemidbar*, there is a passage comprised of two *pesukim* that is surrounded by two inverted regular-sized *nuns*. The passage reads: ויהי בנסע הארן ויאמר משה קומה ה' ויפצו איביך וינסו משנאיך מפניך ובנחה יאמר שובה ה' רבבות אלפי ישראל — "When the Ark would journey, Moshe Rabbeinu said, 'Arise, Hashem, and let Your enemies be scattered, and let those who hate You flee from before You.' And when it rested, he would say, 'Reside tranquilly, Hashem, among the myriads and thousands of Israel'" (*Bemidbar* 10:35–36).

During their travels in the desert, these *pesukim* were said as the Ark containing the Two Tablets, was lifted up, in order to move it to its new location. This acted as a prayer to Hashem to "let Your enemies be scattered and those who hate You flee." The second half of this passage is a prayer for tranquility, when the Torah Ark came to rest again at its new destination.

Rashi explains that the two inverted *nuns* that surround these *pesukim* act as signs indicating that the passage between them is not in its correct place. They are meant to divide two adjoining passages that relate to unpleasant episodes that occurred to the Jewish People. Thus, one would have expected these two *nuns* to face each other, forming a pair of complementing brackets ( [ ] ). However, both of them face backwards in the same direction ( [ [ ), forming two open brackets. The Ba'al HaTurim explains that this indicates that these *pesukim* actually belong fifty paragraphs earlier, before *Bemidbar* 2:17. (In the Torah, a new paragraph is indicated by extra space.)

In the normal alphabetic order of the *alef-beis*, all the letters face away from the first letter, the *alef*— a letter that represents the

Glory of Hashem. The remainder of the letters all face towards the left, away from the *alef*, so as not to stare, so to speak, directly at His Glory. When the Jewish People transgress Hashem's commandments, He hides His *Shechinah* from us — which is the greatest possible punishment. When this happens, then the letters can point towards the right and face towards the *alef*. Thus two *nun*s that face towards the right are now able to stare, as it were, directly towards the letter *alef*, because Hashem's Glory is hidden.

There are differing opinions as to the way these two letters should be written. Normally the נ is wider at the base and narrower at the top. One opinion states that these two inverted letters are actually written upside down, with the wider side at the top. Another opinion maintains that these letters are inverted from back to front but are not written upside down.

The Recanti inverts the letter *nun*s in a different way. He explains that the top part of the letter should be written in the normal format, facing towards the left. The inversion takes place, half way down the leg of the letter, thereby forming a "Z" shape, symbolizing a person kneeling down in prayer, as they did in the *Beis haMikdash*.

The Rokeach, however, is of the opinion that in the second word in that passage (בנסע) the נ is written backwards, with the leg of the letter pointing towards the right-hand side, and no inverted letters surround this passage.

There are eighty-five letters in the above passage, the middle letter being the second ו of the word **וינסו**. The Ben Ish Chai points out that the two inverted *nun*s and the middle *vav* combine to form the full spelling of the fulfillment of the letter נ (נון).

This passage was recited as the appropriate prayer, when the Ark containing the Torah, was moved to the middle of the fifty-*amos*-wide River Jordan, as the Jewish nation were about to conquer the Land of Israel, led by their leader **יהושע בין נון**.

The letter נ, with a numerical value of fifty, represents the fifty gates of wisdom that are incorporated within the Torah that was housed in the Ark. The Rokeach points out that the names of the twelve tribes contain a total of fifty letters. Appropriately, the word תורה (Torah) is mentioned fifty times in the Torah. Furthermore, the collective Torah study of all the members of the tribes of Israel will ultimately reveal all of these fifty gates of wisdom.

It is interesting to note that the first of these two *pesukim* contains twelve words, which corresponds to the last *pasuk* of the Torah, as it also contains twelve words, while the second *pasuk* of the above passage contains seven words, which corresponds to the first *pasuk* of *Bereishis* for the same reason. One would have expected that the first *pasuk* of the Torah would be represented in the first *pasuk* of this passage. However, these inverted letters serve to reverse the logical order, thus placing *Devarim* before *Bereishis* in this context.

The Mesorah writes that there are seven additional occasions where an inverted letter נ is found in Scripture. They all appear in Chapter 107 of *Tehillim*, which begins "*Hodu laShem ki tov*," and is recited on Friday afternoon, shortly before Shabbos. Rashi explains that these inverted letters are used to indicate exclusion.

◇ ◇ ◇

When commenting on *Bereishis* 11:32, Rashi writes that the final letter ן in the word Charan (חרן) should actually be written as an inverted letter.

The Minchas Shai explains that this cannot be taken literally, as the final letter ן is symmetrical along its vertical axis, and inverting it would produce no visible difference. He therefore suggests that originally there must have been an inverted letter נ at the end of the *parashah*, similar to the ones that are found in *Beha'aloscha*.

The Gemara explains (*Sanhedrin* 97a) that the six thousand years of the world's existence are divided into three epochs. The first two thousand years are known as the "years of emptiness," the second as the "years of Torah," and the final two thousand as the "years of

Mashiach." The first epoch ended when Avraham Avinu was fifty-two years old. (He was born 1,948 years after Creation.) The final letter ן in *Parashas Noach* symbolizes the completion of this first epoch. This inverted ן, together with the first letter ב of the Torah, in a sense, create brackets that set off the first two thousand years of Creation. The נ and ב have a combined numerical value of fifty-two — Avraham's age at that time.

It is interesting to point out that the next *parashah* (*Lech Lecha*) marks the beginning of the formation of the Jewish nation through our ancestor Avraham, whose role in life is introduced by the words לך לך. Each of these two words also has a numerical value of fifty, further indicating the natural division in world history.

## ◈ Correlation Between the Representations of the Letter נ

**נ–נון**

The Mishnah (*Rosh Hashanah* 3:3–4) explains that there are two different shapes of the *shofar*. The expansion of the letter נ into נון represents these two different shapes. The bent נ represents the twisted-shaped *shofar* that was used on fast days, while the ן — in essence, a straightened out נ — represents the one used on Rosh Hashanah, as the mouthpiece of that *shofar* is straight.

Alternatively, the letter נ pictorially and numerically represents the fifty loops on the edges of the curtains that were used in the building of the *Mishkan*.

◈ ◈ ◈

When the Jewish nation served the Golden Calf, they rescinded on their previous pledge to follow Hashem's command when they said: **נעשה ונשמע** — "We will do, and we will obey" (*Shemos* 24:7). This undertaking has the acronym of נון, as highlighted above. As a result of this transgression, Moshe broke the Two Tablets containing the Ten Commandments. He then prayed to Hashem for forgiveness, and his prayer mentions the Thirteen Attributes of Mercy. One of these attributes is that Hashem is נצר חסד, the Preserver of kindness, which is spelled with a large letter נ (see ibid. 34:7). The use of the large letter נ hints at their previous willingness to accept His commandments with the proclamation of נעשה ונשמע. Thus, by alluding to the virtues of the Jewish nation, Moshe was attempting to invoke Hashem's kindness.

◈ ◈ ◈

The word "*nun*" in Aramaic translates as "fish." The *mispar katan* of the letter נ is five, and we know that fish were created on the fifth day of Creation. They were the first creatures whom Hashem blessed "to be fruitful and multiply." In nature, fish symbolize reproduction, as this letter is the only letter of the *alef-beis* whose full spelling (נון) is a repetition of itself with an additional letter ו, which, as we mentioned earlier, serves as a conjunction. This spelling represents reproduction, as though to say, "fish and more fish," as reinforced in the *pasuk*: וידגו לרב בקרב הארץ — "May they reproduce like the fish within the land" (*Bereishis* 48:16). Appropriately, the letter ט, which represents the womb where a baby develops during pregnancy, is composed from the letters נ and ו.

## THE LETTER ס

ס

The letter ס has a numerical value of sixty and fulfills as סמך. The numerical value of its hidden fulfillment (מך = 60) equals that of the original letter. The ס is composed from the letters כ and ו, which together have the same numerical value as Hashem's Name (26). The generative process of this fulfillment (ס–סמ–סמך) produces a *mispar katan* of twenty-eight (when the *mispar katan* of each of the letters is added together) and a final *mispar katan* of one (2 + 8 = 10, 1+0 =1) signifying the power (כח) and Unity of Hashem.

The articulated letter סמך translates as "support," as we find in the *pasuk*: סומך ה' לכל הנפלים — "Hashem supports all the fallen ones" (*Tehillim* 145:14). Hashem supports all those who have fallen spiritually, and helps them to return to Him through repentance. The acronym of the letters סמך represents the three forms of repentance that we request from Hashem in the *Vidui* prayer: ועל כלם אלו"ה סליחות סלח לנו מחל לנו כפר לנו — "For all of them, Hashem of forgiveness, forgive us, pardon us and atone for us."

◈ ◈ ◈

The letter ס, with its numerical value of sixty, connects to Hashem's Name of י-ה-ו-ה. Breaking the letter ה into its base composites we end up with two *vavs* and one *yud* (as its foot), which has a total numerical value of twenty-two (6 + 6 + 10 = 22). Using this value for the letter ה, Hashem's Name would produce a numerical value of sixty (10 + 22 + 6 + 22 = 60), the same as that of the ס.

## ◈ The Significance of the Shape of the ס

The entire universe was created through the attribute of kindness, as expressed in the phrase: עולם חסד יבנה — "The world is created through kindness" (*Tehillim* 89:3). This statement encompasses the main principle by which nature functions.

All living matter is composed from cells, consisting of a mass of protoplasm bound by a thin membrane. Life continues to function by the use of the principle of *concentration gradients*, compelling nutrients to pass from one cell to its adjoining one, through its semi-permeable membrane wall. For example, a cell that has a high concentration of water will share with a neighboring cell that has a lower concentration of water. Water molecules will pass through to the poorer cell, through its thin membrane wall. Sharing between cells continues until a state of equilibrium is reached. One could say that constant acts of kindness are performed between cells, during the process of diffusion as part of osmosis. Through this process, fresh oxygen is supplied into the bloodstream, while concurrently extracting any unwanted waste material. Molecular transfer through the semi-permeable membrane of the cell wall continues as long as concentration gradient exists, whereby one cell has more than the other. Thus, the phrase עולם חסד יבנה not only incorporates both the kindness that a person performs for his neighbor, but also the microscopic "kindness" performed in the interaction between two adjoining cells.

Being completely closed on all sides, the letter ס represents the semi-permeable cell walls of all living matter. This is represented in the structure of the word חסד. The ס represents the wall (חסד) separating two cells — symbolized by the letters ח and ד, which have numerical values of eight and four, respectively, representing the concentration gradient between two cells. Together, these two letters form the word חד, which translates as "one" — the state of equilibrium that is eventually reached between adjoining cells via diffusion. These constant acts of kindness, performed even on a microscopic scale, actually maintain the world — for if semi-permeable cell walls are obstructed, diffusion cannot continue to be effective, and life would cease to exist. This membrane obstruction is symbolized by letter ס enclosed within a final ם. Their combination, spells out the word סם — the "poison" that effectively kills life.

### ◈ Correlation Between the Representations of the Letter ס

**ס-סמך**

The ס is the only regular letter that forms a complete circle, both internally and externally. A request for complete forgiveness, represented by the acronym of the fulfillment of סמך and its circular shape, symbolizes a complete return to Hashem. The penultimate *pasuk* of *Koheles* contains a large letter ס, referring to repentance: סוף

סוף דבר הכל נשמע את א-להים ירא ואת מצותיו שמור כי זה כל האדם — "The end of the matter, everything having been heard, fear Hashem and keep His commandments, for this is the entire man" (12:13).

The Alshich points out that this *pasuk* incorporates all the 613 commandments. The phrase "fear Hashem" refers to the 365 negative commandments, which coincide with the number of sinews in the human body. The phrase "keep His commandments" refers to the 248 positive mitzvos, and corresponds to the number of limbs in the human body. Together, these form "the entire man." (As the letter ה represents repentance, it is suitably used to prefix the word **האדם**, at the end of the *pasuk*.)

The ס is composed from the letters כ + ו, which equates to the numerical value of Hashem's Name. *Tehillim* 117:13 expresses our unshakeable trust in Hashem, Who supports us in all circumstances: כוס ישועות אשא ובשם ה' אקרא — "The cup of salvation I will raise, and upon the Name of Hashem, I will call."

When the letter ס is written as כ + ו, the word כוס becomes כו כו. This corresponds to twice the Name of Hashem, as signified by the words בשם ה' — which can be read as ב + שם ה', twice the Name of Hashem. Two times the numerical value of Hashem's Name is fifty-two, the same as אליהו, Eliyahu, who will precede Mashiach and will raise the cup of our ultimate salvation.

The combined numerical value of the letters of the generative process of the word סמך (ס–סמ–סמך) is 280, which equates to the sum of the lower numerical values of the five final letters. As discussed earlier, salvation is effected through the medium of these final letters, which will bring the world full circle back to the ultimate aim of Creation. This is symbolized by the full circle formed by this letter and its close connection to repentance.

Alternatively, the closed circular shape of the letter ס represents **סוד**, the hidden secrets of the Torah, as we find written in the *pasuk*: הלא הוא כמס עמדי חתום באוצרתי — "Is it not stored away with Me, sealed in My treasures?" (*Devarim* 32:34). The word כמס translates as "stored away," and is composed from the same letters as סמך — only in reverse order. As we have mentioned, letters in reverse order indicate strict judgment. In this case, portions of the Torah have been hidden away as a result of Adam haRishon's sin.

These hidden secrets are also alluded to in the *pasuk*: ואתה דניאל סתם הדברים וחתם הספר עד עת קץ — "And as for you Daniel, obscure the matters and seal the book until the end of time" (*Daniel* 12:4). The word סתם, "obscure," incorporates the letters ס and ם, both of which are completely enclosed. Moreover, both are composed from the letters כ + ו, and their hidden fulfillments have the same numerical values as their original letters (מם סמך). The combined numerical value of their fulfillments is two hundred (80 + 120 =200), the same as that of the letter ר. There appears to be a hidden connection between these three letters, מ'ס'ר', as well, in that many *pesukim* that begin with one of these three letters will also end with one of them, as we find in *Ashrei* (*Tehillim* 145) in following the three *pesukim*:

**מ**לכותך מלכות כל עלמים וממשלתך בכל דור ודו**ר**
**ס**ומך ה' לכל הנפלים וזוקף לכל הכפופי**ם**
**ר**צון יראיו יעשה ואת שועתם ישמע ויושיע**ם**

Although I have no rational explanation for this connection, I have pointed it out in order to show the depth that is hidden within different aspects of the *alef-beis* itself.

## ס–סמך–ששים

The enclosed circle formed by the letter ס, with a numerical value of sixty, represents the Holy *Shechinah* of Hashem that surrounds and protects His people, similar to the way that Jerusalem is enwrapped with mountains. This comparison is found in *Tehillim* (125:2): ירושלים הרים סביב לה וה' סביב לעמו מעתה ועד עולם — "Jerusalem is surrounded with mountains, as Hashem surrounds His people, from this time and forever."

Similarly, Shlomo haMelech would protect his couch with sixty mighty warriors, as stated in *Shir HaShirim* (3:7): **הנה מטתו שלשלמה ששים גברים סביב לה מגברי ישראל כלם אחזי חרב מלמדי מלחמה איש חרבו על ירכו מפחד בלילות** — "Behold! The couch of Shlomo, sixty mighty ones surround it, of the mighty ones of Israel. All of them gripping the sword, learned in warfare, each one with his sword on his thigh, from fear of the nights."

This *pasuk* is recited in the evenings, shortly before going to sleep, and is immediately followed by the sixty letters that are contained in the three *pesukim* that make up the Priestly Blessing. Hashem's holy *Shechinah* protects the Jewish nation, which is comprised of a minimum of six hundred thousand adult men. The reason that the circular formation of the letter ס represents His protection can be understood by the fact that the shape of this letter incorporates three different Names of Hashem. Firstly, the fact that the ס is composed from the letters כ+ו, with a numerical value of twenty-six, represents His Name. Secondly, the fulfillment of the letter (סמך) can also be written as כ+ו מך, which has a numerical value of eighty-six, the same as the Name of Elokim. By continuing in a similar fashion for the letter מ, the fulfillment can be broken down further as כ+ו כ+ו ך, which has a total numerical value of seventy-two, corresponding to the *Shem haMeforash*, which contains a total of seventy-two sets of letters.

## THE LETTER ע

The letter ע has a numerical value of seventy and a *mispar katan* of seven, thereby connecting this letter to the holiness of Shabbos — the seventh day of the week. The letter ע fulfills as the word עין, which has a *mispar katan* of thirteen, the same as that of the word אחד, signifying the Unity of Hashem. Its second fulfillment as עין יוד נון contains a total of nine letters, thereby representing the attribute of truth. The generative process of the word עין is ע-עי-עין which has a *mispar katan* of twenty-eight (when adding together the *mispar katan* of each letter) and a final *mispar katan* of one (2 + 8 = 10; 1 + 0 = 1) again signifying the Unity of Hashem. (It is interesting to note that in German the number one is pronounced as *ein*, which sounds similar to the pronunciation of the letter ע.) The generative value of the word עין (280) equates to the generative value of the previous letter סמך, providing a connection between the letters and therefore a possible explanation for their juxtaposition in the alphabetic order.

The Magen David points out that hidden fulfillment of the letter (עין) has a numerical value of sixty (ס), while the actual letter has a value of seventy (ע). He explains that the decrease in numerical values between the letter ע and its hidden fulfillment represents the decrease in the appearance of the size of an object as the distance from that object increases.

## ◈ The Composition of the Letter ע

The letter ע is formed using different combinations of the composite letters י'ו'ז'נ'. Composing the ע from the letters נ'ו'ז' represents Hashem's "watchful eye," as their fulfillments as **נון ואו זין** have a total numerical value of 186, the same as the word מקום, which refers to Hashem, and the עין itself translates as "eye." Of all the five senses, vision is most frequently used to express our desire for the spiritual — for example, in the *Amidah* prayer we request that "our eyes should behold Your return to Zion."

Furthermore, the numerical value of these three composite letters totals sixty-three, which is the same as three times twenty-one. Twenty-one is the numerical value of Hashem's Name of אהי-ה, which is found in the *pasuk*: אהי-ה אשר אהי-ה — "I Shall Be as I Shall Be" (*Shemos* 3:13). This *pasuk* was the sign that Hashem gave to Moshe so that the Israelites would know that the time of the redemption had come. The last two letters of the word **אשר** have a combined numerical value of five hundred, which can also be represented by the final letter ך. By replacing the שר with a ך the word אשר becomes אך, which also has a numerical value of twenty-one. Thus, the original expression אהי-ה אשר אהי-ה can be transformed into the phrase אהי-ה אך אהי-ה, which corresponds to the triplicate numerical value of twenty-one, or sixty-three — the total of the above three composites of the letter ע.

The letter ע can also be composed from the letters of ז and ו. Together these three letters form the word עוז, the strength of the Torah, which is the meaning of the *pasuk*: ה' עוז לעמו יתן — "Hashem gives strength to His people" (*Tehillim* 29:11). The two arms of the letter ע symbolize both the Written and Oral Torah, which must be interpreted and learned in unison. By doing so, one reveals novel interpretations, earning him the title of **מעין המתגבר** — "an overflowing spring of knowledge" (*Pirkei Avos* 2:11).

The use of all four letters (י'ו'ז'נ') to compose the letter ע reveals its full potential. The letter ג is composed from the letters ז and י. From this combination we can spell out the word גנוז, the hidden light of Creation, which remains obscure from the human eye. *Tehillim* 119:18 expresses an appropriate prayer: **גל עיני** ואביטה נפלאות מתורתך — "Unveil my eyes that I may understand the wonders of Your Torah." The fulfillment of the word עין has a numerical value of 130; both eyes together have a numerical value of 260, tenfold the numerical value of Hashem's Name. We, therefore, pray that He should unveil our eyes so that we can fully understand this Divine knowledge and secrets of the Torah.

When the letter ע is composed from the combination of ז and נ, it represents our dependence on Him to provide our זן, nourishment and sustenance, as expressed in *Tehillim* in the *pasuk* beginning with the letter ע (145:15): **עיני** כל אליך ישברו ואתה נותן להם את אכלם בעתו — "The eyes of all, look to You with hope, and You give them their food in its proper time." The Radak points out that even animals instinctively rely on Him for their sustenance — how much more should man recognize the beneficence of his Creator!

The next *pasuk*, *Tehillim* 145:16, states: פותח את ידך ומשביע לכל חי רצון — "You open Your hand, and satisfy the desire of every living thing." The letter ע symbolizes the provision of sustenance. In Hebrew the expression משביע עין is used when referring to someone who is visibly well-off. This is a hint to those who have been blessed with enough wealth to live comfortably, that they should give open-handedly to their less fortunate brethren, viewing the poor man's needs with a generous eye, which is the literal translation of משביע עין.

The eyeball is known as the גלגל עין, the "wheel of the eye." Similarly the wheel (גלגל) of fortune is so named because it is constantly turning.

The Ben Ish Chai connects these two ideas in his explanation of the fulfillment of the letter ע. He points out that the final letter ן of עין has a higher numerical value of seven hundred and a lower one of fifty. If a person gives generously to charity, then the final letter ן in the word עין will have a more generous numerical value of seven hundred. If, however, he is stingy in his charitable contribution, then it will have the smaller numerical value of fifty, like a regular letter נ. In the latter case, the letters of the word עין spell עני, a poor person, as the wheel of fortune will eventually turn against one who is miserly.

## ◈ The Significance of the Number Seventy

The number seventy has great significance in the Torah, for example:

1. The seventy descendants of Yaakov who went down to Egypt
2. The seventy nations of the world and the corresponding seventy oxen sacrificed during the Festival of Sukkos

3. The seventy Names of Hashem (as listed in the Ba'al HaTurim; see *Bemidbar* 11:17)
4. The seventy names that the Jewish nation is known by (also listed in the same Ba'al HaTurim)
5. The seventy names by which Jerusalem is known
6. The seventy members of the Sanhedrin
7. The seventy different ways of interpreting the Torah
8. The seventy years of life that were gifted by Adam to David haMelech
9. The seventy Holy Days in the Jewish Year mandated by the Torah (Shabbosos [52], Rosh Hashanah [1], Yom Kippur [1], Sukkos [7], Simchas Torah/Shemini Atzeres [1], Pesach [7], Shavuos [1])
10. The seventy *pesukim* from the beginning of the Torah until Hashem cursed the snake for instigating the first human transgression
11. The above (#10) corresponds to the seventy *pesukim* from the beginning of the third chapter of *Megillas Esther*, when the wicked Haman rose to power, until he was hanged on the gallows (*Esther* 7:10)
12. The seventy years of the Babylonian exile
13. The first seventy *pesukim* of the Torah contain the Names of Hashem a total of seventy times
14. There are seventy words contained in the Friday night *Kiddush*.
15. The average lifespan of a human being is seventy years.

The seventy different interpretations to the Torah are expounded as understood by the seventy members of the Sanhedrin, who are empowered to reveal its true secrets.

The word סוד, "secret," also has a numerical value of seventy and, as we explained above, these hidden secrets are represented by the enclosed letter ס, which may explain its juxtaposition to the letter ע in the alphabetic order.

### ◈ Correlation Between the Representations of the Letter ע

**ע–עין**

The meaning of the word עין is interconnected to the shape of the ע, as this letter resembles two eyeballs joined to the optic nerve that merge together on their way to the brain. Its foot slants towards the left, pointing towards the heart, symbolizing the *Midrash Tanchuma*'s teaching: העין רואה והלב חומד והגוף עושה את העבירות — "The eye sees, the heart desires, and the body commits the transgression." Furthermore, looking at one eyeball from a side view, the two arms of the ע represent the structure of the muscles that surround each eye — called the superior and inferior rectus muscles. Moreover, the connection of these muscles together with the optic nerve also displays the shape of the letter ע.

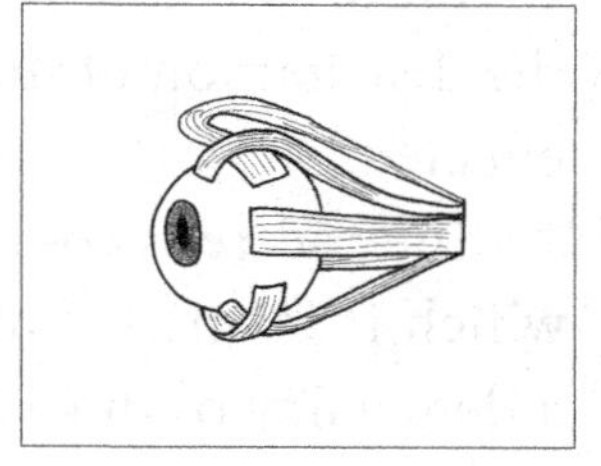

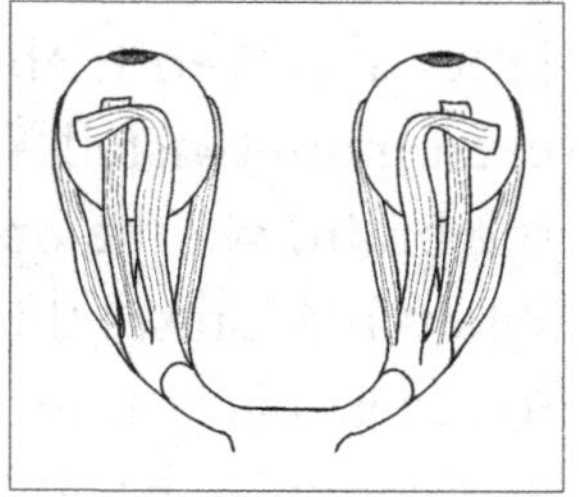

The anatomy of the eye contains two types of photoreceptors, known as rod and cone cells. Each eye contains 120 million rod cells, which are sensitive to light, and another ten million cone cells, which are sensitive to color. Thus, there are a total of 130 million rod and cone cells in the eye, the same as the numerical value of the word עין. The cone cells are concentrated in the central part of the eyeball, known as the macula. These ten million cone cells are situated at the center of the eye, corresponding to the numerical value of the letter י, which appears in the *middle* of the word עין. Both types of cells are represented in the actual shape of the letter ע — the top "v"-shaped part of the letter represents the cone cells, while the straight foot of the letter represents the straight rod cells.

Structurally, the cone cells are in the middle, and they are surrounded by the rod cells which are distributed around the cone cells in a disproportionate fashion, in a 7:5 ratio. The number of cone and rod cells corresponds exactly to the fulfillment of עין, whose letters have numerical values of seventy, ten and fifty, respectively. The ten million cone cells in the middle correspond to the middle letter י, and the 120 million rod cells that surround them in a disproportionate manner correspond to the letters ע and נ, which have numeric values of seventy and fifty, totaling 120 and possessing a 7:5 ratio! Thus the fulfillment of the letter ע corresponds exactly to the distribution of these two types of cells, through which vision is effected.

The rod cells contain a photosensitive pigment called *rhodopsin*, which is formed from Vitamin A. Night blindness develops from a deficiency of this vitamin. The molecular structure of rhodopsin contains seven helixes or turns, the same as the *mispar katan* of the letter ע. When it absorbs light, the molecular structure becomes even more twisted, which triggers electrical impulses to be sent to the brain, via the optic nerve, projecting the image being viewed. Vitamin A causes this twist in the molecular structure of rhodopsin to revert back to its previous position. Retinol, commonly known as Vitamin A, has its source in cream, butter, eggs and fish liver oils. Alternatively, carrots provide carotene which the liver converts into Vitamin A.

We have already mentioned that the juxtaposition of the letters נ'ס'ע' in the alphabetic order symbolizes that fish (which is נון in Aramaic) have therapeutic properties for a person's eyesight (סַמֶךְ עַיִן — can be read as סוֹמֵךְ עַיִן, which literally means "supports the eyesight"). Moreover, fish have an abundant supply of Vitamin A — essential to maintain good vision.

◆ ◆ ◆

The *mispar katan* of the letter ע is seven, and that of its hidden fulfillment (עין) totals six. The Friday night *Kiddush* is recited at the junction between the sixth and seventh day of the week. The Tur Orach Chayim (269) explains that the recitation of the Friday night *Kiddush* over a cup of wine has therapeutic effects on a person's eyesight. Wine (יין) has a numerical value of seventy, the same as that of this letter. Moreover, the Friday night *Kiddush* contains a total of seventy words. This numerical connection is a reason why we look into the wine while reciting *Kiddush* on Friday night.

◆ ◆ ◆

A large letter ע is found in the first word of the *Shema*, whose opening *pasuk* states: **שמע ישראל...אחד**. This is followed by the first paragraph of the *Shema*, which contains a total of five *pesukim*, each of which begin with a letter ו and end with a final letter ך; these two letters have a combined numerical value of twenty-six, representing Hashem's Name. Multiplying that numerical value by the number of *pesukim* produces a total of 130, the same as the numerical value of the word עין.

◆ ◆ ◆

Being that the numerical value of the word עין, "eye," is 130, our two eyes, with a numerical value of 260, are equal to tenfold the value of Hashem's Name. This alludes to the era of Mashiach, when we will be able to perceive His full revelation with intimate eye-to-eye contact, as we find in the *pasuk*: **כי עין בעין יראו בשוב י-ה-ו-ה ציון** — "Eye to eye we shall perceive Hashem when He returns to Zion" (*Yeshayahu* 52:8).

Hashem's Name can be connected to the word עין in another way, as well. The fulfillments of the letters of the generative process of Hashem's Name are: **יוד-יוד הא-יוד הא ואו-יוד הא ואו הא**. The total numerical values of these letters is 130 — the same as that of the word עין.

The above generative process of this fulfillment produces a cone shape, with the initial expansion of יוד at the apex and the final expansion of יוד הא ואו הא at its base, corresponding to the cone-shaped eye cells. We have explained in the section entitled "Triangular Values" that the sum of the triangular values of the four letters of Hashem's Name is 106, the same as that of the word קו — a straight line — an allusion to the straight rod cells. (The numerical value of the fulfillment of the letter נון — which, as we said is "fish" in Aramaic — also totals 106.)

At the first Divine revelation that Moshe received at the burning bush, he turned to see that great sight — a burning bush that was not consumed. The *pasuk* says: וירא ה' כי סר לראות — "Hashem saw that he had turned aside to see [the bush]" (*Shemos* 3:4). The word סר has a numerical value of 260, alluding to the Divine revelation that Moshe saw through both of his eyes. This same sentiment is expressed in *Zechariah* 9:1: כי לי-ה-ו-ה עין אדם — "To Hashem is the eye of a person," as it can be interpreted to mean that the generative value of the fulfillment of Hashem's Name equates to the numerical value of the word עין.

◆ ◆ ◆

The Ben Ish Chai explains the custom of passing *tzitzis* before ones eye's when reciting the words of the *Shema*: וראיתם אתו וזכרתם את כל מצות ה' — "and you shall see it and remember all the commandments of Hashem" (*Bemidbar* 15:39). Good quality *tzitzis* strings are made from eight-ply wool. Since each corner of the garment contains eight strings, each corner has a total of sixty-four-ply wool (8 x 8). The complete four-cornered garment will therefore have a total of 256 (64 x 4 = 256) ply in all their strings. The numerical value of the fulfillment of the word עין also totals 256 (עין יוד נון). The optic nerve, which transports the visual image to the memory cells in the brain, contains a total of 256,000,000 cells. The ply that are contained in the *tzitzis* strings correspond to the numerical value of the fulfillment of "eye," and to the number of cells in the optic nerve that ensure that the image seen by the eye is stored in the brain's memory. Thus, looking at the *tzitzis* strings and passing them over one's eyes to remind us of the mitzvos is a fulfillment of the above *pasuk*: "and you shall see it and remember all the commandments of Hashem."

## THE LETTER פ

פ

The letter פ has a numerical value of eighty and a *mispar katan* of eight, a number that signifies the Unity of Hashem. It can be written in its fulfilled form in three different ways, either as פא, פה or פי. Both the fulfillments of פא and פי have a *mispar katan* of nine, representing the absolute truth. The *mispar katan* of the fulfillment of פה is thirteen, the same as that of the word אחד, representing the Unity of Hashem. All of the fulfillments of the letter פ represent the mouth.

Collectively, these three different fulfillments of the letter פ use as their hidden fulfillments the letters א'י'ה', which are the same as the three hidden fulfillments of the letter ה. These same three letters form the different fulfillments of the ה in Hashem's holy Name (see p. 223). Together the פ and ה form the word פה, "mouth." When the mouth is used correctly, it has the potential power to imbue the speaker with spiritual holiness, as expressed in the concept of פה קדוש — a holy mouth. Since the פ and ה share the same fulfillments as those used in the fulfillments of Hashem's Name, it is appropriate that they are used in the highest form of spiritual communication — that which was between Hashem and Moshe, as we find in the *pasuk*: פה אל פה אדבר בו — "Mouth to mouth I speak to him" (*Bemidbar* 8:8).

In the human facial profile, the eyes are the uppermost feature, with the nose and mouth, being progressively lower down. In the alphabetic sequence, the letter ע, representing the eye, precedes the letter פ, representing both the nose (אף) and mouth (פה).

The juxtaposition in the *alef-beis* of the letters ס'ע'פ' conveys the fact that, in Jewish Law, witnesses are only relied upon if they have personally witnessed the event. The fulfillment of the letter ס translates as "rely," the letter ע translates as "eye" and the letter פ translates as "mouth." In a *beis din* (Jewish court of law), one can only rely on the testimony of a witness who has actually seen the event.

### ◈ The Composition of the Letter פ

In the Torah script, the letter פ is written in such a way that the white space in the interior of the letter forms the shape of the letter ב. This serves to remind us to think twice before opening our mouths to speak. Furthermore, the entire Torah is hinted at in the letter פ. Being that the פ represents the mouth, it signifies the Oral Torah. The ב in the white space represents the Written Torah, which begins with the letter ב.

◈ ◈ ◈

The letter פ itself is composed from the letters כ and י.

The Holy of Holies in the Temple contained the Ark, which was composed of three open boxes, one inside the other, with a lid on top. The Two Tablets were housed within the interior box. The composition of the letter פ represents the Ten Commandments — the ten (י) which are housed in a box-shaped Ark, which pictorially is represented by the letter כ (lying on its side). It can also represent a bird that sits inside its nest, a concept that is an allegory to the holy *Shechinah* dwelling in the Temple. Alternatively, it can also represent, the Divine spark of the human soul — which is the י — that enters the body through the nostrils, the אף, as the *pasuk* tells us: ויפח באפיו נשמת חיים — "and He blew into his nostrils the soul of life" (*Bereishis* 2:7).

In the section dealing with the five final letters, we have already explained how the letter פ represents the redemption of the Jewish nation from their Egyptian exile. At the age of eighty, Moshe Rabbeinu redeemed them from their bondage, received the Torah for them on Mount Sinai, and led them through the desert. At the age of 120, as the Jewish People reached the borders of the Land of Israel, Moshe passed away. The numerical value of the letter פ corresponds to Moshe's age at the time of the Exodus. The total numerical value of the fulfillments of the letters כ and י — כף and יוד, respectively — is 120, the age at which Moshe Rabbeinu completed his mission.

### ◈ Correlation Between the Representations of the Letter פ

**פ–פא**

The fulfillment as פא has a numerical value of eighty-one, equal to that of the word כסא, a reference to Hashem's Throne, and also equal to that of the word אנכי, the first word of the Ten Commandments.

As stated above, the letter פ is composed from the letter כ and an inverted letter י. The shape of the כ represents the Throne, and the letter י alludes to the tenth *Sefirah* of מלכות. Combined together, the letter פ represents the כסא מלכות — the Divine royal Throne. When the פ, the mouth, is used incorrectly, it causes Divine anger, אף, which is a reversal of the spelling פא. The word אף also refers to the nose, a part of the body through which anger is expressed. In combination, the mouth and nose are represented by different fulfillments of the letter פ. Through these two organs a person breathes in and expels air, enabling him to remain alive. Furthermore, just as through the *Sefirah* of מלכות the benefits of all the other *Sefiros* are filtered into the physical world, similarly, a person's inner thoughts and feelings are expressed through his power of speech.

**פ–פה**

The fulfillment as פה produces a numerical value of eighty-five, the same as the word מילה, "*milah*." Part of the *bris milah* (circumcision) ceremony is performed with the mouth. *Bris milah* is associated with the ninth *Sefirah* of יסוד, which has a numerical value of eighty, the same as the letter פ itself. The second fulfillment into פה הא, has a total numerical value of ninety-one, the same as the combination of Hashem's two Names of י-ה-ו-ה and אדנ-י, which are, as we have said, the written and articulated forms of His Names, thereby representing a mouth that is used to sanctify Hashem.

**פ–פי**

The fulfillment as פי has a numerical value of ninety, the same as that of the word מלך, "king." Kingship is attained through a total of thirty attributes — thirty being the total numerical value of the letters (כ + י) which form the shape of the פ. The כ represents the mouth and the י the lip.

## THE LETTER צ

The letter צ has a numerical value of ninety, and a *mispar katan* of nine, thereby representing the truth. This letter צ fulfills as either צדי or צדיק. When spelled as צדי, it translates as "hunting" and has a progressive fulfillment of צ–צד–צדי, which also has a final *mispar katan* of nine. The numerical value of the fulfillment as צדי is 104, which is four times the numerical value of Hashem's Name.

The letter צ is composed from the combination of the letters נ and י, where the neck of the letter נ is bent forward, representing humility. This bent נ represents the righteous person subjugating himself to Hashem's will. Such a person draws down the *Shechinah*, which is symbolized by the letter י, placing it above him. This is represented by the י being placed atop the נ.

Since the צ is the eighteenth letter of the *alef-beis*, it has an ordinal value of eighteen, the numerical value of חי — life.

Shlomo haMelech said: צדיק יסוד עולם — "The righteous are

the foundations of the world" (*Mishlei* 10:25). This can also be interpreted literally to mean that the foundations of the world took place through the power of the letter צדי (צדיק). For this reason, the ninth *Sefirah*, יסוד, is represented by the letter צ, and it is therefore appropriate that the letter צ has a *mispar katan* of nine.

The shape of the letter צ represents the ideal compromise between good and evil influences, in that the left and right arms meet at the center of the letter and continue together. The foot of the letter is bent back, representing the righteous person's complete control over his evil inclination.

There is a concept in Jewish Law called *psharah* which in essence means "a fair compromise." This is part of the Jewish system of justice. We see this reinforced by the fulfillment of צדי, which is composed as a combination of the words צדק + דין, "fairness" and "justice."

### ◈ Correlations Between the Representations of the Letter צ

**צ–צדיק**

When the צ fulfills as צדיק, it translates as "a righteous person" and has a *mispar katan* of fifteen, the same as the numerical value of Hashem's Name of י-ה. Adding the numerical value of the letter itself (90) to that of its fulfillment as צדי (104) produces a total numerical value that equates to the word צדק (194) — "righteousness."

## THE LETTER ק

ק

The letter ק has a numerical value of one hundred, and a *mispar katan* of one, representing the Unity of Hashem. The fulfillment as קוף can mean "to round off" or "strength," as in the *pesukim*: לא תקפו פאת ראשכם — "You shall not round off the edge of your scalp" (*Vayikra* 19:27), and וכל מעשה תקפו וגבורתו — "And all the acts of his strength and might..." (*Esther* 10:2). The fulfillment can also mean "monkey."

The letter ק is composed from either a combination of the letters of ן + כ or ן + ר, with the final ן acting as its foot. The ק is one of only two letters (the other being the letter ה) that are composed from two disjointed parts.

The Gemara (*Shabbos* 104) explains ק as קדוש, attributing holiness to the letter ק, and we know from the Torah: "Every tenth one shall be holy to Hashem" (*Vayikra* 27:32). The letter ק, with a numerical value of one hundred, thereby represents a ten-fold degree of extreme holiness.

Through its numerical value the letter ק is closely connected to Hashem's Name. As explained earlier, in the section dealing with the letter כ, Hashem's Name of י-ה-ו-ה can be divided in two halves (יה + וה), which have special grouping values totaling forty-five and fifty-five respectively (see p. 269 for clarification). These two values total one hundred — the numerical value of ק. Our daily requirement to recite one hundred blessings, through which we praise Hashem, is hinted at in the phrase: **הן הם** יודו ויברכו — "All of them shall thank and praise [Hashem]." The numerical values of these two highlighted words are fifty-five and forty-five, respectively.

## ◈ Correlations Between the Representations of the Letter ק

### ק–קוף

The fulfillment of the letter ק as קוף, has a numerical value of 186. We have already explained how the number 186 connects to Hashem's Name of מקום (see p. 153). The hidden portion of the fulfillment (ק**וף**) has a numerical value of eighty-six, the same as the Name of Elokim. The *mispar katan* of the fulfillment is fifteen, the same as the numerical value of Hashem's Name of י-ה. These two letters fulfill into **יוד הא** and have a total numerical value of twenty-six, the same numerical value as His complete Name, י-ה-ו-ה.

## The Letter ר

ר

The letter ר has a numerical value of two hundred and fulfills as ריש, ראש or רש — meaning "beginning," "head" or "a poor man," respectively. The double fulfillment of the word ריש becomes ריש יוד שין, and has a total *mispar katan* of twenty-six (when adding the *mispar katan* of each individual letter), the same as the numerical value of Hashem's Name. This double fulfillment is made up of nine letters, thereby symbolizing the truth.

It seems incongruous that a letter that appears towards the end of the *alef-beis* would itself denote "head" or "beginning." One would think that it should appear early in the alphabetic order. The answer is that these connotations of the letter ר do not refer to its juxtaposition in the *alef-beis*. Rather the meaning of this letter alludes to the "heads" of the first thirty-four *pesukim* of *Bereishis*, which contains the entire narrative regarding Creation. With the exception of the first *pasuk* — which begins with the letter ב — these *pesukim* all begin with the letter ו. The numerical values of ב and ו are two and six, respectively. Thus these thirty-four letters, which form the "head" of each *pasuk*, have a total numerical value of two hundred (33 x 6 = 198 + 2 = 200), the same as that of the letter ר.

Thus, we have established that the final letter ץ corresponds to the Final Redemption (see p. 19), the letter ר symbolizes the entire Creation, and the format of the letter א represents the Omnipresence of Hashem (see p. 194). Their combination spells out the word ארץ — Earth. The supreme power of Hashem (represented by the א) will be acknowledged by all of Creation (symbolized by the ר) with the arrival of Mashiach (which corresponds to the ץ).

◆ ◆ ◆

We have already explained, in the section dealing with the letter ה, how both the letters ה and ק represent different aspects of repentance. The letter ק is followed by the ר in the alphabet. A wicked person (רשע) turns his back away from the numerous opportunities to repent. This is symbolized by the fact that the format of the letter ר is facing away from the previous letter ק. A רשע deserves Divine punishment, which is carried out through the Name of Justice, that of א-להים, which also equates to two hundred in its generative value. However, when the wicked person repents, there is a reversal of the spelling of the word ריש into שיר, a welcoming song as he begins again with a clean slate. The hidden portion of the fulfillment as **ריש** has a numerical value of 310, alluding to the ultimate reward that lies ahead for a repentent sinner, for he is destined to inherit 310 worlds.

### ◈ The Shape of the Letter ר

The shape of the letter ר represents the profile of a poor man, the רש, with a bent back, collecting charity.

Yet the ר is very similar to the letter ד, the only difference being in the upper right hand corner of the letters. The letter ד has a sharp corner and signifies a strong allegiance to Hashem and His commandments. In contrast, the letter ר curves to accommodate itself into a new direction, symbolizing idolatries that easily bend to accommodate the wishes of their followers. In order to emphasize this difference, the Torah uses a large letter ד in our proclamation of "Hashem is One," in the *pasuk*: שמע ישראל ה' א-להינו ה' אחד. Conversely, the large letter ר in *Shemos* 34:14 is used to warn us against serving idols and alien gods, with the words of אל אחר.

The Vilna Gaon points out that these two large letters represent the first two of the Ten Commandments. The first commandment obligates us to believe in His Omnipresence, as represented by the large letter ד. The second one prohibits idol worship, as represented by the large letter ר. After the Jewish nation served the Golden Calf, having ignored the warnings and lessons that were taught by these two large letters, Hashem commanded Moshe Rabbeinu: לך רד — "Go, descend..." (ibid. 32:7). The Gemara in *Berachos* (32a) explains this command as לך רד מגדולתך — "Descend from your greatness." Since the Jewish People had interchanged the lessons taught by these two large letters — by serving the Golden Calf in exchange for Hashem — there was no purpose in writing them in a larger size. Therefore, the Gemara is saying that Moshe is told לך ר'ד' מגדולתך, "go decrease the letters ר and ד from their original large sizes in which you wrote them."

*Osios d'Rabbi Yitzchak* explains that the changing the ד for a ר is alluded to in the *pasuk*: ויקב חר בדלתו — "He made a hole into the doorway" (*Melachim* II 12:10), which can be interpreted to mean that he has made a hole at the corner of the letter דלת, thereby transforming it into the rounded shape of the letter ר.

As mentioned elsewhere, the Rokeach enumerates, in his *Sefer HaChochmah*, the seventy-three methods of interpreting the Torah. One of those methods is that the first and last letters of every *pasuk* form an acronym, each one with a specific lesson. The *Midrash Talpios* brings an interesting correlation between the similarity in shape between the two letters ד and ר, by pointing out that the *pasuk* that prohibits us from partaking of blood (דם) begins and ends with the letter ר. It reads as: רק חזק לבלתי אכל הדם כי הדם הוא הנפש ולא תאכל הנפש עם הבשר — "Only be strong not to eat the blood, for the blood is in the soul, and you shall not eat the soul with the meat" (*Devarim* 12:23). The two *reish*s indicate a connection between the message of not interchanging a ד for a ר and the context of the *pasuk*. Thus the lesson here is: Just as one must be careful not to exchange the ד for a ר (i.e. to engage in idolatry rather than serving only Hashem), one must likewise be careful to extract the blood of an animal before consuming it.

## ◈ Correlations Between the Representations of the Letter ר

### ר-רש-ראש

The letter ר fulfills as either ראש, which translates as "head," or as רש, which means poor or impoverished. These two translations seem to be diametrical opposites, as a poor person is at the bottom of the economic ladder and not at its head. Yet there is an underlying message in their similarities, for in fact the only difference in their spellings is that the רש lacks the letter א that the ראש has. We have previously explained that the letter א represents Hashem, and it is He Who determines whether a person is a רש or a ראש. All progress, both in material wealth as well as spiritual growth, emanates only from Hashem.

The translations of the fulfillments of the letter ר as "head" and "a poor man," represent two opposite extremes. Shlomo haMelech mentions both of these extremes — poverty and wealth — but desires only to have sufficient bread to eat: ראש ועשר אל תתן לי הטריפני לחם חקי — "Give me neither poverty nor wealth; provide me with my allotted bread" (*Mishlei* 30:8). These two extremes are represented by the phrase **ראש ועשר**, "poverty and wealth," which begins and ends with the letter ר, representing the two opposite ends of this gamut. Preference should always be given to the "golden path" — the middle road in life.

We also find that the word רש is used to encourage a poor person to perform some action that will enhance his financial status and move him towards the ראש — the head of the financial ladder. One example of this is found in the *pasuk*: עלה רש כאשר דבר ה' וכו' — "Go and inherit [the Land] as Hashem has spoken to you" (*Devarim* 1:21). Thus, the fulfillments of רש and ראש correlate through their interconnection to Hashem.

◈ ◈ ◈

The fulfillment of ר as ראש, meaning "head," also refers to Hashem — as He is the Source of all Creation. The fulfillment as רש has a numerical value of five hundred, a number which is connected to Hashem's Name of שד-י — the Name that was used to give the world its finite size — Hashem said "*Dai*" and caused the world to cease expanding.

The Gemara states that the circumference of the earth is a distance equivalent to a five-hundred-year walk. The Maharsha points out that the hidden fulfillment of the Name שד-י (**שין דלת יוד**) has a total numerical value of five hundred (60 + 430 + 10 = 500), hinting that the latent power contained within the Name שד-י produced a universe that would be measured in units of five hundred.

It is interesting to note that the *pasuk* which first introduces this Name, states: ויאמר אליו אני א-ל **שד-י התהלך** לפני והיה תמים — "And Hashem said to him (Avraham), I am *Kel Shakkai*; walk (*his'halech*) before Me and be perfect" (*Bereishis* 17:1). The Name *Shakkai* is juxtaposed with the word "walk." The boundaries of the expanding universe — which were established by the use of the Name of *Shakkai* — are measured by units of "walking distance." When ascending into the celestial spheres, the standard unit of measurement is that of a five-hundred-years' walk.

The Gemara in (*Chagigah* 12a) teaches us that there are seven firmaments, having a total of six spaces in between them. Each firmament, together with its intermediate space, is five-hundred-walking-years' distance in size. This provides a different interpretation to the phrase שד-י התהלך לפני in the above *pasuk*: As we ascend into the celestial spheres, figuratively reaching closer to Hashem (לפני), we express our measurements by the time it takes to walk (התהלך) in increments of five hundred, which is extrapolated from the latent power in the hidden fulfillment of the Name of שד-י.

Furthermore, on the *pasuk*, השקיפה ממעון קדשך מן השמים וברך את עמך את ישראל — "Look down from Your Holy abode, from the heavens, and bless Your people Israel" (*Devarim* 26:15), the Ba'al HaTurim comments that השקיפה, the word used to request Hashem's blessings for the Jewish People, has a numerical value of five hundred, alluding to the distance between the firmaments through which His blessings filter down to us.

Similarly, we are required to pursue our Torah learning with the same vigor that one pursues silver treasures, as is states in: אם

תבקשנה ככסף וכמטמנים תחפשנה אז תבין יראת י-ה-ו-ה ודעת א-להים תמצא — "If you seek it like silver and hunt it like treasures, then you will understand the fear of Hashem, and find the knowledge of God" (*Mishlei* 2:4).

In order to reach the required degree of fear and knowledge of Hashem through the medium of Torah study, one must be prepared to seek it (**תבקשנה**) in the same manner that he pursues money. The Rokeach points out that the letters of the word **תבקשנה** spell out **בְּת"ק שנה**, as one must be prepared to travel a distance equivalent to **ת"ק שנה**, five hundred years, in order to climb to a higher spiritual level in his Torah learning.

In his commentary to the *siddur*, the Shlah points out that the opening words of *Kaddish* — our prayers for the speedy restoration of Hashem's dominion on Earth — are: **יתגדל ויתקדש שמה רבא** — "May His great Name grow exalted and sanctified." The second word, **יתקדש**, incorporates Hashem's Name of **שד-י** (**יתקדש**) with the remaining two letters (**יתקדש**) having a total numerical value of five hundred.

## The Letter ש

The letter **ש** has a numerical value of three hundred. It fulfills as the word **שין** which has a numerical value of 360 and a *mispar katan* of nine, the number that represents absolute truth. The second fulfillment (**שין יוד נון**) also has a final *mispar katan* of nine.

The first fulfillment translates as either "tooth" or "ivory," or "to replace" — when taken from the root **שינוי**. These alternative meanings are interrelated in that tooth enamel is a material similar to ivory. Teeth are also the only part of the body that are replaced — one's primary teeth fall out and permanent ones grow in their stead.

### ◈ The Four-Armed ש

The ש letter is unique in that it is the only regular letter that is found in two different formats. On the *tefillin* that are worn on the head (*tefillin shel rosh*), one side contains the usual three-armed letter, whereas the opposite side has a four-armed one. We find a hint to these two different *shins* in the Torah itself. The first word of the Torah, בראשית, can be written as ש + ב + יראת — "the fear of two letters ש," a reference to the two *shins* on either side of the *tefillin shel rosh*. This interpretation of the word בראשית is reinforced in the *pasuk*: וראו כל עמי הארץ כי **שם** י-ה-ו-ה **נ**קרא עליך ויראו ממך — "And all the nations of the world will recognize that the Name of Hashem is proclaimed over you and they shall fear You" (*Devarim* 28:10). The Gemara explains that this *pasuk* refers to the time when the nations of the world will acknowledge the Name of Hashem, as proclaimed by the performance of the commandment of *tefillin* — an act that will cause the nations to revere the Jewish People. This is derived from the above *pasuk*, as the acronym of the words **ש**ם **י**-ה-ו-ה **נ**קרא spells out the fulfillment of the letter ש, referring to the *tefillin shel rosh*.

Moreover, the latter part of the *pasuk*, that the nations shall fear (יראו) you, gives further meaning to the above explanation of the meaning of בראשית as ש + ב + יראת — interpreting it as "the fear of the two letters ש, that will result in a universal fear of Hashem."

A further allusion to this idea is found in the *pasuk*: כי ביתי בית תפילה יקרא לכל העמים — "My House is a House of Prayer, a meeting place for all the nations" (*Yeshayahu* 56:7). The double expression of **ביתי בית** is a reference to the large ב of **בראשית** (as large letters are written *double* the size of the regular ones). The word *tefillah* in the phrase כי ביתי בית **תפילה** refers to the *tefillin*, as these words share the same root. The fear of Hashem that will result from the performance of the commandment of *tefillin* will occur during the epoch that will coincide with יקרא לכל העמים, the Ingathering of the Exiles.

The Rokeach points out that the letter ש, with a numerical value of three hundred, equates to the value of the words נורא גדול — "a great awe," referring to the reverence that the nations will have for those who wear *tefillin*. The straps that hold the *tefillin* firmly on the head are tied with a knot at the back of the neck. This knot is known as the קשר של תפילין. The word קשר has a numerical value of six hundred, the same as the total of the two *shins* that are embossed on the *tefillin*.

The letter ש also equates to Hashem's Name of י-ה-ו-ה, when this Name is converted via the At–Bash alphabetic transformation:

| | | | | |
|---|---|---|---|---|
| י | → | מ | = | 40 |
| ה | → | צ | = | 90 |
| ו | → | פ | = | 80 |
| ה | → | צ | = | 90 |
| | | **Total** | **=** | **300** |

Moreover, the numerical values of the fulfillments of the letters that spell the Name of Elokim also total three hundred:

| אלף | למד | הי | יוד | מם | |
|---|---|---|---|---|---|
| 111 + | 74 + | 15 + | 20 + | 80 | = 300 |

These two Names of Hashem (י-ה-ו-ה and א-להים) can both be represented by the two different formats of the letter ש. The Name י-ה-ו-ה is comprised from four letters, and thus there are a total of three gaps in between these letters. Likewise there are four gaps housed in between the letters of the Name א-להים. These correspond respectively to the three- and four-armed formats of the two *shins* of the *tefillin shel rosh*. The two *shins* on the *tefillin* therefore represent both Names — Hashem and Elokim.

With the arrival of Mashiach, all the nations of the world will realize the importance of the commandment of *tefillin*, will acknowledge Hashem's Kingship, and will fear those who worship Him. This coincides with the proclamation of **י-ה-ו-ה הוא הא-להים**, as represented in the two *shins* on the *tefillin shel rosh*.

Although these two *shins* represent two different Names of Hashem, the prophet warns us not to mistakenly attribute them to two different deities, as he states: כי אני יהוה לא שניתי — "For I, Hashem, have not changed" (*Malachi* 3:6). These two *shins* are alluded to in the word **שניתי**, as it incorporates the fulfillment of שין. We must realize that any deviation in our perception of Hashem, as understood through his various Names, is only as a result of our limited human understanding. Hashem Himself has not changed in any way.

The shape of the letter ש represents a flame, which produces light. There are three primary colors and seven rainbow colors inherent in light. These two aspects are incorporated in the three-armed letter, and the seven arms of both letters on the *tefillin*. The faculty of sight is housed in the skull of the head, and appropriately, the four-armed ש appears only on the *tefillin* worn on the head. (Those worn on the hand represent the sense of touch.)

When the fulfillment of ש translates as "change," it can represent the positive effect of giving generously to charity. The act of giving charity causes a positive change in the donor. Charity is separated from one's earnings, similar to the separation of tithes (מעשר) from produce. The resulting blessing is that Hashem recompenses the donor with a commensurate amount of wealth (עשר). The spelling of the word **מעשר** incorporates the word עשר, alluding to the fact that one who gives מעשר will be blessed with עשר.

◈ ◈ ◈

The two *shins* on the *tefillin shel rosh* together spell out the word שש, which translates as the number six. When joined together to form the word שש, these two letters have a total of five spaces between their respective sets of arms, alluding to the teachings of the Mishnah (*Kilayim*, Ch. 3) that states that in a patch of field that has a minimum size of six square *tefachim*, one can plant five different species without transgressing the prohibition of planting *kilayim*. This is represented by the composition of the word שש, "six." These contain five separate spaces between the arms of the letters, in which to plant these individual species. Interestingly, the very shape of the ש is similar to that of a growing vegetable, with the bottom point of the letter being at ground level.

The combination of these two formats also represents the Four Species that we wave together during the Festival of Sukkos. Of these four species, the *lulav*, *hadas* and *aravah* are bound together, which is represented by the three-armed letter ש. In order to fulfill the mitzvah one takes one *lulav*, one *esrog*, three *hadasim* and two *aravos*, making a total of seven individual pieces, which are waved together in six directions — correlating to the two different formats of the ש on the *tefillin shel rosh*, which together have seven arms, and translates as the number six.

Using the At–Bash transformation, the letter ש converts into a ב, thereby connecting it to the first letter of the Torah. This is written as a large letter, known as the בית רבתי ("the large letter ב") an expression that has a numerical value of 1,024, which equates to the combined numerical value of the Four Species — לולב, אתרוג, הדס and ערבה. Furthermore, the Magen David explains that since a large letter is written twice the standard size, it is considered equal to two normal-sized ones. Thus the large letter ב in בראשית represents both of the two *shins* on the *tefillin shel rosh*.

## THE LETTER ת

ת

The letter ת has a numerical value of four hundred and fulfills as either the word תיו or תו. The double fulfillment, spelled as תיו יוד ואו, contains a total of nine letters, representing the attribute of truth. The final *mispar katan* of this second fulfillment is eight (when adding the *mispar katan* of each of the fulfillments), while its first fulfillment as תו has a final *mispar katan* of one — both of these numbers represent the Unity of Hashem. Even the ת, the final letter of the *alef-beis*, continues to display the Unity of Hashem.

The numerical value of the fulfillment תיו is 416, which is a multiple of thirteen and thirty-two (13 x 32 = 416). Thirteen is the numerical value of the words אהבה, "love," and אחד, "one," and thirty-two is the numerical value of the word לב, "heart." Being the final letter of the *alef-beis*, the ת displays the לב אחד, representing a loving heart, which has the power to unify the complete nation in our service of Hashem.

The letter ת translates in Hebrew as "sign" or "mark," and in Aramaic as "continuously." The shape of the letter is composed by combining the letters ד and נ together, whose letters also spell out the word דן, "judgment." This final letter thereby represents the final judgment that Hashem will bring upon mankind after the resurrection of the dead. It is also indicative of the fact that the tribe of Dan (דן) traveled at the rear of the encampment in the wilderness, as stated in *Bemidbar* 2:31.

The Ohr HaChayim explains that the Creation of the universe took place in six days, and ended with the day of Shabbos. The merit of honoring the Shabbos empowers Creation to exist another week. The narrative of Creation, therefore ends with the phrase: אשר ברא א-להים **לעשות** — "which Hashem creates *to do*." This verb is in the infinitive, which incorporates the simple present tense of the verb, indicating that Creation continues on a weekly basis. Shabbos is the eternal sign between Hashem and the Jewish People, and through its observance a further week is created. These concepts are expressed in the passage: ושמרו בני ישראל את השבת לעשות את השבת לדרתם ברית עולם ביני ובין בני ישראל אות היא לעלם — "And the Children of Israel shall keep the Shabbos, to make the Shabbos an eternal covenant for their generations. Between Me and the Children of Israel it is a sign forever..." (*Shemos* 31:16–17).

Both translations of the fulfillment of the letter ת ("sign" and "continuously") apply concurrently and are appropriate with reference to Shabbos.

◆ ◆ ◆

Rabbeinu Bechaye points out that the letters ת and ה are sometimes interchanged when used at the end of a word, as both letters are used for the feminine form of words. For example, in the *pasuk*, ישימו קטורה וכו' — "And they shall place incense..." (*Devarim* 33:10), the word for incense, **קטורת**, is written as **קטורה**.

It is appropriate that the ת, which has a feminine connotation, is the last letter of the *alef-beis*, for it represents the *tznius* (modesty) that a Jewish woman displays in not wanting to draw attention to herself.

# CHAPTER 7
# Vowels

MIDRASH TALPIOS EXPLAINS THAT the letters of the *alef-beis* have their source in the third *Sefirah*, that of בינה, the vowels in the second *Sefirah*, that of חכמה, and the cantillation marks in the highest *Sefirah*, that of כתר. Since the vowels have their source in a higher *Sefirah* than that of the letters, they are correspondingly more spiritual in nature and therefore occupy less physical written space than the letters they accompany.

However, since the vowels emanate from a higher *Sefirah*, they cannot be comprehended on their own and must be placed in proximity to one of the letters of the *alef-beis*. Only by their relative position to the letters can they produce different meaningful sounds. For example, the *cholom*, *shuruk* and *chirik* are all single dots, each producing a different sound depending on its relative position to a letter. By the same token, without the use of vowels, letters on their own cannot be expressed verbally. Vowels are best compared to the soul inside a human body that provides life and movement.

The Ginas Egos devotes the final chapter of his book to the topic of the Hebrew vowels. He divides them into four distinct groups, a division that we have adopted here, as well. (It should be noted that

Rabbi Moshe Cordovero, in Chapter 28 of his *Pardes Rimonim*, explains the vowels differently, dividing them into three sets that are termed as "five major vowels, five minor vowels and two servants." The serious reader is referred to that chapter for a fuller discussion on this approach.)

Here, the names and spellings of the vowels are also according to the Ginas Egos (the letter ו is used to show their positioning):

| VOWEL | EXAMPLE OF USE | PRONUNCIATION |
|---|---|---|
| חלם *cholom* | וֹ | **o** as in fl**ow** |
| שרק *shuruk* | וּ | **oo** as in f**oo**d |
| קבץ *kubutz* | וֻ | **oo** as in f**oo**d |
| חרק *chirik* | וִ | **i** as in mach**i**ne |
| צרי *tzerei* | וֵ | **ei** as in sl**eigh** |
| סגול *segol* | וֶ | **e** as in b**e**d |
| שוא *shva* | וְ | silent or short e |
| פתח *patach* | וַ | **a** as in h**a**d |
| קמץ *kamatz* | וָ | **aw** as in s**aw** |
| *chataf patach* | וֲ | **a** as in f**a**ther |
| *chataf segol* | וֱ | **e** as in b**e**d |
| *chataf kamatz* | וֳ | **aw** as in s**aw** |

In the system of vowels, there are eight major and four subsidiary ones which are used to punctuate the letters. The major ones are the *cholom*, *shuruk*, *chirik*, *tzerei*, *segol*, *shva*, *patach* and *kamatz*. The auxiliary ones are the *kubutz*, *chataf patach*, *chataf segol* and *chataf kamatz*.

## The Cholom, Shuruk, Kubutz and Chirik

This first set consists of three different vowels, known as the *cholom*, *shuruk*, and *chirik*, while the *kubutz* is a subsidiary of the *shuruk*.

Each of the vowels in this first set represents different aspects associated with one of the three spheres of Creation. The highest sphere, occupied by Divine angels, corresponds to the *cholom*; the next lower sphere, occupied by the planetary orbits, corresponds to the *shuruk*; while the lowest sphere, our physical world, corresponds to the *chirik*.

### ◈ The Cholom

The *cholom* (חלם) occupies the highest position of all the vowels and is always placed above the letter, representing the formation of the Divine and Angelic sphere. The numerical value of the word חלם is seventy-eight, which is three times the numerical value of Hashem's Name. As explained earlier, the alphabetic order of the letters signifies the Kingship of Hashem as a proclamation of י-ה-ו-ה מלך י-ה-ו-ה מלך י-ה-ו-ה ימלך. The *cholom* reinforces this both in its numeric value and by its regal stature as it coronates the top of the letters.

The חלם also represents the eternal nature of Hashem, as expressed in the phrase: הוה והיה ויהיה — "[Hashem Who] Is, Was and Will Be [the eternal Ruler]." The numerical value of these three words also equals seventy-eight.

Chapter 136 of *Tehillim*, known as *Hallel haGadol* (הלל הגדול), is made up of twenty-six *pesukim*, all ending with the phrase כי לעולם חסדו — "for His kindness endures forever." The word חסדו, "His kindness," has a numerical value of seventy-eight. The lofty position given to the חלם vowel symbolizes Hashem's great kindness.

The letters of חלם also spell out the word חלם, "dream," a state in which one may experience lofty Divine disclosures. It can also spell out the words מחל (forgiveness), חמל (pity) and מחל (a circle) — words which are connected to the events of the end of days. At the time of Mashiach, Hashem will have pity on His People and forgive them for all their transgressions; world History will then commence a new cycle in the circle of Time.

The letters that spell the חלם vowel also spell out the words מלח (salt) and לחם (bread), all of which symbolize eternity. The latter two both played important roles in the *Beis haMikdash*. Every sacrifice brought required *melichah*, "salting," before being offered up on the Altar, as we find in the *pasuk*: ברית מלח עולם — "An eternal covenant of salt" (*Bemidbar* 18:19). Similarly, the לחם הפנים, the twelve loaves of Shewbread had to remain continuously on the *Shulchan* (Table), as stipulated: ונתת על השלחן לחם פנים לפני תמיד — "And on the Table you shall place the Shewbread before Me, always" (*Shemos* 25:30).

It is interesting to point out that the word לחם has a numerical value of seventy-eight, which, as stated earlier, is three times the value of Hashem's Name. The first fulfillment of His Name (יוד הא ואו הא) has a total numerical value of forty-five, the same as that of the letters מ"ה. The number forty-five tripled is 135, the same as that of the word מצה, the unleavened bread. The first of the Four Questions which is asked during the Pesach Seder is:

> מה נשתנה הלילה הזה מכל הלילות שבכל הלילות אנו אוכלים חמץ ומצה הלילה הזה כלו מצה — "Why is this night different from all other nights? For on all other nights we eat leavened and unleavened bread, yet on this night only unleavened bread (matzah)."

This question is appropriately introduced by the word מה which has one-third the numerical value of the word מצה, and equates to the first expansion of Hashem's Name.

### ◈ The Chirik

In contrast, the *chirik* represents the sphere of this physical world, which is the lowest of the three spheres of Creation. This vowel is therefore always placed at the lowest point, below the letter. The letters of חרק also spells out the name of קרח (Korach), who was buried alive underground. They also spell out the word רחק (distant), as the חרק vowel is the furthest away from the חלם, in this specific set. This idea is confirmed in the *pasuk*: מרחק ה' נראה לי — "from afar Hashem appears to me" (*Yirmeyahu* 31:2). The highlighted letters of the word **מרחק**, "from afar," spell out the vowel חרק. The חלם vowel represents the Spirit of Hashem that sits above the letter, and the חרק is situated in a diametrically distant position, below the letter, which provides a literal meaning to the phrase: "from *afar* Hashem appears to me."

Alternatively, the letters of חרק also spells out the word חקר — to investigate and question. In this physical world, the human mind continuously explores new frontiers of knowledge.

### ◈ The Shuruk

The שרק vowel is always placed in a central position, as it represents the middle celestial sphere of the planets. The letters of the שרק vowel spell out the word קשר (a knot), alluding to the fact that its positioning ties together the חלם and חרק.

The spelling of the vowel שרק also spells the word שקר — lies and falsehood. The first *pasuk* of the Torah contains all the major vowels, apart from the *shuruk*, as falsehood has no place in a Torah of absolute truth, as is reinforced in the *pasuk*: ראש דברך אמת — "Your very first utterance is truth" (*Tehillim* 119:160).

The pronunciation of the שרק is the same as that of the קבץ, as they both represent the same central planetary sphere. The קבץ is used to stress this central position relative to the other two spheres. This is displayed in the fact that the *kubutz*'s three dots are placed one above the other, diagonally. When this contrast is not required, the single dot of שרק is sufficient. The Ginas Egos explains that these two vowels, which produce a similar phonetic sound, are connected in another way as well. The three dots of the קבץ vowel form the shape of a diagonal letter ו, which has a numerical value of six. The name of the similar sounding vowel, שרק, has a numerical value of six hundred (300 + 200 + 100 = 600), the same as that of שש, which translates as six.

## THE TZEREI, SEGOL AND SHVA

The *tzerei*, *segol* and *shva* form the next set of vowels, and symbolize the actual construction of these three different spheres of creation. The *tzerei*, composed from two dots placed horizontally, represents the building process of the spiritual and angelic sphere. Spiritual angels are not jealous of each other and are able to coexist peacefully side by side.

The *shva* is on the lowest spiritual level of this group, as it represents the building process of the physical world. These two vertical dots duplicate a building format, where foundations are laid below and the actual buildings on top of them.

The *segol*, as the middle vowel of this set, is comprised of three dots that form the shape of an equilateral triangle. They are in fact, a fusion of two horizontal dots of the *tzerei*, and two vertical ones of the *shva*, representing a complete cycle.

The three dots of the *segol* vowel represents a complete cycle, which connects them to the three alphabetic structures — Al–Bam, At–Bash and Ach–Bi — as they form a triangular transformation ring. In other words, in any of these structures, the results of transforming letters using any two of the above alphabetic structures will result in the third one (see p. 83).

The combination of the *segol* (the middle sphere) and the *shva* (the lowest sphere) forms the *chataf segol* vowel, whose format is symbolic of a servant standing by his master, ready to serve him. This is also indicative of the way that the lower forms of creation fulfill their purpose by being subservient to the higher forms.

◇ ◇ ◇

The *tzerei* appropriately symbolizes the higher spiritual spheres of creation. Owing to its elated nature, the *tzerei* has a softer pronunciation than the corresponding *segol* vowel. Because the *segol* and *shva*, symbolize lower spheres of creation, they can be combined to form a composite vowel known as the *chataf segol* and *chataf shva*. In contrast, the *tzerei* is never combined with another vowel, because of its elated nature. We see this manifested in the word אש (fire). Flames from a fire will always ascend upwards, and thus it is appropriate that the word אש be punctuated with a *tzerei*.

◈ ◈ ◈

The numerical value of the vowel צרי is three hundred, which equates to the numerical value of Hashem's Name of י-ה-ו-ה when transformed by using the At–Bash method, and also to the total numerical value of the fulfillment of the Name of Elokim.

The letters of the word צרי also spell out יצר, "[evil] inclination." Thus, both are connected to Hashem through their numerical values, alluding to the fact that Hashem helps a person overcome his evil inclination.

Every person possesses a good inclination (יצר טוב) and an evil inclination (יצר הרע), which have similar but opposite persuasive powers. The good inclination will encourage a person to follow the correct path, while the evil one will try to do the opposite. A person has free will to choose between good and evil. These inclinations are represented by the צרי vowel, as evidenced by the fact that the letters of this vowel also spell out the word יצר.

These inclinations are part of a person from birth. However, during childhood only one's evil inclination is active; his good inclination remains dormant. It emerges only when he reaches the age of puberty. For boys this occasion is known as the bar mitzvah (בר מצוה), when he is obliged to keep all the Torah commandments.

This idea is alluded to in the first word of the Torah, בראשית.

The first two letters also spell out the word "bar" (בר). The word בראשית is vowelized with a *shva* under the ב, and a *tzerei* under the ר. The construction of *shva* vowel, with one dot placed vertically one above the other, alludes to the power of the evil inclination overshadowing that of the dormant good inclination during childhood. The construction of the *tzerei*, with both dots lying next to each other, alludes to the equal strength of both inclinations at this second stage in life — when the child reaches the age of bar mitzvah.

◈ ◈ ◈

*Osios d'Rabbi Yitzchak* explains that the combination of a ב and a *shva* (שוה) implies שְׁו בָּה — an invitation to the poor man to come inside into the comfort of the rich man's home, to take a seat and make himself comfortable; whereas the combination of a ב and a *tzerei* (צרי) alludes to a homeowner who is a צער עין — a stingy person. The first letter of the Torah could have been punctuated with either a *tzerei* or a *shva*, yet the *shva* is the one used, in order to show the correct way; the *tzerei* would have been an unsuitable choice, since the ב in בראשית represents a house (בית), and the Torah teaches us the correct way of utilizing one's home and worldly possessions. Moreover, the letter בית represents the acronym of י"ב תנועות — the twelve vowels that are required to articulate the Hebrew *alef-beis*, and portray the correct intended message conveyed in the Torah.

## The Patach and Kamatz

The *patach* vowel, which translates as "opening of a doorway," complements the *kamatz*, which means "gathering into" or "closing." The Ginas Egos explains that the word *kamatz* derives from the word *kamitzah*, which is the measure of flour that was required for the *minchah*-offering in the *Beis haMikdash*. The *Kohen* obtained this measure by opening his hand (*patach*), dipping it into the flour and closing his hand in order to gather in (*kamatz*) the flour. Both of these vowels are a horizontal line, representing the letter ו, with the *kamatz* having the addition of a dot connected below.

The true Name of Hashem of י-ה-ו-ה remains a hidden one, as it is pronounced as *A-donai*. This concealed name is normally punctuated with the vowels *shva* (שבא), *cholom* (חלם) and *kamatz* (קמץ). Together these spellings have a total numerical value of 611, the same as that of the word תורה, alluding to the fact that Hashem's Divine wisdom is concealed within the Torah itself.

## The Numerical Values of the Vowels

In addition to the significance of the numerical values of their spellings, the vowels themselves possess a numerical equivalency. In his commentary to the *siddur*, the Shlah explains that all the vowels are composed from either dots, lines or a combination of both. Each dot corresponds to the smallest letter י and thus has a numerical value of ten. A line represents the letter ו and therefore has a numerical value of six.

The *cholom*, *shuruk* and *chirik*, each comprising of a single dot, all have a numerical value of ten; the *tzerei* and *shva*, with two dots, each have a corresponding numerical value of twenty; and the *segol* and *kubutz*, with three dots, each have a corresponding numerical value of thirty. The *patach* is composed from a single line, and has a numerical value of six, while the *kamatz* combines the line with a dot below it, to produce a numerical value of sixteen.

The Magen Avraham, commenting on *Orach Chayim* 187:3, makes use of these numerical values to clarify the correct pronunciation of certain words. Quoting from the Shlah, he discusses the correct vowelization of the words in the first passage of the Grace after Meals: תמיד לא **חסר** לנו ואל **יחסר** לנו מזון לעולם ועד—"we have never lacked and may we never lack nourishment for all eternity." The first highlighted word, חסר, is vowelized with a *kamatz* and *patach*, which together have a total numerical value of twenty-two (16 + 6). The second highlighted word, יחסר, uses *segol*, *shva* and *patach* vowels, which have a total numerical value of fifty-six (30 + 20 + 6). These two words together have a value of seventy-eight, the equivalent to the numerical value of the word לחם, "bread." We ask Hashem that we should never be lacking the basic requirement of bread to eat.

◈ ◈ ◈

As mentioned earlier, the fulfillment of the letter א (אלף) can represent both the number one and one thousand, depending upon its vowelization. The Chasam Sofer points out that the vowels of the fulfillment as אַלֵף have a numerical value of twenty-six. Thus, the אלף, as the number one, represents the Unity of Hashem in its composition as well as the numerical value of its vowels. Vowelized as אֶלֶף — the number one thousand — it has two *segols*, equating to sixty, which corresponds to the unity of the six hundred thousand men present at the time of the birth of the Jewish nation — the nation that is charged with the task of proclaiming the Unity of Hashem to all mankind.

◈ ◈ ◈

The letters א'ה'ח'ע' all belong to the Gutturals group as they are formed in the גרון, the throat. These letters fulfill as אלף, הה, חית, עין, and when articulated they have under their first letters a *patach*, *tzerei*, *tzerei* and *patach*, respectively. These four vowels have a total numerical value of fifty-two (6 + 20 + 20 + 6 = 52), while the four guttural letters have a total numerical value of eighty-four (1 + 8 + 5 + 70 = 84); together these total 136, the same as the word קול — the sound that originates from the voice box in the throat.

# Afterword

THE RAMBAN, IN THE introduction to his commentary on the Torah, writes that there are a total of fifty gates through which one can obtain different types of בינה (understanding), appropriately known as the נ' שערי בינה, "the Fifty Gates of Wisdom." This wisdom is incorporated into the actual letters of the *alef-beis* — in their shape, size, crowns, numerical value, or juxtaposition in the alphabetic order — some examples of which have been mentioned in this book.

The Torah teaches us regarding the creation of the initial light: וירא א-להים את האור כי **טוב** ויבדל וכו' — "And Hashem saw that the light was good and He separated it..." (*Bereishis* 1:4). Rashi explains that Hashem saw that this initial light was unsuitable for the wicked's use, so He set it aside for future use by the righteous. This hidden light contains the secrets of the Torah embedded within the letters of the *alef-beis*. The Ben Ish Chai comments on the word טוב, pointing out that its hidden fulfillment (**טית ואו בית**) spells out the word **אתיות** — the letters of the *alef-beis*. Thus the hidden light — the ultimate goodness — is incorporated within the word טוב.

In *Tehillim* 119:18 we ask Hashem to allow us to view this hidden wisdom: **גל** עיני ואביטה נפלאות מתורתך — "Unveil my eyes that I may understand the wonders of Your Torah." It is appropriate to express our prayers for this revelation by using the word גל, "unveil," which has a numerical value of thirty-three, and thus corresponds to the thirty-third word of the Torah, טוב, which stores this hidden light.

These concealed treasures will be revealed to us with the advent of Mashiach, when all will see the fulfillment of the *pasuk*: ביום **ההוא** יהיה ה' אחד ושמו אחד — "On that day, Hashem will be One and His Name will be One" (*Zechariah* 14:9). The numerical value of the word ההוא is seventeen, the same as that of the word טוב, alluding to the fact that the goodness hidden within each letter of the *alef-beis* will be revealed to us "on *that* day," when Mashiach arrives.

◈ ◈ ◈

The Chasam Sofer explains that our understanding of the profundity of the hidden spiritual wisdom is compared to our perception of the stars. The sheer number of stars that exist in the universe is beyond our comprehension, and the naked eye cannot see a star's true size and luminosity because its distance from us is so great. The Hebrew word for star, כוכב, can be read as כו + כב, with numerical values of twenty-six and twenty-two, respectively. Twenty-six symbolizes Hashem, and twenty-two refers to the twenty-two letters of the *alef-beis.*

Just as we are unable to perceive the true luminosity of a star, the true greatness of the Divine wisdom that is embedded in each of the twenty-two letters of the *alef-beis* is far removed from our perception.

# Glossary

The following glossary provides a partial explanation of some of the Hebrew, Aramaic (A.) and Yiddish (Y.) words and phrases used in this book. The spellings and explanations reflect the way the specific word is used herein. Often, there are alternate spellings and meanings for the words.

**AKEIDAH:** the binding of Yitzchak on the altar.

**AL HANISIM:** an additional prayer said on Chanukah and Purim acknowledging the Divine miracles.

**AMAH (PL. AMOS):** a Biblical measure of length.

**AMEN:** a response uttered after hearing a blessing being pronounced.

**AMIDAH:** lit., "standing"; a reference to the SHEMONEH ESREI prayer which is recited while standing.

**ARAVAH (PL. ARAVOS):** a willow branch used on the Festival of Sukkos as part of the Four Species.

**ARON:** the rectangular-shaped box in which the Ten commandments were housed in the Holy of Holies.

**AVODAH:** lit., "work"; worship; service.

**BA'AL TESHUVAH:** a penitent; formerly non-observant Jew who returns to Jewish practice and tradition.

**BEGED:** an article of clothing.

**BEIS DIN:** a court of Jewish law.

**BEIS HA-MIDRASH:** a Torah study hall.

**BEIS HAMIKDASH:** the Holy Temple in Jerusalem.

**BERACHAH (PL. BERACHOS):** blessing(s).

**BERAISA (A):** a compendium of Biblical teachings of the Oral Law.

**BIRCHAS HAGOMEL:** a special blessing of thanksgiving after having been saved from danger.

**BNEI YISRAEL:** the Children of Israel.

**BRIS MILAH:** the ritual of circumcision.

**CHACHAMIM:** wise and learned people; Torah authorities.

**CHAZAL:** a Hebrew acronym for "our Sages, of blessed memory."

**CHAZAN:** cantor, who leads the congregation in prayer.

**DAVENING (Y.):** praying.

**DIN:** law.

**DREIDEL (Y.):** a six-sided die with a pointed bottom on which to spin it.

**ECHAD:** one; unity.

**ESROG:** a citron, one of the Four Species taken on the Festival of Sukkos.

**GAN EDEN:** the Garden of Eden; Paradise.

**GEHINNOM:** Purgatory.

**GET:** a Jewish legal divorce.

**HADAS(IM):** myrtle branches, one of the Four Species taken on the Festival of Sukkos.

**HALACHAH:** the entire body of Jewish law; a specific law.

**HAMAKOM:** lit., "the place"; a term used to represent a holy place or God.

**HAR HABAYIS:** the mountain in Jerusalem on which the Holy Temple was built.

**HASHEM:** God.

**HEICHAL:** the outer courtyard of the Holy Temple.

**KADDISH:** a prayer sanctifying God's Name; the mourner's prayer.

**KIDDUSH:** the blessing over a cup of wine recited on Shabbos and Festivals.

**KILAYIM:** The prohibition of planting two different seeds or trees too close to each other.

KODESH HAKODASHIM: the Holy of Holies.

KOHEN: a Priest, a member of the priestly clan, a direct descendant of Aharon.

KOHEN GADOL: the High Priest.

KORBAN PESACH: an offering brought in the Holy Temple before Pesach.

LASHON HA-RA: evil speech, which is forbidden by the Torah.

LEVI: a descendant of the tribe of Levi.

LULAV: a palm branch, one of the Four Species taken on the Festival of Sukkos.

MA'ASER RISHON: the first tithe from produce that was given to the KOHEN.

MACHATZIS HA-SHEKEL: a half a *shekel*; a monetary yearly contribution given by every Jewish person to the BEIS HAMIKDASH.

MALCHUS: kingship.

MELICHAH: the salting of meat in order to remove its blood.

METZORA: a person suffering from TZARA'AS.

MEZUZAH: a rolled parchment containing the prayer *Shema Yisrael* which is affixed to the doorposts of Jewish homes.

MIDDOS: character traits; attributes.

MIKVEH: a special pool of water for spiritual purification.

MINCHAH: the afternoon prayer service.

MINYAN: a quorum of ten adult Jewish men required for public prayer.

MISHKAN: the temporary Tabernacle used after the Exodus from Egypt, before the Holy Temple was built.

MUSAF: an extra prayer said on Shabbos and Festivals.

NE'ILAH: the concluding prayer of the Yom Kippur service.

NUSACH ASHKENAZ: the prayer text used by Jewish people of European descent.

OLAH: a burnt-offering.

PARASHAH: a portion of the Torah.

**PASUK (PL. PESUKIM):** Scriptural verse(s).

**PIYUT(IM):** liturgical poem(s).

**PSHARAH:** a compromise.

**ROSH CHODESH:** the beginning of a new Hebrew month.

**RUACH HA-KADOSH:** lit., "a spirit of holiness"; Divine inspiration.

**SATAN:** the evil spirit.

**SEFER:** a book.

**SEFIRAH (PL. SEFIROS):** channels through which spiritual forces descend to the physical world.

**SELICHOS:** special penitential prayers.

**SHACHARIS:** the morning prayer service.

**SHECHINAH:** the Divine Presence.

**SHEM HAMEFORASH:** the esoteric Name of Hashem, which is comprised of seventy-two letters.

**SHEMA:** the verse, "Hear, O Israel..." the opening words of the fundamental Jewish prayer which proclaims the Unity of God, and is recited by Jews morning and evening.

**SHEMITTAH:** the seventh year in the Jewish calendar during which all fields lie fallow.

**SHEMONEH ESREI:** lit., "eighteen"; the eighteen blessings of the AMIDAH prayer, the central part of our daily prayers.

**SHOFAR:** a ram's horn, blown on Rosh Hashanah.

**SIDDUR(IM):** prayer book(s).

**SIMAN:** a sign.

**SIYUM:** the completion of studying a complete section of the Torah.

**SUKKAH (PL. SUKKOS):** booth(s); the temporary dwelling where Jews reside during the Festival of Sukkos.

**TAGIM:** the crowns that adorn some letters in the Torah script.

**TEFACHIM:** a Biblical measure of length. (There are 6 *tefachim* in one AMAH).

**TEFILLAH:** prayer.

**TEFILLIN:** boxes of leather encasing specific verses of the Torah written on parchment, worn by Jewish adult men on the head and arm during morning prayers.

**TEFILLIN SHEL ROSH:** the TEFILLIN worn on the head.

**TERUMAH GEDOLAH:** *see* MA'ASER RISHON.

**TERUMAS MA'ASER:** a tithe that the LEVI gives to the KOHEN.

**TESHUVAH:** repentance, and return to the way of life prescribed by the Torah.

**TZARA'AS:** A disease of the skin which is a punishment for LASHON HA-RA.

**TZEDAKAH:** charity; righteousness.

**TZIMTZUM:** a constriction of spiritual forces.

**TZITZIS:** knotted fringes attached to a four-cornered garment worn by Jewish males to remind them of God and His commandments.

**TZNIUS:** modesty.

**VIDUI:** the confession of sins.

**YETZER HA-RA:** the evil inclination.

**YETZER HA-TOV:** the good inclination.

**YOVEL:** the fiftieth year in the Jewish calendar.

**ZEMIROS:** songs of praise.

**ZT"L:** a Hebrew acronym for "may the memory of the righteous be for a blessing."

# Sources

ARUCH: R. Nasan ben Yechiel (1030–1106).

BA'AL HATURIM: R. Yaakov ben Asher (1269–1343).

BEN ISH CHAI: R. Moshe Chaim of Baghdad (1832–1909).

BNEI YISASCHAR: R. Tzvi Elimelech of Dinov (1783–1841).

CHASAM SOFER: R. Moshe Sofer (1762–1839).

DEGEL MACHANEH EFRAYIM: R. Moshe Chaim Efrayim (died 1800).

GINAS EGOS: R. Yosef Giktilia (1248–1323).

IBN EZRA: R. Avraham ben Meir Ibn Ezra (1092–1167).

KLI YAKAR: R. Shlomo Efrayim ben Aharon (1545–1619).

KUZARI: Yehudah ben Shmuel haLevi (1075–1141).

MACHZOR VITRI: R. Simcha ben Shmuel (1075–1141).

MAGEN DAVID: R. David ben Zimri (1480–1573).

MAHARAL OF PRAGUE: R. Yehudah Aryeh Loeb (1512–1609).

MAHARSHA: R. Shmuel Eliezer ben Yehudah haLevi Edels (1555–1631).

ME'OR V'SHEMESH: R. Klonimus Kalman Epstein (1751–1823).

MEGALLEH AMUKOS: R. Nasan Neta Shapiro (1585–1633).

MIDRASH TALPIOS: R. Eliyahu haKohen (died 1729).

MINCHAS SHAI: R. Yedidyah Shlomo Rafael of Nortzi (17th century).

OSIOS D'RABBI YITZCHAK: R. Yitzchak Eizik, Rav of Zorovitz (18th century).

PANE'ACH RAZA: R. Yitzchak ben R. Yehudah haLevi (mid-13th century).

PARDES RIMONIM: R. Moshe Cordovero (1522–1570).

**PIRKEI D'RABBI ELIEZER:** R. Eliezer ben Hyrcanus (circa 1st–2nd centuries).

**RABBEINU BECHAYE:** Bechaye ben Asher (1260–1340).

**RADAK:** R. David Kimchi (1160–1235).

**RAMBAM:** R. Moshe ben Maimon, a.k.a. Maimonides (1135–1204).

**RAMBAN:** R. Moshe ben Nachman, a.k.a. Nachmanides (1194–1270).

**RASHI:** R. Shlomo Yitzchaki (1040–1105).

**ROKEACH:** R. Elazar ben Yehudah Kalonymus (1176–1238).

**SAADIAH GAON:** R. Saadiah ben Yosef (892–942).

**SEFER CHAREIDIM:** R. Elazar Azkari (1533–1600).

**SEFER HASHORASHIM:** R. David Kimchi, a.k.a. the Radak (1160–1235).

**SHACH:** R. Mordechai haKohen Mikoriel (16th century).

**SHLAH:** R. Yeshayahu Horowitz (1560–1630).

**TORAS CHAIM:** R. Avraham Chaim Shor (died 1632).

**VILNA GAON:** R. Eliyahu ben Shlomo (1720–1797).

**YALKUT REUVEINI:** R. Avraham Reuven Katz (1600?–1673).

# Index

## CHAPTER 4:
## Numerical Methods for Interpreting the Torah ..... 131



## CHAPTER 5:
## Attributes of the Letters and Their Usage in Words ..... 157

# Alef-Beis Chart
## (According to the Beis Yosef)

לעילוי נשמת

**אאמו"ר ר' חיים אריה בן ר' משה דוד ז"ל**

**נפטר בשם טוב כ"ז אלול תשמ"ח**

ולעילוי נשמת

**זוגתו אאמו"ר מרת הינדא בת ר' מרדכי ז"ל**

**נפטרה בשם טוב ה' אייר תשמ"ט**

**ת. נ. צ. ב. ה.**

לעילוי נשמת

**ר' שמואל בן ר' יהודה בלוך ז"ל**

**נלב"ע כ"ז אדר א' תשי"ט**

לעילוי נשמת

**זוגתו מרת ייטל בת ר' אורי שרגא צבי ז"ל**

**נלב"ע ח' תמוז תש"מ**

לעילוי נשמת

**החבר ר' יוסף בן מו"ר אברהם ז"ל**

**נלב"ע א' תמוז תרפ"ה**

לעילוי נשמת

**זוגתו מרת פרל בת החבר ר' מאיר ז"ל**

**נלב"ע א' תמוז תשל"ג**

**ת. נ. צ. ב. ה.**

לעילוי נשמת

**מורינו הרב ר' אברהם בן הח' ר' שמעון ארלנגר ז"ל**
נלב"ע כ"ג כסלו תרצ"ב

**וזוגותו מרת בילה בת ר' משה יהושוע ארלנגר ז"ל**
נלב"ע י"א מרחשון תרע"ט

**האשה גיטל בת מור' ר' אברהם ארלנגר ז"ל**
נלב"ע י"ד אייר תשל"ט

**הרב שמשון רפאל בן מוה"ר אברהם ארלנגר ז"ל**
נלב"ע כ"ט שבט תשל"ג

**וזוגתו מרת גיטל בת ר' רפאל יצחק ארלנגר ע"ה**
נלב"ע ט"ז אלול תשל"ט

ת. נ. צ. ב. ה.

לעילוי נשמת

**דוד בן מאיר צבי** ע"ה

***Dr. Dovid Osterreicher***

**וזוגתו מרת מלכה בת יחיאל** ע"ה

***Mrs. M. Osterreicher nee Leitner***

**ת. נ. צ. ב. ה.**

לעילוי נשמת

**שרה** ע"ה **בת ר' עזריאל הכהן מונק** נ"י

**ת. נ. צ. ב. ה.**

לעילוי נשמת

**בלומה בת זאב** ע"ה

***Bluma Lachterman***

***St. Louis, Missouri USA***

**ת. נ. צ. ב. ה.**

לעילוי נשמת

**הרה"ח ר' יוסף בן הגאון רבי שמואל**
**היילפרין** זצ"ל
**ממייסדי ק"ק מחזיקי הדת במנשסטר**
**נלב"ע י"ח תמוז תשנ"ט**

**ת. נ. צ. ב. ה.**

**ולעילוי נשמת האשה החשובה**

**מרת פריידא היילפרין** ע"ה
**בת הרה"ח ר' אליעזר** ז"ל
**נלב"ע ביום ה' מנחם אב תש"ס**

**ת. נ. צ. ב. ה.**

לעילוי נשמת

**ר' ראובן גרשון בן ר' שלמה ע"ה**
**ואשתו מרת רבקה בת ר' מנחם ע"ה**
**ר' אלכסנדר בן ר' מרדכי ע"ה**

ת. נ. צ. ב. ה.

לעילוי נשמת

*Jack Harris*

**ר' יעקב ב"ר מאיר ע"ה**

נפטר ב' סיון תשס"א

ת. נ. צ. ב. ה.

לעילוי נשמת

**ר' שמעון הכהן בן ר' משה** ע"ה

ת. נ. צ. ב. ה.

לעילוי נשמת

**החבר ר' משה בן מוהר"ר ישראל יצחק** ע"ה
**ואשתו מרת יכט בת החבר ר' מרדכי** ע"ה

***Manfred & Edith Lewin*** **(London)**

ת. נ. צ. ב. ה.

לעילוי נשמת

**הרב רפאל ב"ר שמחה מרדכי ז"ל**

**ת. נ. צ. ב. ה.**

לעילוי נשמת

**ר' דוב ארי"ה בן משה צבי ע"ה**

**ת. נ. צ. ב. ה.**

Made in the USA
Middletown, DE
08 March 2025